WORKING MEN'S COLLEGE.

LIBRARY REGULATIONS.

The Library is open every week-day evening (except Saturday), from 6.30 to 10 o'clock.

This book may be kept for three weeks. If not returned within that period, the borrower will be liable to a fine of one penny per week.

If lost or damaged, the borrower will be required to make good such loss or damage.

Only one book may be borrowed at a time.

VOLUNTARY
SOCIAL SERVICES
since 1918

INTERNATIONAL LIBRARY OF SOCIOLOGY
AND SOCIAL RECONSTRUCTION

Editor: Dr. Karl Mannheim

VOLUNTARY SOCIAL SERVICES
since 1918

by

HENRY A. MESS

in collaboration with

CONSTANCE BRAITHWAITE, VIOLET CREECH-JONES, HILDA
JENNINGS, PEARL JEPHCOTT, HAROLD KING, NORA MILNES,
JOHN MORGAN, GERTRUDE WILLIAMS AND W. E. WILLIAMS

Edited by
GERTRUDE WILLIAMS

LONDON
KEGAN PAUL, TRENCH, TRUBNER & CO., LTD.
BROADWAY HOUSE : 68–74 CARTER LANE, E.C.4

First published 1947

PRINTED IN GREAT BRITAIN
BY WESTERN PRINTING SERVICES LTD., BRISTOL

*Owing to production delays
this book was not published
until 1948*

~~CON~~TENTS

	PAGE
INTRODUCTION BY GERTRUDE WILLIAMS	vii

CHAPTER

I. WHAT IS MEANT BY VOLUNTARY SOCIAL SERVICE? .	1
By Henry A. Mess	
II. THE POSITION OF VOLUNTARY SOCIAL SERVICES IN 1918	8
By Nora Milnes	
III. VOLUNTARY SOCIAL SERVICES IN URBAN AREAS .	28
By Hilda Jennings	
IV. SOCIAL SERVICE WITH THE UNEMPLOYED . .	40
By Henry A. Mess	
V. VOLUNTARY CASE-WORK SOCIETIES	55
By Hilda Jennings	
VI. COMMUNITY CENTRES AND COMMUNITY ASSOCIATIONS	69
By Henry A. Mess and Harold King	
VII. THE NATIONAL COUNCIL OF SOCIAL SERVICE WITH APPENDIX ON WORK IN RURAL AREAS . 80, 99	
By John Morgan	
VIII. THE WORK OF VOLUNTARY SOCIAL SERVICES AMONG CHILDREN BEFORE SCHOOL-LEAVING AGE . .	106
By Violet Creech-Jones	
IX. WORK AMONG BOYS AND GIRLS	129
By Pearl Jephcott	
X. ADULT EDUCATION	146
By W. E. Williams	
XI. THE GREAT PHILANTHROPIC TRUSTS . . 172, 183	
By Henry A. Mess and Constance Braithwaite	
XII. THE FINANCE OF VOLUNTARY SOCIAL SERVICES 188, 195	
By Henry A. Mess and Constance Braithwaite	
XIII. THE PLACE OF VOLUNTARY SOCIAL SERVICE IN THE LIFE OF THE NATION	204
By Henry A. Mess	
XIV. THE TRAINING AND RECRUITMENT OF SOCIAL WORKERS	214
By Gertrude Williams	
INDEX	247

CONTRIBUTORS TO VOLUNTARY SOCIAL SERVICES IN GREAT BRITAIN SINCE 1918

CONSTANCE BRAITHWAITE. Lecturer in Social Studies. Author of *The Voluntary Citizen*.

VIOLET CREECH-JONES. Magistrate and Member of Lambeth Borough Council and of Home Office Advisory Committee on the Treatment of Offenders. Author of pamphlet in the Fabian Research Series, *Nurseries and Nursery Schools*.

HILDA JENNINGS. Warden of the University Settlement, Bristol. Author of *Brynmawr*, etc.

PEARL JEPHCOTT. Formerly member of the staff of the National Association of Girls' Clubs and Mixed Clubs. Author of *Girls Growing Up* and *Clubs for Girls*.

HAROLD KING. Publications Officer, National Council of Social Service.

H. A. MESS. Formerly Reader in Sociology, University of London.

NORA MILNES. Reader in Social Studies and Head of the Department of Social Study, University of Edinburgh. Author of *A Study of Industrial Edinburgh*, etc.

JOHN MORGAN. Formerly Community Centres Officer and Publications Officer of the National Council of Social Service. Lecturer and Research Associate of the School of Social Work. University of Toronto, Canda.

GERTRUDE WILLIAMS. Lecturer in Economics, Bedford College, University of London. Author of *The Price of Social Security*, *Women and Work*, etc.

W. E. WILLIAMS, C.B.E. Director of the Bureau of Current Affairs, Editor-in-Chief, Penguin Books.

INTRODUCTION

by

GERTRUDE WILLIAMS

A WORD of explanation about this volume is necessary. It was originally planned by Henry Mess who, in the early years of the war, realized that the development of the statutory social services—one of the outstanding features of the twentieth century and quickly gathering speed—would be immensely accelerated by the urgency of problems thrown up by war conditions. Feeling convinced that the post-war world would necessitate some radical reorganization he thought that he could perform a useful service by setting forth clearly the work that had been done by the voluntary social services in the period between the two wars, so as to make clearer the lines of demarcation between statutory and voluntary methods of providing for social needs. He was peculiarly fitted for such a task. The greater part of his adult working life had been spent in social work, including a very fruitful and constructive decade as Director of the Tyneside Council of Social Service during the worst part of the inter-war depression ; whilst his appointment as Reader in Sociology in the University of London in 1933 gave him the opportunity to look at the work in perspective, with a greater degree of detachment than is common to those faced with day-to-day problems in the practical field. Unfortunately the pressure of other work prevented Mess from pushing on with the book as quickly as he had intended and death overtook him in 1943 before he had completed more than a few chapters.

Both the editor and publisher of the series were anxious that the plan should not be abandoned and invited me to get together a group of contributors who between them might cover the various topics that should be included in a survey of voluntary work. By the time, however, that these arrangements were made it became evident that some alteration of the original plan was essential for the inter-war years no longer represented a clearly marked period of development as they had seemed to do when the scheme was first designed. The problems thrown up by the war were a challenge to voluntary effort as well as to statutory provision and not only did the existing social agencies undergo considerable changes in their response but also completely new organisations had to be established to deal with unprecedented situations. I came to the conclusion that no good purpose could be served by breaking off in mid-story and that, to be really valuable, the history of the voluntary social services must include some account of war time developments. Of the chapters that Mess had already written, one— What is meant by Voluntary Social Service?—is concerned solely with definitions and a second—Social Service with the Unemployed—dealt with one particular period, so that this change of plan did not here introduce any serious difficulty ; as regards the others, Miss Constance Braithwaite agreed to expand and bring up to date the chapters on Philanthropic Trusts and the Finance of Voluntary Social Services, where the retention of 1939 as the end date might have forced this part of the volume out of line with the remainder and Mr. Harold King largely rewrote the chapter on Community Centres.

A book written by a number of persons cannot hope, of course, to have the same underlying unity as one which has a single author ; nor is it possible to prevent altogether some slight amount of overlapping. There is, on the other hand, compensation to be found in the wide field of experience and knowledge that can thus be utilised and, in dealing with problems many of which are still highly controversial, it is often of value to have light thrown from many different angles.

No attempt has been made in these chapters to give a detailed factual account of the history of the different social organisations ; the aim has rather been to try and discover the main lines of development in the various fields of voluntary effort since the end of the first world war. During this period two outstanding factors have played a decisive part. In the first place, the growth of statutory social services—health and unemployment insurance, widows and orphans pensions, unemployment allowances, old age pensions with the possibility of supplementation and so on—has made routine provision for an immense proportion of the cases of poverty that would otherwise have come for help to the charitable bodies and one might justly ask the question, " Have the voluntary social services

outlived their usefulness?" There is always a danger of a
social institution going on when the purpose for which it
originally came into being is being served by some other means,
and, in such circumstances, its existence means nothing less
than a waste of effort, time, and money that could better be
devoted to other ends. Has this position been reached with the
voluntary agencies or is there still a field which can best be
cultivated by them?

The second important factor that has played a part during
the last thirty years is the deepening understanding of the
nature of society. Until the end of the first world war organised
social effort was concerned primarily to help the social casualty
—the individual who, for one reason or another, proved unable
to maintain himself on the minimum standards demanded by
the community. Since then, more and more attention has come
to be paid to the normal, rather than the abnormal, and a
wealth of effort is now directed towards helping the ordinary
member of society to live as rich, full, and satisfying a life as
he is capable of.

These essays are intended, then, as a form of stocktaking of
the present position. From one side the scope of voluntary
effort has been greatly narrowed, from another, it has been
immensely widened. How have the voluntary agencies responded to the changing circumstances? What changes are
discernible in their outlook and methods? Is it possible to see
in which direction they can most usefully expand? Is there,
indeed, a permanent place for them at all or is it merely a
matter of time before statutory agencies take over all their
functions? These are some of the questions that the authors
of the following chapters have set themselves to answer.

A*

Chapter I

WHAT IS VOLUNTARY SOCIAL SERVICE?

by

HENRY A. MESS

SOCIAL Service, like many other terms in common use, is very hard to define satisfactorily. It is used in a number of different senses in different connections and by different persons. The only satisfactory procedure is to sort out the different senses, and then to see whether the term " social service " can be reserved for any one of them, and whether we can find distinguishing terms for the others. Social service is a modern term, virtually a twentieth-century term.[1] Older terms in use were " charity," " philanthropy," " poor relief," " social reform." To what extent " social service " corresponds to these, and to what extent it has a different and a new connotation, should appear in the course of analysis.

The first sense in which the term is sometimes used is when the claim is made that anyone who is doing honestly work which is useful to others is rendering social service. Thus one hears it sometimes said that a great firm of popular caterers, or of cheap tailors, has rendered conspicuous social service ; and the statement conveys something which is true and important. In this sense a good ironmonger or a good accountant renders social service. Often the adjective is omitted. (" All service ranks the same with God " ; cf. the Rotary motto " Service not Self.") The bulk of such service is rendered in the ordinary way of industry or of professional work. It is doubtless a good thing that stress should be laid on the element of service in all honest and useful work, though one knows that the phraseology can be associated with a good deal of cant. In any case such use of the term " social service " is too wide to be of much value, and for the most part the term is used and understood in a narrower sense.

The connotation of the term " social service " often includes the idea of supererogation. Social service is here regarded as

---

[1] See *Encyclopædia of the Social Sciences*, q.v. "Social Work".

being something extra to the ordinary work of the world, something which need not be done, but is actually done because of
men's overflowing goodness and enthusiasm.   In this sense
social service is primarily a matter of volunteers ; aims are
formulated, organisations are founded and directed, money and
service are provided by volunteers.

If this be accepted, it follows that activities cease to be social
service when they become statutory obligations.

Social service in the past has been much concerned with, and
by many identified with, the relief of distress, especially material
distress, and the combating of evils.   It is one of the outstanding
changes of recent decades that the emphasis, is coming to be
laid more and more on the enrichment of normal life.   Yet
the former objects remain, and are likely to remain for a long
time, a large part of what is called " social service " and
" social service " is still identified in the minds of many with
them.

Many of the risks of life are met by mutual aid.   Mutual aid
is to be contrasted with help rendered by the privileged to the
unprivileged.   Many of our social services to-day are a mixture
of the two ; help is given by those who have means or leisure
to spare on such terms and in such a manner as to stimulate
mutual aid among the recipients.   It is important to note that
mere mutual aid without any help or stimulation from outside
is seldom thought of as social service.   Thus a middle class
amateur dramatic society, entirely spontaneous and self-
supporting, is not usually thought of as " social service," but
the dramatic societies fostered by Rural Community Councils
or by similar agencies are thought of as being in the field of
social service.

If this be accepted, it indicates that whilst the promotion of
mutual aid is an important part of social service, and whilst
such mutual aid is included in social service, it is still implicit
in the notion of voluntary social service that some help shall be
given by the privileged to the unprivileged.   It seems impossible
to escape the conclusion that this is an intrinsic part of the idea
of voluntary social service, as the term is understood today.
Such help is certainly an important part of the realities of
voluntary social service, as it is today.

The case of propagandist and vigilance societies offers peculiar difficulties.   Some of them exist to combat acknowledged

evils or supposed evils, e.g. the National Anti-Gambling League, the Anti-Vivisection Society. It seems clear that they come within the field of social service. Others exist for the enrichment of life of some part or the whole of the community, e.g. the British Institute of Adult Education ; the Commons, Open Spaces and Footpaths Preservation Society.

It is more doubtful whether these are usually thought of as social service.[1] Foreign missionary societies have the marks of voluntariness, supererogation, of service rendered by the privileged to the unprivileged ; yet it is doubtful whether foreign missionary societies are usually thought of as social service and the foreign missionary as a social worker. The medical missionary would, I think, be considered more closely akin to a social worker than a missionary without such a special qualification.

So far we have been concerned with the voluntary social services. There are other ambiguities to face when we come to examine the term " statutory social service " (or " public social service "). The term has come into use because historically the State has taken over a great deal of social work initiated by voluntary organisations. To some extent, not entirely, work which was previously performed by voluntary associations, but which has now been taken over, is regarded as statutory social service. But as such work becomes part of the normal functioning of the State, it tends to be thought of less and less as social service. Thus the provision of schools in the early part of last century, was social service, or, as the term was then, " philanthropy " ; and Lancaster, Bell and others were social workers. But the educational service of today is not popularly thought of as " social service," nor are the school teachers usually thought of as " social workers," except in respect of their works of supererogation. Certainly we know what is meant when, as sometimes happens, a school teacher says that she wishes to train to become a social worker.

Yet it is true, and it is an indication of the confusion attaching to the interpretation of the term, that education is included in the annual Treasury White Paper, commonly known as the

[1] The latter is listed in the *Annual Charities Register and Digest*, the former not ; but the World Association for Adult Education is listed. A study of the *Annual Charities Register* shows how uncertain and arbitrary the line is. Thus, training colleges are included, but not the university colleges. The Town and Country Planning Association appears, but not the Council for the Preservation of Rural England.

Drage Return, whose official title is the *Annual Return of Expenditure on Public Social Services.*[1]

It is impossible, however, to maintain that the Drage Return is logical in its inclusions and exclusions. It includes war pensions ; it excludes expenditure on the welfare of the blind ; and there are other inconsistencies. There is no legal definition of social service ; the May Committee sought for one in vain.[2] Lord Eustace Percy has suggested that what people usually think of as social services are those services " which are designed more directly to benefit the citizen as an individual."[3] The P.E.P. Report on the British Social Services excludes the impersonal environmental services, such as street lighting and sewage disposal, and includes in its survey a wide range of personal services.[4] These it classifies as (1) constructive community services (such as the provision of public elementary education) open to everyone, (2) social insurances, and (3) social assistance.

It is to be noted that most of the statutory social services which the P.E.P. Report includes were taken over by the State from pioneer voluntary social service organisations. It is further to be noted that they are mostly social services which are used, and are intended to be used, by the poorer section of the community. It is true that legally the public elementary schools are open to all children, but in fact the children of the well-to-do go elsewhere. And there is considerable feeling that they ought to go elsewhere, that the provision is not meant for them. The constructive community service which is most used by the well-to-do is the hospital service, but with regard to that also the feeling lingers that it is primarily intended for the poor. The social insurances and social assistance are limited to those whose means are below a certain level. It is obvious that there attaches at present to the statutory social services the idea that they are provided for the less well-off members of the community. But an increasing use is made of some of them, e.g.

---

[1] The term " public social services " seems to have been first used in this connection. What Mr. Geoffrey Drage, M.P. asked for in 1913 was a return of expenditure under certain Acts of Parliament providing "direct beneficiary assistance." It was at the suggestion of the Registrar-General, Sir Bernard Mallet, that the term " public social services " was substituted. See *P.E.P. Report on the British Social Services*, p. 36, and W. H. Wickwar, *The Social Services*, p. 228.

[2] See T. S. Simey, *Principles of Social Administration*, p. 4.

[3] Lord Eustace Percy, *Government in Transition*, p. 126.

[4] *P.E.P. Report on the British Social Services*, pp. 36–8.

of public elementary schools and of municipal hospitals, by members of other sections of the community, and this is likely to increase rapidly.

There are those who hold that the term " social service " should be restricted entirely to service which, so far as those who control and finance it are concerned, is freely and voluntarily given and is without the spur or compulsion of economic motive.

In other words, they hold that " statutory social service " is a contradiction in terms. The adjective " voluntary " is therefore superfluous as applied to social service ; social service is voluntary (so far as the organisers are concerned, though not necessarily in the case of all agents,) or it is nothing. They hold that the expression " public social service " was an unfortunate invention of Sir Bernard Mallet and is a misnomer, and that the original expression, "direct beneficiary assistance", was preferable.

But the term " statutory social service " is now too well established to be set aside. Moreover, to confine the term "social service" to that which is done by voluntary associations would land us in fresh difficulties. We should have to say that the maintenance and direction of a nursery school ceased to be social service at the moment when a local education authority took it over ; that a hospital almoner was engaged in social service if she worked in a voluntary hospital, but that she was not engaged in social service if she worked in a municipal hospital ; that a woman property manager was a social worker when she worked for a philanthropic trust, but that she was not a social worker when she transferred her services to a local authority. Such a distinction runs strongly against convenience as well as against common usage, though, as noted above, there is still a feeling that voluntary social service is more essentially social service than is statutory action of a similar kind.

It will be seen that there is not at present any one agreed definition of " social service " ; the expression is used in a number of senses. It would probably be impossible to frame an acceptable definition ; the best that can be done at present is to bear in mind the different connotations, and to be clear in what sense the term is used on any particular occasion. I think we have to admit, whether the admission be palatable or not, that there attaches at present to the term a strong presumption that a benefit is being conferred on those who are relatively less well off or relatively unprivileged in some way. Mutual aid societies pure and simple are not usually regarded as social service agencies, though they are so regarded when they are stimulated or subsidised or otherwise aided by a social service agency. Also they are often brought into consideration along with undoubted social service agencies when they share a field with them. It is also to be noted that agencies dealing with distress or defect or concerned with morally redemptive work are more certain of classification as social services than agencies which aim at the enrichment of normal life. Work of super-erogation of the privileged, aiming at relieving the distresses of the unprivileged, has been in the past the core of social service ; and it still is, though the proportion and the emphasis are altering in favour of common effort to enrich normal life. To discuss the ethics of social service would be to raise a large issue, which will not be treated at this point. But two remarks may be allowed, the first being that it is foolish to confound what might be, or what ought to be, with what is ; and the facts are that at present a great deal of service is rendered by the more privileged to the less privileged, and that this is generally re-garded as being typical social service ; the second being that it is probable that there will be always, in some form or other, the giving of help by the more fortunate to the less fortunate.

There still remains to be cleared up some confusion with regard to the term " voluntary." Fortunately it can be cleared up quickly. " Voluntary " may refer to an organisation or it may refer to a worker for that organisation. In the former case " voluntary " is contrasted with " statutory " ; in the latter case " voluntary " is contrasted with " paid." Statutory organisations employ salaried workers, and may also make use of the services of volunteers ; so also voluntary organisations employ, in most cases though not invariably, salaried workers, and they also make use of volunteers. There are therefore :—

Salaried workers for statutory organisations
Voluntary workers for statutory organisations
Salaried workers for voluntary organisations
Voluntary workers for voluntary organisations

It seems clear enough ; yet there is undoubtedly a good deal of confused thinking on the subject, which works out sometimes badly in action. The confusion arises from carrying over some of the idea of " voluntary " from the organisation to the worker, so that it is thought that the worker, like the promoters of the organisation, should be making a sacrifice of time and of money. Behind this there is a good deal of history. Whilst some of the early philanthropic associations employed salaried agents, yet social work as a profession did not arise until comparatively recently. The bulk of the work of the earlier charitable societies was done by unpaid amateurs. Occasionally an honorarium would be given, or some small stipend, but it was regarded as a supplement applicable to marginal cases of persons just not able to give their services. Or sometimes very small stipends would be paid to persons to do the more mechanical parts of the work. The presumption was that the income was of small importance ; that voluntary societies did not pay salaries in the ordinary sense of the word, and ought not to do so. This point of view has changed slowly, but still lingers ; it is being superseded by the view that the voluntary and philanthropic nature of an association gives that association no warrant to underpay those who serve it for wage or salary.

Chapter II

THE POSITION OF
VOLUNTARY SOCIAL SERVICES IN 1918

by
NORA MILNES

THE social services, whether voluntary or State, are in a large measure a reflection of the contemporary social philosophy, and therefore can only be rightly understood and properly estimated by those who have knowledge to see the services against the right background. When, therefore, voluntary social services held the field we know it was because the prevailing social philosophy was based on beliefs which supported the view that voluntary action was infinitely better for man and for society than was a large measure of State interference and State control. It is not, however, the purpose here to discuss prevailing philosophies, but the relation between these philosophies which seek ends and the means which are adopted at any age to remedy social ills and thus to achieve ends is so close, that to think of the one must mean to think of the other.

The historian of the future interpreting events in the first forty years of this century, will probably be no less intrigued in seeking explanations for the extraordinary growth of the British public social services during this period, than he will in finding reasons for the outbreak of the two Great Wars. He will not fail, however, to notice the close connection which exists between the two. War throws a searchlight on social evils which during peace may be but the study of a few interested individuals who have striven, perhaps for years, to arouse a wider interest in social wrongs, and have sought to bring home to the public in general that no country could hope to retain a pre-eminent position while social conditions, undermining social strength, were allowed to persist. Frequently, however, it is only the urgency caused by wars that awake the majority to the seriousness of the situation. In spite of other more immediate pre-occupations, social reforms are, during wartime, warmly debated and thus strange to say the war period becomes an era of

8

almost Utopian planning in the social sphere. Development
in the State social services in the first eighteen years of the
century gained impetus from the two wars of the period in
which this country was engaged, the Boer War and the Great
War—or as it is now more often called the first World War.
A few examples will serve to support this argument.

It is perhaps not sufficiently appreciated that the numerous
public services now concerned with the welfare of children were
largely the result of the revelations as to the poor physical condition of many who volunteered for service at the time of the
Boer War. While voluntary organisations had been at work
doing what they could to remedy undernourishment, from
which many children suffered as a result of the poverty of their
parents, it was largely the finding of the Committee set up to
enquire into the causes of the physical deterioration of the race
as revealed by the medical examination of recruits, that gave
us two pioneer acts, the one for the provision of meals for necessitous school children, the other for the medical inspection of
all children of school age. So also the Great War of 1914–18
with its tragic loss of adult life, tended to concentrate attention
on the need to preserve infant life ; and the various voluntary
organisations which had been active in measures aimed at reducing the unnecessarily high infant mortality rate, found much
support in the " Save the Children " campaign. This campaign in its turn helped to make widely known how great was
the unwarranted wastage of infant life, a wastage which, if it
were to be avoided, required the far-reaching all inclusive efforts
which can only be made available through State intervention.

These examples are noted in order to indicate one of the many
reasons for the rapid growth of our State social services, a
growth which needless to say has profoundly affected both the
field and the method of voluntary agencies. The development
is probably best appreciated by reference to the increase in
expenditure upon these services. Whereas at the beginning of
the century the public social services entailed an outlay of
19s. 2d. per head of the population, by 1920 the expenditure had
doubled, an increase which became even more rapid in the
inter-war period, in spite of, or maybe because of, the great
industrial depression of the thirties.[1] Quite obviously such a
development, though hastened by wars, could not have been

[1] Between 1900 and 1934 the net increase was sevenfold.

caused by wars. It shows an entire change in public opinion, a dissatisfaction with the action being taken by the State to remedy social ills, and equally a growing doubt as to the validity of the assumption which underlay so much voluntary effort, that the individual should be made to accept responsibility for his own failure. The propaganda of the Fabians, led by the Sidney Webbs, in making known the inadequacy of the Poor Law in dealing with distress and its causes, led to the appointment of the famous Commission which sat from 1905 to 1909, and producing as it did two divergent reports enabled the powers that be to postpone taking action. But if the Commission led to little being done at the moment it indicated as has been said, a growing dissatisfaction with things as they were, a dissatisfaction which was largely the cause of new measures of State assistance, the Old Age Pension Act of 1908 and the Insurance Acts of 1911.

Thus before 1914 the view was becoming more generally accepted that while voluntary agency can point the way, voluntary agency, having proved the need, must stand down in favour of something more all embracing. The discovery, for instance, that through child welfare schemes not only infant life could be saved but that unnecessary physical suffering among children could be reduced, was bound to lead to an insistence that measures which could have this desired result must be made available for all who needed them and not left to the whims of voluntary agency. While, therefore, there was this changing public opinion demanding more and more State action, those responsible for voluntary organisations believed that in consequence the days of voluntary effort were numbered ; for it was frequently asked, how could they hope to continue to raise the funds necessary for their existence when those who were able and ready to give would be the victims of high direct taxation, which taxation was in part due to the need to meet the expenditure entailed by new public social services.

Perhaps one of the most surprising and interesting features in in the development of our social services, has been the extraordinary power of survival of voluntary organisation in face of this threat. It seems obvious, therefore, that voluntary service must possess some special qualities which are generally recognised to be worth preserving, however much it may be agreed that State intervention is necessary. Maybe it is but another example of the British genius for compromise which enables the public and the voluntary services to develop side by side and in fact to seek and discover a basis of co-operation.

But if, with our growing experience of the State social Services, this compromise is recognised today as not merely a possibility, but as a desirable method of dealing with the social problems, such was not the attitude in the first years of the nineteenth century. Many of those working for voluntary organisations viewed with alarm the various proposals for further State intervention. To many, the introduction of school meals, old-age pensions, health and unemployment insurance were measures which, in their view, could but result in the demoralisation of individuals. All such measures, therefore, were strenuously opposed by those who sincerely believed that no society could continue to survive if the individuals forming that society ceased to be responsible for their own lives. Such measures, it was maintained, undermined individual responsibility and thus could only be regarded as a menace to society.

These were the views held by many who had the welfare of human beings so much at heart that they were ready to give, not merely their money, but also largely of their time to some field of voluntary social service. It would, in fact, be wrong to assume that those who opposed State intervention were indifferent to the terrible conditions and the no less terrible suffering which poverty in their time entailed, but they were convinced that voluntary agency could best deal with the situation, if for no other reason than that with voluntary agency none could claim assistance as a right, and all were encouraged to do their utmost to be self-supporting. Let men realise that they had a claim on society for maintenance unaccompanied by severe deterrents, then the idle and the vicious would be afforded an easy way of living, while those whose failure was due to weakness of character rather than any moral defect, would soon find life comparatively easy, and all incentive to effort on their part would be removed. In fact, it can be stated without gross exaggeration that at the beginning of the century, failure to be able to maintain oneself was regarded as being due to some fault in the individual rather than to any defects in the environment, and though the influence of environment was coming more and more to be appreciated as a determining factor, the prevailing idea seems to have been that a firmly defined line could be drawn between those whose failures might be attributed to ill luck (and they were the province of voluntary organisation) and those whose failure was due to character defects and for them there existed a Poor Law. A further corollary of such ideas was that the ill-luck category was not so large that voluntary organisation could not quite well meet all that was required, while the larger group of character failures were rightly those for whom a Poor Law based on the principle of less eligibility existed.

Today such an attitude seems so lacking in understanding and knowledge as to be almost barbarous, and it is only right again to insist that those working for the voluntary organisations, many of whom held these views, were themselves anything but inhuman. They were firmly convinced that State social services were based on a determinist philosophy, based that is on the assumption that man was a victim of his environment and could do little to control it, whereas they at least paid man the compliment of assuming that being above the animals and possessed of free will, he could largely mould the environment to his liking.

Here one sees the opposition between the two schools of thought—the new school growing up and winning more and more adherents, a school which stressed the power of environment in determining the conditions of a man's life; and the old school continuing to insist that these conditions were controllable by man. Nor must it be assumed that voluntary organisation failed to take cognisance of environment. The work of Octavia Hill in what is today called house property management, the skilled apprenticeship associations, the police court missionaries who were the forerunners of our probation system, to say nothing of the famous voluntary hospitals, all these and many others were engaged in tackling environmental forces ; but always from the standpoint of the individual. And while it is true that many social workers were coming to believe that only by State intervention could many of our social ills be remedied, more maintained that such State intervention should be resisted whenever possible.

These general introductory remarks must be borne in mind if the position of voluntary organisations at the close of the last war is properly to be appreciated. To understand the aims and methods of voluntary organisations, it is essential that they should be studied against the background of the constantly developing State function. To many the fact that during the last war there was no Ministry of Health, no Ministry of Labour until 1916 (though there were employment exchanges under the Board of Trade), no Assistance Board, comes somewhat as a surprise. How, it may be asked, was it possible to deal with the numerous emergencies brought about by the outbreak of war in the absence, for example, of an Assistance Board which in the last war carried on such varied functions. To recall that between 1914 and 1918 families of men who joined the services had to turn to voluntary agency, the S. & S.F.A., for maintenance until such time as their allowances came through, may serve to indicate the point which is being made. Before 1914 voluntaryism reigned more or less supreme. By 1918 its position was seriously assailed.[1]

As has already been indicated, before 1914 signs were not wanting that the tide had set towards State intervention, of which perhaps the most significant movement was to be seen in the passing of the Insurance Act of 1911, part II of which gave the world the first experiment ever made in compulsory insurance to meet certain types of unemployment. But generally speaking the position in 1914 was that a Poor Law, and a deterrent Poor Law at that, represented the province of State help, while voluntary organisations dealt with all hard cases.

So long then as State assistance was largely limited by a less eligible Poor Law system, so long was voluntary effort chiefly concerned with dealing with those persons who, through ill fortune, were lacking in the bare means by which to live. Relief societies of one sort and another were the main feature of voluntary organisation in the pre-1914 era. This is not to ignore the fact that many individuals and many societies were doing work of a different kind, as for instance the various settlements and those concerned with leisure activities of youth. Nevertheless many appreciated that first things must come first, and that it was little use providing for man's recreation if that man were without the means by which he could provide himself with food and shelter.

This then very briefly stated, was the background against

---

[1] Yet in the last war in spite of the remarkable growth of our State social services, so numerous were the gaps in State provision that the W.V.S. an entirely new voluntary organization, came into existence.

which voluntary social service must be seen, and we may now consider these services in more detail classifying them in accordance with the age groups of the population.

While by 1914 voluntary organisation no longer had to carry the entire burden of the sick, the aged, and the unemployed, nevertheless the amount of help obtainable under the State schemes was so slight that relief societies had still much to do. An examination of the case papers of these societies on which were recorded the circumstances of the applicants for assistance, would reveal that the main causes of distress still were unemployment, sickness, accident, old age, widowhood ; in fact, those causes of insecurity which the Beveridge Plan aims at remedying.

With our knowledge of the cost of the Beveridge Scheme, one may well ask how the voluntary services could have been expected to deal with the numerous families who were in need of assistance. They had to find some answer to the question— What was to be their policy ? Were they to give help to all who seemed deserving, or should they leave the majority to the tender mercies of the Poor Law. The former plan would have placed an intolerable burden on their funds if the families were to receive adequate assistance. Either they would have been compelled to have given inadequate doles which would have been unsatisfactory both to the giver and the recipient, or they would need to find some basis of selection by which they would be justified in helping some, and helping them adequately, while leaving the rest to State agency.

The C.O.S. which was the most famous of the relief agencies in the pre-1914 era, had since its foundation in 1869 set its face against indiscriminate charity.[1] It therefore adopted the latter of the two alternatives and by so doing faced the odium of all those who could see no reason why a man, finding himself in need through no fault of his own, should be refused help. But the C.O.S. maintained its ground in an attempt to establish scientific philanthropy—something of a contradiction in terms. To help adequately, and only to help those who by the assistance given would be restored to independence appeared to them the only rational plan to adopt. Since also it was a basic principle of the society that the family must be considered as a

---

[1] The full name of this Society was The Society for the Organisation of Charitable Relief and the Repression of Mendicity.

whole, they and other societies working on similar lines came to be known as Family Case Work Agencies.

The position then taken up by the C.O.S. was that voluntary organisation should be used to help the helpable ; that was the test. To discover which families fell into this category entailed elaborate enquiry, which was directed not so much to separate the sheep from the goats, as to discover which families could be helped to independence by voluntary agency. The enquiry into circumstances should in fact be regarded as an attempt at diagnosis, and the recording of the results on a case paper was part of a technique by which causes could be arrived at and thus remedy planned.

It was this enquiry system which became so repellent to many who disliked refusing any appeal for help, especially when, as might happen, after the enquiry had been carried out, the decision come to was that the family should be referred to the Poor Law. It was not surprising that the enemies of the C.O.S. maintained that it was a society which spent 19s. 11½d. out of every £1 subscribed in order to discover why the remaining ½d. should not be distributed among the applicants for assistance. Yet the use of case papers and the general recognition given today to the need for family case work in dealing with many social problems seems a somewhat belated recognition that C.O.S. methods were justified even if at the times of which we are writing, they appeared to be somewhat crudely applied.

As part also of the policy of helping adequately those people who after enquiry were considered suitable for voluntary assistance, every effort was made to avoid any overlap between voluntary and State agency and thus to prevent the risk of the one leaving too much to the other, so that the applicant for assistance found himself with his essential needs unprovided for.

With the introduction of Old Age Pensions and Insurance Schemes this sharp division of the field of service between State and voluntary, became untenable. The amount of assistance obtainable under the State scheme was generally inadequate, but was frequently available and accepted by many of those who formerly would have come within the province of voluntary agency. It was not long, therefore, before the boundary line between State and voluntary help became blurred and families who would have been considered suitable for voluntary assistance were now granted assistance to make more adequate what they could derive from the State scheme. No one could believe this to be a satisfactory state of affairs. It was the result of the somewhat tentative efforts made by the State in this new era of social reform, for certainly in 1911 it would have been impossible to get through the House a proposal comparable to the Beveridge Plan.

An Old Age Pension of 5s. per week was utterly inadequate for anyone who had no other source of income. Hundreds of elderly people, however, wishing to live out their lives in independence preferred semi-starvation on the pension to accepting food and shelter in a workhouse. Again it was impossible for voluntary societies to supplement the pensions of all who needed help. While some societies adopted a rule by which they distributed bags of coal and a few grocery tickets to eke out the meagre State pension, others like the C.O.S. organised regular supplementary pensions and from among their helpers obtained a visitor for each pensioner they assisted. But again this involved a policy of selection and meant saying " no " to many, and to many who probably had never earned sufficient to make any provision for their old age.

It must not be forgotten that the Old Age Pension was not obtainable below the age of seventy and numbers of men and women were unable to remain self-supporting until that age. Thus it frequently happened that those who were no longer able to work largely because younger people were preferred, were forced to seek the shelter of the workhouse where they remained until they arrived at the age when they were entitled to their pension. Then they discharged themselves, to enjoy their so-called freedom on 5s. per week, often with no home to go to and no furniture even if they could find shelter. For those who had sons or daughters who were ready to receive them the position was not so hopeless, but for the rest it meant a struggle against overwhelming odds, trailing from one charitable agency to another and finally, when all hope was dead, returning in misery to the workhouse. Surely before we criticise the voluntary agency for its failure to deal with these problems, we may ask ourselves in what way they really could have provided a solution. In fact, the only criticism that could be made was that knowing as they did from direct contact with the sufferers how great was the need, they so often opposed those who were urging State intervention in order to deal more humanely with these elderly victims of an imperfect social system.

But if the elderly could get 5s. per week from the State service, for the widow there was nothing but the Poor Law and many a family was broken up when the so-called bread-winner died too young to have made any provision for his family. Even had he lived to be a little older, with wages as they were, to make adequate provision for a young family was well nigh impossible. Here again the family case-work agencies sometimes helped until such time as the widow could obtain work, or the children between them could provide for the family needs.

Not the least of the difficulties with which the adult worker was faced arose from changes in the industrial system by which his particular type of work became redundant. The idea of rehabilitation is comparatively new and even with men disabled in the War of 1914–18 the provision to train them for new occupations was inadequate. Before 1914 it was not considered to be the duty of the State to provide the facilities by which men whose particular skill was no longer required, could be trained for work of a different kind. The writer well remembers the tragic position which arose for many when motor transport began to displace the horse-drawn vehicle. Numbers of " cabbys " found their livelihood gone with only a workhouse existence in front of them. Nor was it an easy problem for a voluntary agency to decide whether such a man would, if trained, be a success as a driver of a motor. While a " cabby " in a city like London at least had the advantage of knowing his streets, it did not follow that he who had made the horse his friend, could be made mechanically minded, and since reliability was hardly a feature of the early motor vehicle, some mechanical capacity was essential if a man was to be certain of employment as a driver of what later came to be known as a taxi. This was not, however, the end of the difficulties. The self-propelled vehicle was somewhat of a mystery and the idea of training a man for what was regarded as the nerve-racking occupation of driving a contrivance which might go at the dangerous speed of fourteen miles an hour was not to be lightly contemplated. Before deciding to help him to learn this new occupation, it was essential to have him thoroughly overhauled by a doctor to be sure that his nervous system could stand up to the strain. Added to all this, it has to be borne in mind that it took time to learn the new job and during that time the man and his family had to be provided with a means by which to live.

The voluntary agency which undertook work of this kind could obviously only assist the few, but their deeds should not be measured merely by the number helped. Anyone who chooses to study the old case papers of the C.O.S. might be surprised to find how many had been assisted in this way when society as a whole was blind to the problem. What is no less surprising is that faced with the individual man so obviously a victim of the industrial system, the C.O.S. did not sooner start a campaign to demand public assistance and training for all such people.

Changes in the industrial system invariably produce a long train of individual problems. The disappearance of the "cabby" was noticed by thousands, but how many also thought of the stableman whose lot was no less tragic. Progress hits hard the deserving and the undeserving alike and the public enjoying the fruits of this progress seldom stops to think of the tragedy which may be behind it. The " cabby " was seen, the stableman was unseen and the effects of industrial changes are such that the unseen is invariably greater than the seen.

The introduction of motor traffic was one cause of improvement in our roads and this improvement meant the disappearance of many an individual who was frequently a friend in need, the crossing-sweeper. What we may ask became of him who day in and day out, in all conditions of weather, cleared the mud away so that we might cross without too seriously soiling our shoes. A man whose earnings were likely to rise when the weather was at its worst but a man exposed as he was to all the rigours of the climate, making his very irregular and inadequate living, became frequently the victim of one of our national diseases.

These instances have been cited because they are examples of men who were the victims of changes observable to most of us in our daily lives, but in each such case that we saw one has to remember the numerous cases of individuals working in the factories who were faced with the same problem of finding that their skill was no longer required. Such men if unable themselves to acquire new skills, often turned to our voluntary organisations for help, which organisations in many cases were able to see them through hard times. For those working for these organisations, it was a heartbreaking business when they were compelled to admit that some man in whom they had been interested, could no longer be included in the category " helpable " and for his own sake must be recommended to apply to the Poor Law for assistance.

Sufficient has perhaps been said to indicate the range of voluntary organisation as it affected the adult man and woman in need. Let us now turn to consider voluntary agency in its relation to the problems of children.

For this purpose children may be classified as (a) infants, that is to say under one year old ; (b) toddlers, children between one year and compulsory school age ; (c) children of school age ; (d) children who have left school but are not old enough to be considered adult.

Throughout the period under consideration voluntary organisations were largely responsible for what must be regarded as one of the most important of our social services, recognising as they did the need for some special provision to promote the welfare both of the infant and of the child of pre-school age.

Infant Welfare Clinics staffed with trained doctors, sometimes with trained nurses and always with a large number of voluntary workers, were doing all they could to ensure infant health and to lessen the terribly high infant mortality rate which was found among certain sections of the community. To us it seems astounding that State intervention did not come sooner in an effort to give to the babe born of the poorer classes the same chance of survival that it would have had had it been born of parents belonging to one of the better-off sections of the community. Surely here was a case where State intervention was unquestionably justified since it would be directed to the elimination of an obvious inequality. The child born into surroundings typical of the life of an unskilled and casual worker was obviously starting with so serious a handicap that if he survived he might be left with his physical condition so undermined that he had little prospect of developing into a healthy adult.

Nevertheless, voluntary organisation, whose aim was to bring to the poorer mothers not only the elementary knowledge so necessary if their children were to be given a chance of health, but no less the facilities by which such knowledge could be translated into practice, were slow in urging the State to intervene, and it was only during the last war and in the early post-war period that there was any considerable development in the child welfare services as we know them today. The voluntary infant welfare centres were in many ways similar to the child welfare centres now so important a part of the Public Health Services but they were often less well equipped and were not sufficiently all-embracing and in many areas were non-existent. But if they had these defects they made up for many of them by the enthusiasm which they brought to their work, and the travelling exhibitions did much to spread throughout the country a knowledge first of the seriousness of the problem and secondly, the means by which it might be combated.

Interest in the baby led naturally to interest in the ex-baby and it was soon recognised that the good done for the infant might be rapidly undone when a new baby meant that a harassed mother had little time to devote to the needs of a child who having got over the first difficult period might be left to fend for itself. Provision for the toddler necessarily followed provision for the infant, and day nurseries, nursery schools, and kindergartens were included in the pioneer work of the voluntary societies who sometimes employed a staff of salaried and qualified workers, assisted by a number of volunteers, while in other cases the staff was entirely voluntary.

The passing of the Education (Provision of Meals) Act of 1906 and of the Education (Administration Provisions) Act of 1907, afforded an opportunity for co-operation between voluntary and Public Social Services of an entirely new kind and in some ways marks an epoch in the history both of the public and of the voluntary social services. Probably the best example of this form of co-operation is seen in the Care Committee system in the schools for which the London County Council is responsible. The fact that this system has survived two wars, which made so many calls on voluntary services, is sufficient to indicate that here is to be found something which may prove a most valuable form of co-operation between the State and the voluntary services. A plan was worked out for the administration of the 1906 and 1907 Acts which sought to combine the advantages both of State and of voluntary action.

The area for which the London County Council was responsible was divided into districts and for each district a central
office staffed with a District Organiser, Assistant Organisers and
Clerks was established. These organisers were responsible for
the administration of these Acts in their district, but a general
plan to which they were expected to work was laid down.
Each school was to have its voluntary Care Committee which
in many cases would carry on work already done by voluntary
agencies. In fact the Secretary of many of these Committees
who was unpaid, was often and whenever possible, drawn from
the voluntary workers who had already interested themselves
in the welfare of school children. Obviously with so extensive
a plan it became necessary to attract new voluntary workers
and it was one of the many duties of the District Organiser to
initiate the new volunteer into the functions of the school Care
Committee. The members of these Committees visited parents,
collected information about the economic circumstances of
parents whose children appeared to need free meals, assessed
contributions from those parents who were in a position to pay
something towards the cost, and paid follow-up visits after
school medical inspection in order to ensure that the advice of
the doctors was being carried out. In fact, on the health side,
the Committee was engaged in a great educational crusade
bringing into the homes of many parents a knowledge of what
steps they must take to enable their children to grow into
healthy adults.

Obviously had the London County Council relied on its
salaried staff the task would have been an impossible one except
at a very heavy cost, but by inviting the co-operation of the
voluntary worker and giving to that voluntary worker a share
in responsibility, numbers of children could be dealt with individually in a manner impossible with a State scheme dependent entirely on its paid staff. Since the work was largely
educational its success would depend on the opportunity the
worker had of really getting to know the families and of being
recognised by them as a friend whose advice was worth seeking.
For this it is essential that no one worker should be expected
to carry a heavy case load.

So successful has been the Care Committee system in London
that one is only surprised that similar plans have not been more
generally followed in other areas. It may be that the very size

of London calls for a special type of organisation and that smaller cities can achieve the same ends in other ways. Admittedly as a plan it has its weaknesses, as for instance the difficulty of finding a sufficient number of volunteers able and ready to give regular service in an area which is far from what is commonly described as " a good residential part." But with our present-day plans for development in social security, it would seem that this type of co-operation between State and voluntary agency should be further developed since it makes possible that personal touch, the absence of which is so frequently recognised as one of the chief defects of State action. That the personal touch must be free of all taint of patronage goes without saying and to be sure that this will be so is far from easy. In fact, it seems probable that one of the chief reasons why the Care Committee system is not more widely used is the fear on the part of many that it may tend to perpetuate patronage, so characteristic of many voluntary services and so loathed by those who have to suffer it.

The Care Committee dealing as it did with the child of school age, became a centre from which much might be done to assist the school leaver in choosing his future work and getting embarked upon a career. From care to after-care was a natural progression. With the coming of the Juvenile Advisory Committee and the Juvenile Labour Exchange the after-care became another example of co-operation between the State and voluntary service. Often parents anxious to do their best for their children had little knowledge how to proceed especially when a child wished to branch out in a line quite new to his parents. To be able to talk all this over with a member of the Care Committee who perhaps had been visiting the family over a period of years, was a real comfort to many a parent. The Care Committee visitor might not be an expert on jobs, but she often knew to whom to turn to get the necessary information and many a parent has valued the opportunity of thrashing out the whole question with someone he knew and thrashing it out in his own home instead of in the somewhat unfriendly linoleum atmosphere of many official organisations.

Many a child expressed a wish to enter a trade which entailed not only an expensive apprenticeship, but often meant low earnings for a number of years. Here again the Care Committee worker would assist with encouragement and do all that was possible to deter parents from seeking for their children the highest possible wage at the earliest possible age. If a child had really the ability to train for a skilled job the apprenticeship he would have to serve might entail the payment of a premium beyond the parents' ability to meet. Once again voluntaryism with its skilled apprenticeship associations, stepped into the breach long before such type of assistance could be obtained through State agency. But while these voluntary agencies could claim to have started many a lad who otherwise might have drifted into a blind-alley job, the numbers they helped were pitifully small compared with the number who required guidance and assistance.

It is quite impossible in a short review of this nature, to deal with all the numerous voluntary agencies which were concerned with children. Naturally and rightly the child has always had a special appeal to those who are moved with a desire to perform some social service. But mention must be made of the organisations which provided homes for the orphans and for other children needing care and protection. While some of these homes were sadly inadequate, strangely unimaginative as to the needs of a child deprived of the natural affection of its parents, others were doing all they could to keep up with the times and certainly were providing as good a substitute as possible for home life. To name any may be invidious but there probably is good reason why Dr. Barnardos has attained world-wide fame. The reason probably is that it has attempted to cast old-fashioned ideas and to incorporate as far as possible the best teachings in the requirements of the child. But it must be recognised that all such institutions are faced with special problems, dealing as they do with many who have a bad heredity, and have known and been influenced by an environment which can only be described as evil. While others of the little inmates are merely the children of ill-luck the attempt to cope with them all together, the lack of facilities for classification, even if a basis of just classification could be arrived at, produces bewildering problems.

Here again there is much to be said for retaining voluntary action for if there is one thing these children require it is individual interest. To keep homes comparatively small is essential from the point of view of the welfare of the child and

B

this is no less true of children in such institutions because they have no one to care for them than it is of children who have got out of control and joined the ranks of young delinquents.

In regard to the latter, strides have been made since many " reformatory " schools have become " approved " schools, approved, that is, by the Home Office as falling in with certain required standards. Such schools can obtain grants through the Home Office and thus while retaining a large measure of independence are helped to bring their buildings more in accordance with modern ideas and to pay salaries which should attract a staff properly qualified for the work. But the word " should " has been used with intent. The whole question of finding suitable staff for these institutions remains somewhat baffling and while much concern is today felt in regard to our responsibilities towards children in these institutions, many are still far from assured that in all homes the children are getting the type of care which will enable them to develop into adults with a proper sense for the rules of society. If this is true today it was no less true in 1918 when the plea could always be put forth that the war had stopped building and that such Institutions must wait their turn since there were more pressing needs. On the other hand some of the management committees of these schools, anxious to introduce improvements, found that they were hampered by too high costs, insufficient financial support and much red tape. Others, however, suffered from what is frequently a weakness of voluntary organisation—an undue sensitiveness to criticism and the feeling that their excellent and pioneer work was unappreciated. All voluntary organisations and all social services should aim at destroying the need for their existence for since such services are dealing with social ills their success should be judged by the rapidity with which the need for them dies. Much of the objection to criticism arises from their failure to appreciate this fact.

A further example of the manner in which voluntary agency has so frequently filled in a gap in the State services is seen in their work for invalid children. The National Health Insurance Act of 1911 provided no benefits for the children of an insured man, with the result that the serious illness of a child involving long and specialised treatment was more than many could afford out of their wages. It was here that the Invalid Children's Aid Association stepped in and arranged convalescence or long periods of stay in the country with families well known to them, helped in the provision of invalid chairs and surgical appliances, and frequently collected from the parents small weekly sums which were banked so as to build reserves ready to meet the cost of the numerous repairs which the surgical instruments required. A State Medical Service will have to go far before the need for such voluntary services as this ceases to exist.

Before leaving this review of the voluntary services, mention must be made of their pioneer work in assisting both the physically and mentally disabled. Institutions for the training of the blind and the deaf were certainly not the least important of the activities carried on by voluntary organisations and these preceded any provision made by the State for the education of children thus handicapped. But even if the entire care of the blind and the deaf during the school ages became the province of the State there would remain that special type of service so important with the handicapped, the placing of them in employment, the maintaining of their hopes when, as must frequently happen, they find themselves left on one side by employers who feel they cannot undertake the responsibility of employing those who may so easily become a liability. If after-care is needed for the normal child it is needed tenfold for those who are outside the normal group.

Mention of the blind and the deaf calls attention to the cripples and also to the mentally defectives. It is perhaps the last who produce the most difficult problem and one with which voluntary agency showed great courage in tackling. It would be beyond the purpose of this chapter to enter into all the special difficulties concerned with the problems of mental deficiency. These are admirably set out in the Faversham Report on the Voluntary Mental Health Services. But the Mental Welfare Association of the pre-1914 era had so well established itself as an authority on these problems and on the means of dealing with them, that after the passing of the Mental Deficiency Act of 1913 the Association was given a special type of recognition by the Board of Control. The various County Welfare Associations of this voluntary body were associated with the State schemes in making provision both for the defectives and for the borderline cases.

.   .   .   .   .   .

The original idea of this chapter was that it should give a picture of the voluntary social services as they were in 1918. But 1918, or in fact any particular year, is not easy to consider when thinking in terms of change. It therefore appeared better to try to produce a sketch of the voluntary services in the first eighteen years of the twentieth century, indicating the kind of change which was being brought about as a consequence of the altered idea of the responsibility of the State for the welfare of its members.

Although a number of new ministries was established in the war years[1] there was, during that period, comparatively slight development in the public social services. An extension of the employment insurance scheme to cover munition workers appears today to have been a singularly inadequate and unimaginative measure. Men on demobilisation qualified for out-of-work donations which it was hoped would tide them over short periods if they were unable quickly to obtain employment. Not until 1920 was there any considerable development in the scope of the Unemployment Insurance Act. Voluntary organisations were called upon, therefore, to fill the numerous gaps in State provision just as the same voluntary organisations dealt with cases of men who had suffered war injury or shell shock and were unable to find suitable employment when passed by the medical boards as fit for work. That the medical boards were right in signing up such men as fit for employment need not be questioned but that many of these men needed further assistance in what today would be described as rehabilitation is no less true. Without the voluntary organisations many would have drifted till they had become social wrecks.

During the war years numerous special committees were " exploring " the field of social needs, and " adumbrating " schemes, two words which became anathema to those who were painfully alive to the need for immediate action. In the future it will probably seem that the State social services grew with remarkable rapidity. To those trying to cope with the frequently insoluble problems of families whose life had come so near disaster as a consequence of the war, it appeared that organised State efforts of assistance were chiefly remarkable for the slowness with which they came into being.

[1] This refers to the years 1914–18.

Yet one fundamental change was taking place : a growing degree of co-operation between the voluntary and the State social services and the recognition of the need to establish some kind of machinery which would facilitate this new partnership. The setting-up of the National Council of Social Service will be dealt with elsewhere in this volume and therefore need not be further considered here, although it has probably proved one of the most important developments in the voluntary services of the war period.

Finally then, it may be said that the year 1918 viewed from the year 1945, was a year of transition. To those living and working in 1918 the movements of the transition were hardly visible. It was not, in fact, until the industrial depressions of the twenties and thirties were upon us that the changes which had been gradually taking place in the fields and methods of the voluntary services became apparent.

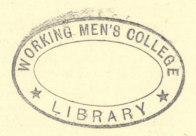

Chapter III

VOLUNTARY SOCIAL SERVICES IN URBAN AREAS

by

HILDA JENNINGS

OTHER chapters of this book contain accounts of some of the main types of voluntary social services. Here, it is intended only to suggest briefly certain common lines of development and to show how these general trends have been brought about. How far, in fact, are the characteristics of different types of service determined by their historical origin ? Are they capable of change with changing conditions and social ideas ? What has been the interaction between them and the public social services which have grown up alongside of them ? Above all, is there any permanent principle which animates them and will continue to find expression ? It is only by attempting to throw light on these questions that it is possible to see any meaning in what at first sight appears to be a bewildering medley of agencies, often having different, or even contradictory, aims and methods.

In some sense the impulse which moves men to the service of their fellows is always philanthropy. In different ages, the love of man for man has been ascribed to different causes. It may be attributed to a common membership of a divine family, involving the kind of all-pervading relationship recognized in Christianity. It can be thought of as social in origin and explained as an expression of the social conscience and sense of social obligation. Often the two conceptions are united in the same individual. Nevertheless, during the present century, those organised social services, which are not directly promoted by institutional religion, have tended to shift the emphasis of their appeal from the super-social to the social plane. It is a corollary of this, that personal and financial aid has been extended far beyond the direct service of the individual and his family. There is very little emotional appeal to the numerous busy men and women who give, not only subscriptions, but a considerable amount of time, as members of such bodies as

28

Councils of Social Service or other co-ordinating agencies. This change in what are, at any rate, the avowed objects of the social services must be to some extent reflected in the nature of their work.

The development of voluntary services even in urban areas, has been very unequal. Even substantial towns are often lacking in some recognized types. Some, indeed, have very few of the facilities which social workers in the great cities take for granted. There are County Boroughs and Boroughs, for instance, which are devoid of organized case-work societies, and many other large areas where both old-established and newer types of facility are lacking. On the other hand, the initiative and specialized interests of a few local residents may easily lead to the promotion of a pioneer service in an area with comparatively few other agencies. Sometimes an acute local problem of a particular kind leads to an experiment, which is later found to have a wider application. This haphazard and partial distribution of services is a natural result of dependence on local initiative and self-support. As will be seen later, the invention of new forms of organization is gradually leading to more equal and widespread provision.

The scope and general line of development of voluntary social services are most easily discerned if they are studied where they are most concentrated, in the great cities which are the natural focal points for surrounding districts and smaller towns. Especially in the older cities of this type, the aggregation of population had similar results in the fields of social service to those brought about in the sphere of education by the massing of children in the early Board Schools, or, in another field, by the concentration of unemployed men in the Special Areas. Misfortunes which in a small community might be looked upon as due to exceptional causes, began to be seen as part of a large-scale problem. Individual assistance to a neighbour or dependant in distress gave place to concerted effort and philanthropy began to express itself through organized social services.

In the great cities there can be seen at one and the same time old-established charities founded by individual benefactors ; the great network of voluntary hospitals ; a number of agencies dating from the time when the provision for material needs—blankets, surgical instruments, free meals, and clothing or monetary assistance—was the most obvious outlet for benevolence ; organised services of the family case-work and medico-social kind ; services for children and adolescents, some of which arose at a time when " slum " conditions and the accompanying moral degradation made it imperative for philanthropists to keep young people " off the streets," and others which, like the Scouts and Guides and the present-day boys' and girls' clubs, were founded when the conception of educating for citizenship had ousted the old ideas. There are settlements and social centres, which cater for educational and leisure-time interests, but often had their origin in days when the cleavage between the East and West ends of the cities and the difference in their amenities were even more pronounced than they are to-day. There are the established branches of the Workers' Educational Association, and the pre-war examples of Community Centres, as well as other bodies providing leisure-time facilities. In addition to all these field services are a growing number of promoting and co-ordinating bodies.

Nor can it be assumed that agencies ostensibly for the same purpose necessarily date from the same period, or that the date of their origin must determine their outlook and methods. All that can be said is that from a wide survey there tend to emerge distinctions between the types of service, the initiation of which has been the characteristic expression of different periods. From this point of view, the various kinds of social agency can be looked on as tide-marks in the ebb and flow of social thought as it plays on changing social and economic conditions. It is worth while, therefore, to divide the agencies which exist to-day into the types which first sprang up in the period of individual benevolence ; in the age of organised charity dating from 1869 ; in the post-1918 era, when the relief of distress became increasingly the business of the various departments of public service ; and in the period beginning with the second war.

The endowed charities, dating from the age of individual philanthropy, are necessarily the least susceptible of change and development. The pious founders, who perpetuated them through their wills or by the formation of Trusts, sometimes, indeed, impaired their usefulness in a changed society by laying down too rigid conditions. It is not always easy to find a one-legged tailor born in a certain parish, nor a sea captain's spinster daughter who wants to live in an almshouse. Never-theless, many of the municipal and parochial charities, the almshouses, annuities, and dispensaries with their visiting doctors, continue to meet real needs. Indeed, the philan-thropic impulse, providing for the kind of emergency of which the donor had first-hand knowledge, may point the way to satisfy desires which seem to be inherent in human nature, where large-scale and impersonalised services fail.

Up to the end of the 1914–18 War, the typical voluntary social services were the case-work agencies. The original aim of the London Charity Organisation Society and its provincial fellow-societies was to mobilise philanthropic effort so that it might be most effective in restoring to self-reliance and self-sufficiency families which had failed in their economic function. They re-acted strongly against the danger to the existing social structure and *laissez-faire* doctrines, which they considered inher-ent in the multiplicity of isolated charities. Thus, they were early pioneers in the movement towards co-ordination, which other bodies carried into wider fields of social service at a later date. They were also fertile in ideas and bold in experiment, and many new types of social service, such as that of the Hospital Almoners, owed their initiation to them. Later still, newer case-work services were able to help the parent family case-work societies to adapt themselves to ideas and methods more suited to the needs of a society organised as a social service state.

Social workers and social reformers are concerned with the same economic conditions and social phenomena, and naturally follow parallel lines of thought and action. In the present century, the works of supererogation of the few have been trans-formed by an active social conscience into the common obliga-tions of the whole body of citizens. The growth of the public social services was both influenced by the pioneer voluntary services and reacted on their thought and work.

It follows that forms of voluntary service initiated since 1918 have been mainly in other fields than that of material relief. A quickening of the sense of social obligation in the general public was brought about by the 1914–18 war. There was a natural desire to build up a society which should be worthy of the ideals and sacrifices made by those who had fought in it. The instinctive reaction of the ordinary citizen was expressed

B*

in such slogans as " Homes for Heroes," and in the general determination that ex-service men should not be forced to have recourse to the Poor Law. Reconstruction groups and societies, such as C.O.P.E.C., put forward schemes which involved public planning and action. Thus, when the great depression came, although clothing depots and free meal centres still afforded outlet for some philanthropy, it was recognised that the provision of basic material needs was the business of the State. The voluntary social services were free to turn their attention to the psychological and personal effects of unemployment. It was in the attempt to mitigate these that their main contribution was made.

Often, as in the coalfields distress work of the Society of Friends, which included not only relief but allotments schemes, and experiments in industry and subsistence production, a strong religious motive persisted. The most widespread voluntary organization in the field of unemployment was, however, that of the Unemployed Men's Clubs. The origin and methods of promotion of these were significant of another trend of development.

National as opposed to local responsibility was by then covering a wider field both in public and voluntary social service. On the public side there were already a national service of Employment Exchanges, national Old Age Pensions, and national Insurance Schemes both for sickness and unemployment. Long-term unemployment, with its obvious origin in causes beyond individual or local control, brought into being the Unemployment Assistance Board and thus removed persons who were the victims of long-term unemployment from the local Poor Law.

The voluntary social services were influenced by the same movement of thought to fit current conditions ; they realized also the need to devise effective machinery through which to put forward suggestions and programmes to the powerful Government Departments. Hence, while occasionally the local pride and tradition of some of the large cities brought into being a wholly independent unemployed welfare service, the National Council of Social Service played the main part in initiating clubs and centres throughout the country. It also successfully negotiated with the departments for grants in aid of the new service, and fortified by these, began to emulate the public authorities in an attempt to secure comprehensive service.

In other fields of social work also, such as the youth movements, there was a swift growth of national co-ordinating or promoting bodies, with financial aid sometimes from the big charitable Trusts, and sometimes from public funds. The Government Department with its large administrative staff and travelling inspectors, now had its counterpart in the headquarters and organisers of the National Association. The local and piecemeal voluntary services in many fields were stimulated by an army of travelling officers ; grant-aid was made the incentive to fill in gaps in provision and to improve standards of efficiency. The Government Departments' circulars to Local Authorities found their counterpart in pamphlets, circulars, and questionnaires, issued from the national headquarters to affiliated local voluntary bodies.

One result of this tendency was that the individual supporter of the National Association became yet further removed from the persons who ultimately benefited by his goodwill. Another was that the appeal had to be so broad-based that the common social obligation to fellow citizens was emphasized rather than the religious bond, the recognition of which varied from individual to individual.

The tide was now flowing so swiftly in the direction of public provision that the responsibilities and powers assumed by Government Departments still left the Local Authorities with an increasing volume of services to administer. There was a consequent movement towards larger areas of local government and finance. The work and influence of the County Borough Councils, in particular, grew rapidly, as one new public service after another was provided for by Act of Parliament and fell to the Local Authorities to implement. On the voluntary side, locally as well as nationally, there was a corresponding incentive to provide a mouthpiece for ideas and, if necessary, an agency for negotiating with the elected public representatives. Local Councils of Social Service were initiated or greatly developed their work in a number of urban areas. Local Associations of District Nursing Committees, of Boys' and Girls' Clubs, and of other specialised voluntary services, grew in effectiveness and range of work.

Wherever there was a group of voluntary services with

similar aims and functions, the tendency was to form local associations, often affiliated to national bodies, in order to give expression to a particular point of view or interest and to plan for comprehensive service in the local sphere. National and local voluntary finances began to intersect, as the local associations, whether nationally or locally grant-aided or wholly dependent on local subscribers and the support of affiliated units, were called upon to raise money for national purposes.

The public social services not only co-operated with and aided the voluntary agencies, they actually created new problems which called for voluntary pioneer work. The acute apprehension of the social evil of poverty and unequal opportunity in an age of ever-increasing productive capacity led to an unbalanced view of men's needs. It seemed to social reformers, and for a time to social workers also, that the provision of a high standard of living, of healthy physical environment and of security against the economic effects of the common contingencies of life, were all-important.

The assumption of responsibility in the material sphere by the State released the volunteers from the burden of obsession with poverty. Soon they were able to lead the way to new forms of service, such as psychiatric social work, and to pioneer in new institutions of the case-work type, such as child guidance and later marriage guidance clinics, where social adaptation was the aim. In such new forms of service there was at least an attempt to integrate the sciences in the service of the individual, and to give to the different sides of his nature their due weight.

It was the large-scale rehousing of the working population which perhaps did most to convince public authorities and social workers that physical and economic welfare were only part of the necessary make-up of a healthy society. Housing enthusiasts had failed to observe that even the under-privileged slum-dwellers had created for themselves compensatory features which played a highly important part in their lives. Amid the overcrowded and sordid streets, in the homes huddled together, in the little shops and favourite public-houses, as well as in churches, chapels, co-operative guilds, and Friendly Societies, had grown up an intimate and deeply rooted society with well-established traditions and standards and a wealth of neighbourhood and family associations. The enthusiasts for fresh air, open spaces and houses with bathrooms and gardens were painfully surprised to find that other non-material values did not automatically spring up among them.

The residential settlements had already spread to most of the big cities in this country and to America as well as to the Continent. Their work had been based on the perception of the social evil of the segregation of the privileged and un-privileged in one-class areas and on the need to provide for a diversity of people and experience in every neighbourhood, as well as the necessary facilities for social intercourse and the following up of awakened interests.

Yet the new housing schemes followed the old tradition, and added to its evils a wholesale uprooting and transplantation of large numbers of families. It was not a matter for surprise, therefore, that the word " Community " took on a new sig-nificance, and that a deliberate attempt was made to foster the neighbourhood values which had slowly grown up in the old areas. The Community Centre movement was promoted eagerly, both by the National Council of Social Service, by voluntary groups in different localities, and by some local authorities. The war prevented its development. It has now been officially sponsored by the Ministry of Education and it seems probable that the possibility of obtaining grants, both from national services for capital expenditure and from the local authority for maintenance and staffing, may once again stimulate an extension of voluntary social service.

The provision of community or neighbourhood centres and the promotion of local Neighbourhood Associations is inti-mately connected with the use of leisure. The Unemployed Men's Centres were handicapped in their experiments by the fact that they were not catering for true leisure, but for persons suffering from enforced idleness. Spontaneous groups, sports associations, dramatic and literary or debating societies, either in isolation or fostered by churches, chapels or co-operative societies, have been initiated and organised by their own members on mutual-aid lines. The organised social services have so far done relatively little to cater for the leisure-time needs of adults outside the realm of formal education. Excep-tions to this are to be found in some of the settlements, which provide Neighbourhood Centres with varied and informal pro-grammes, the Townswomen's Guilds, and the Family Clubs,

and in the widespread facilities provided by the Y.M.C.A. and
Y.W.C.A.

Adult education, whether provided by the Local Education
Authorities through evening institutes and technical colleges, or
by the Workers' Educational Association and extra-mural
departments of the universities, has appealed to the self-
selected minority. It is easy to account for this failure of the
majority to participate in it by the early school-leaving age and
by long working hours. Since the principle of free choice is
inherent in the conception of leisure, the voluntary organisations may have a special part to play in implementing the provisions of the 1944 Education Act. New forms of voluntary
service and a new approach may be needed to help the un-
touched majority to develop creative interests through free
association and a further measure of mutual aid.

The war, while it inevitably postponed certain developments
which seemed about to take place at its outbreak, strengthened
other existing tendencies in the public and voluntary social
services. In particular, the field of partnership between them
was widened. There continued also the parallel movements of
ever-increasing provision by the State, and the growth of co-
ordinating machinery to enable the voluntary service to meet
the national and local authorities on less unequal terms.

Wartime emergencies were so numerous and had to be met
so swiftly that the State not only called on the ordinary citizen
to undertake air-raid precautions and fire-prevention duties,
and to man rest centres for homeless persons, but also was glad
to foster newly organized voluntary services, such as the
Citizens' Advice Bureaux and Women's Voluntary Services.
Characteristically, these were designed to cover the nation-
wide field and embraced and catered for members of society
irrespective of their economic status. As in the case of the
Unemployed Men's Clubs, the National Council of Social
Service was the main body which was concerned to secure a
comprehensive service of bureaux and was the channel through
which government aid was secured. The need to secure
immediate and official information on the ever-growing
volume of regulations and official provision meant that contact
had to be more continuous and intimate than in previous
experiments. Possibly this accounted in part for the speed
with which the State set up a parallel public service in the

Resettlement Advice Centres, officially launched after only five years of pioneer voluntary experiment on similar lines. At present the two services function side by side and both seem to be meeting needs and to be largely used by the public. It is interesting also that in the Housewives' Service, the W.V.S. created an organisation in which there was no distinction of privilege between the helper and the helped, but rather a new kind of mutual aid incorporated in a social service setting.

For other personal services, the State called on existing voluntary agencies and their workers. The old and new case-work services found themselves required to deal with countless problems arising out of evacuation and billeting. The difficulty of meeting individual needs by mass provision of a uniform kind, and the social problems arising from the failure to do so, were more clearly demonstrated than ever before. At the same time, such studies as *Our Towns* undertaken by the Women's Public Welfare group sponsored by the National Council of Social Service, and the Cambridge Evacuation Survey, revealed how much still remained to be done in making social service effective and relating it to individual needs and standards of living. As a result of the *Service of Youth* circular issued by the Board of Education soon after the outbreak of war, partnership between voluntary agencies and public authorities dealing with the needs of young people was made more effective and far-reaching. The principle of co-ordination received practical recognition, not only in the voluntary sphere but also over the whole field shared by public and voluntary services. The voluntary youth organisations were given a voice in the distribution of grant-aid and the direct expenditure of public funds, this time mainly from the local authority's purse and without the intervention of the national voluntary bodies. Among the many interesting points in these developments is the fact that the religious bodies, even though given direct representation on the Youth Committees, themselves set up co-ordinating and promoting bodies whose function it was to ensure that their special point of view and aims found practical expression.

The representatives of the voluntary agencies on the local Youth Committees, or on some other co-ordinating committees often maintained first-hand contact with organisations doing the actual field work. Their personal knowledge of field problems and of individual young people thus served to keep their human sympathies alive, and to give meaning and understanding to their Youth Committee work.

The great new projects put forward during the war in the fields of education, public health, social security through a comprehensive insurance scheme, and the provision of National Assistance, point the way to a far wider measure of national provision and influence in the public services. On the other hand, the initiation of the Service of Youth and, more recently, the definition of policy with regard to Community Centres, seem to indicate that there may be a movement to restore to the local authorities responsibilities and powers which the Physical Training and Recreation Act had tended to divert from them. The recent pronouncement of the Ministry of Health with regard to grant-aid to Citizens' Advice Bureaux also involves consultation between voluntary and public bodies at the local level. Such consultation and mutual appreciation can more easily be made intimate and continuous in the large urban areas than in scattered rural areas. It may lead to the transfer of some of the functions of the national voluntary associations to co-ordinating agencies whose boundaries are co-terminous with those of the grant-aiding local authorities.

If the proposals now under consideration for ensuring comprehensive services, paid for by all and intended to be used by all, materialise, the field of privilege will necessarily shrink in the personal as well as in the economic sphere. In what ways, then, can it be expected that the philanthropic impulse or social conscience will find expression? Even the brief and scanty allusion made here to the diversity of voluntary social services, which function where large numbers of people are gathered together in our great cities, serves to indicate the persistence of the impulse. For the most part, too, the main voluntary agencies have shown the capacity to adapt themselves to new ideas and conditions, and to devise new machinery to fit those conditions. It is impossible to determine in what proportions personal philanthropy, humanitarianism, religious motives, social conscience and the desire to rationalise or to find outlet for organising ability, make up the impulse to works of supererogation. Often several of these motives are present in one individual, and the supporters of the same agency may be actuated by different motives. We can only say that a glimpse of the history of voluntary social services in the great cities over the last century shows no failure to respond to the call to service. We can be sure that the ideal still looms ahead and that there is still room for adventure in the service of mankind.

Chapter IV

SOCIAL SERVICE WITH THE UNEMPLOYED

by

HENRY A. MESS

UNEMPLOYMENT is far from being a new phenomenon, but it took on some new features in the period between the two wars. In the first place it was better recorded than in the past, since the majority of the unemployed were receiving payments from the State or from local authorities. It was on a very large scale. We have no accurate records of the volume of unemployment in years before 1914, but it is doubtful whether it ever reached the high level of post-war years. It had the feature of being very uneven in local incidence, being very acute in the heavy industries areas. There was the new feature that the bare livelihood of the workers and of their families was provided by the State, so that philanthropy did not have to attempt to deal with a task which would have been hopelessly beyond its strength. And there was more social conscience about unemployment than there had been in the past.

The causes of the post-war unemployment are well known. The heavy industries had been swollen during the war for war purposes ; after the war the demand for their products dropped but many of those who had come into them stayed on in their districts. Foreign countries, deprived during the war of access to British supplies, had in many cases developed their own supplies or alternatives. Moreover they were impoverished, and therefore they were bad buyers. Finally, a series of disastrous labour conflicts did much harm to this country in foreign markets.

It was in the heavy industry districts, therefore, in the coalfields and in the shipyard and steel smelting areas, that distress developed first and most acutely. At a later date Lancashire and its cotton industry went the same dismal road. And after the American crash of 1929 practically the whole of the country was involved. How long and how severe unemployment was in some areas can be illustrated by a few facts. In Jarrow the percentage of insurable men out of work did not fall below 30 between 1921 and 1931, and at one time it was as high as 89. In 1935 there were close on 2,000,000 men unemployed at one time ; and since many men passed in and out of employment, far more than 2,000,000 men experienced unemployment during that year. Of these men 400,000 had been out of work continuously for a whole year, and of these 400,000 no fewer than 50,000 had been out of work continuously for four years.

The perception of unemployment and the response to the need were curiously tardy and uneven. For several years after 1921 the country lived in a state of false hope ; the turn of the tide was continually expected. It was about 1925 that a realisation began to come that this was no ordinary trade depression, no phase of a normal trade cycle, but that this country had come into a new industrial situation from which it would require great efforts to extricate it. The disastrous year 1926, with its coal stoppage and its general strike, made many persons realise the gravity of the situation ; and it was after 1926 that the unemployed began to migrate in considerable numbers. From 1926 to 1931 there was some slight recovery, but in 1931 the tidal wave of trade depression which had begun in America spread over this country, and the numbers of the unemployed rose steeply.

It was after the 1926 coal strike that there began those efforts to help the unemployed which developed into such a big movement. A group of Quakers founded a settlement at Maes-Yr-Haf in the Rhondda Valley ; another group of Quakers settled down in the town of Bryn Mawr. At Lincoln the local W.E.A. founded a club and workshop for its un-employed members. In 1927 the Coalfields Distress Fund was launched by the Lord Mayor of London ; it amounted in all to nearly £2,000,000. The Coalfields Distress Fund distributed considerable sums of money in cash, made gifts in kind, and spent a certain amount of money in encouraging music and drama. It is a curious fact that at this time it was almost impossible to get help for the shipyard towns, so obsessed was the public by the misery of the coalfields; yet the unemploy-ment in Jarrow was already as high as that in any mining town.

The example of starting clubs for unemployed men was fol-lowed rather slowly. In 1933 an immense impetus was given to it by an Albert Hall meeting, organised by the National Council of Social Service, at which the Prince of Wales spoke. Shortly afterwards the Prince of Wales started on a series of tours of the heavily hit areas. Towards the end of the same year the Government announced an experimental grant of £20,000, a sum to be much exceeded before long, for social work to help the unemployed ; and it requested the National Council of Social Service to undertake the general direction and supervision of such work. Before long clubs were springing up all over the country, and by 1935 there were said to be 400 of them in existence with a total membership of 250,000 persons.

Consider the necessity for some such provision. When trade was good, the men who were now unemployed had been busy all day in buildings provided by their employers, working on materials provided by the employers at tasks prescribed by the employers ; and all their working hours were organised and supervised by the employers. From all this they were ejected to be placeless, toolless, workless, left suddenly to manage their own lives, with no obvious purpose and with no facilities. They were not wanted in their cramped homes during the day time. They hung about streets, crowded the reading rooms of public libraries, poured into any kind of shelter, if they could find it. There were buildings where you could see two or three hundred shabby and dispirited men sitting at rough wooden tables, shuffling greasy cards from eleven or so in the morning, till late in the evening.

The first object of many of those who set out to help the unemployed was just to get them off the streets, to give them somewhere where they could be. Committees were formed which got the use of church halls ; in the early stages there was often a rota of halls in use, but this was soon found to be unsatisfactory. Later on a great variety of buildings were pressed into service : derelict chapels, empty warehouses, empty shops. It was at a considerably later stage that some clubs were planned fairly carefully, and from first to last most premises were makeshift. Most of the permanent buildings were rented at nominal figures. The next step was to equip them with some rough furniture and to make some provision for recreation. But fairly early the need and opportunity were perceived of enabling unemployed men to meet the most pressing needs of themselves and of their families by work in their enforced leisure. Usually this took the form of providing cobbling bench and tools, and arranging for the supply of leather at wholesale prices ; the mending of shoes is a heavy item in the budget of a working man. The making of furniture was a second common occupation. Other forms of self help were facilitated later. Another development was in the direction of doing useful work for the community. It will be convenient to examine the development of the unemployed clubs and kindred associations under these five heads :—

(*a*) provision and equipment of premises.
(*b*) recreation ;
(*c*) activities directed to supplying material needs of unemployed men and their families ;
(*d*) activities directed to supplying the neighbourhood with amenities.
(*e*) education.

PROVISION AND EQUIPMENT OF PREMISES

The size and quality of premises differed much at different times and in different places. After the very early days it was generally accepted that an unemployed men's club, to be effective, needed to have the sole use of premises and some security of tenure. The latter was often difficult to get; industrial and commercial buildings were let at a nominal rent on condition that they should be vacated promptly if the owners were able to get a commercial let. The men occupying them had therefore the discouragement of knowing that any work put into improving the premises might be thrown away, and those who provided money for improvements had the same discouragement. And occasionally a group of unemployed men were dispossessed ; in one case the site was sold to be cleared for the erection of a new school after a good deal of work had been put into making an old and unsuitable building habitable as a club. But usually in the worst areas the likelihood of the building being required was small. Some were small and cramped, others were too big. Among the buildings utilised in the Tyneside area were two disused police stations, one block of offices belonging to a gas company, the offices and yard of a dismantled shipyard, a disused Methodist chapel, a derelict papermill, a large private house, and the former canteen of a large steel works. Several clubs were housed, for a time at least, in wooden huts. Several groups of men built their own premises, and these were by no means the worst premises, since they were designed for their purpose. Some of the premises had grounds attached to them, and these were sometimes laid out tastefully, sometimes not. On the whole the adaptation and unkeep of the premises did great credit to the club members, who put a good deal of energy and of ingenuity into the work. But as a rule the work was done by a mere handful of members. Advice was very freely and generously given by the local professional men : architects, solicitors, members of the staffs of Schools of Art.

RECREATION

In the early days men spent an immense amount of time playing cards and dominoes, darts and quoits. Gradually the range of recreation was increased ; draughts and chess became popular. In the Tyneside clubs there was at one time a furore for chess, fanned by the visits of a retired doctor with whom chess was a passion. Matches and championships were arranged, clubs sent teams to other clubs. In the same way football matches, more seldom cricket matches, were arranged. Keep fit classes were also arranged. And in the summers there were holiday camps to which a succession of men went. In most clubs there were wireless sets. Of the concerts and dramatic performances something is said later.

ACTIVITIES DIRECTED TO SUPPLYING MATERIAL WANTS OF UNEMPLOYED MEN

Practically all the unemployed men were receiving weekly sums of money from the Ministry of Labour or from a Public Assistance Committee, or, after 1934, from the Unemployment Assistance Board. These sums kept them and their families from starving, enabled them to maintain a threadbare existence, but that was all. Clothing was a perpetual trouble, diet was meagre. Clearly if unemployed men could turn their enforced leisure to account, it would be of immense advantage. Most club premises, as has been indicated, offered facilities for cobbling and for woodwork. At various clubs a number of other useful occupations were encouraged, e.g. tailoring, haircutting. Some of the Tyneside clubs acquired fishing-boats and brought home useful catches from the North Sea. A national Allotments for the Unemployed Scheme, of which the Quakers were the main initiators, encouraged the cultivation of allotments and subsidised the supply of tools, of seeds and of fertilisers. Very large numbers of men raised useful crops. Poultry rearing was also started, but did not develop to the same extent ; the usual course was to supply the men with one-day-old chicks, and to arrange for the supply of food on easy terms. Poultry rearing requires considerably more skill than growing vegetables, and in not a few cases the young chickens succumbed to disease; but a number of men made quite useful additions to their resources.

The poultry and allotment schemes were usually distinct from the schemes for unemployed men's clubs, but as a high proportion of members of clubs belonged to them, there was naturally close collaboration between the clubs and the associations responsible for the allotment and poultry schemes.

AMENITIES

The unemployed men lived, in many cases, in dreary districts where social provision was poor. Since they had a good deal of unoccupied time, they felt the need of amenities more than they would have done in normal times, and also they were in a position to give their labour, if they liked, to improving the condition of their neighbourhoods, and so improving the lots of themselves and their neighbours. There came into existence —and it must be regarded as one of the most remarkable and encouraging features of those dismal years—a number of schemes carried out by unemployed men for the improvement of their neighbourhoods. One of the best known of such schemes was the conversion of an old mining tip into a park, with open-air swimming bath, at Brynmawr, and a similar scheme was carried through at Tow Law. At Lincoln unemployed men built a holiday bungalow, made lockers for the inmates of the local poor law institution, and made a communal garden. At Hebburn a number of unemployed men converted a derelict power-house into a really beautiful institute. And in many places throughout the country amenity schemes were carried out.

All this work was done without pay. Materials were usually

either given or purchased out of grants made by the National
Council of Social Service.   Expert advice was given freely by
professional men.   The labour was given by unemployed men ;
all they received was boots for heavy work, sometimes overalls
or working clothes, and in many cases a meal during the day.
It may be said at once that only a minority of men participated
in these amenity schemes.   Those who did found a great
satisfaction in the work ; and they set a magnificent example
of cheerful and generous service when they might well have
nursed their grievance against society.   And they placed their
fellows under lasting obligation.

EDUCATION

It is not easy to draw the line between recreation and education, because much recreation has an educational value and
much education is also recreation.   There was nothing new
in a certain number of unemployed men obtaining cultural
education ; the W.E.A. has always had a proportion of its
students out of work, and doubtless this was true of the earlier
Mechanics Institutes.   These are the scholarly minority to be
found in any society.   What was new, interesting and important about the unemployed men's clubs was that a large
stratum of population was reached which had never contributed hitherto, except very slightly, to the membership of adult
education classes, and that new techniques of adult education
were evolved to deal with them.

At most unemployed men's clubs it was useless in the early
days to attempt formal classes ; the men were not used to
them, were in no mood for them, and could not profit by them.
Short lectures and informal talks they might or might not
appreciate ;   more depended upon the personality of the
speaker than on his subject.   The quite informal talk was best
of all ; a man dropping in to discuss the events of the day, and
taking his start from the morning newspaper might get a hear-
ing, and might, if he were successful, do real educational work.
Informal talks on hygiene went down well.

Two of the most successful modes of approach were through
drama and music.   Wherever there was a skilful instructor,
dramatic groups did well ; a good deal of latent talent was
discovered ; performances were creditable.   Nor was there any
need to choose plays of poor quality ; such plays as the

Green Goddess, Arms and the Man, The Romantic Young Lady, were presented and were well performed, as amateur acting goes.

Music can be an important form of cultural education ; and in some areas where the incidence of unemployment was heavy, there was much progress made. This was notably so in South Wales. In some areas it was harder to develop music than to develop drama, for whereas drama was a barren field which only needed to be tilled, music was by no means a barren field, but a field bearing a plentiful crop of weeds. There was positive bad taste to reckon with ; the men liked music, but it was bad music. Remarkable tact and skill of music instructors led gradually to the disappearance of bad concert parties and their replacement by good male voice choirs ; and sometimes small orchestras were built up. Musical recitals with exposi- tions, the kind of thing which Walford Davies used to do so skilfully, were also successful.

And the day-to-day business of the clubs was of itself a valuable kind of informal education. Many of the men had never before had the opportunity to take responsibility. The committee meetings, often incredibly bad in the early stages, became more orderly and more competent. The planning and carrying out of the amenity schemes had its educational value, not least in aesthetics. In general, it may be said that the unemployed men's clubs resembled on their educational side the leisure institutes which some local authorities have deve- loped rather than any organisation for formal education. That it was sound education, that the approach was right, there can be little doubt.

In some cases unemployed clubs were a spontaneous creation of the unemployed men, were financed entirely by them, and remained entirely under their control. But these were a minority. In a much greater number of cases the initiative came from a group of middle-class persons, and after 1933 the initiative often came from an official of the National Council of Social Service. The usual thing was for a committee to be formed by middle class persons anxious to be helpful ; and this committee found premises, raised funds, and acted as adviser and guarantor to the unemployed men, who had their own committee. The government of the clubs was in these cases a dyarchy. Those who provided premises and equipment exercised some control ; as trustees they were bound to do so ; funds and premises would not have been forthcoming otherwise. But usually within a framework of conditions the men's clubs were free to manage the clubs as they thought fit. Often there were representatives of the trustees on the men's committee, sometimes the men had their representatives on the trustee body. It was a relationship which might easily become awkward if there were bad feeling, and in a few cases this happened. But on the whole there was a pretty smooth adjustment and division of functions.

In many districts, and especially in large towns, it was found necessary at an early date to put in a salaried man as manager of the club. Many of the unemployed, it must be remembered, were unused to self-discipline ; in not a few cases there were bad elements. There were unfortunate examples of groups of men being granted the use of buildings and turning them into gambling dens and rough houses, the right to use the building being only saved by the trustees stepping in and exercising a firm control. The paid managers were usually called " supervisors " and in course of time there came to be something like a hundred paid supervisors in the country. Wages ranged from £2 a week to £4 a week ; probably £3 a week was the modal figure. It was an arduous office, well deserving of a greater reward. The supervisor was the servant of the trustees and the leader of the men. The success of a club depended in no small measure on his initiative, his tact, his popularity, his firmness. Supervisors came from many previous walks of life and were of very varying education and ability. A small amount of training became available for them as time went on, but for the most part they had to pick up their jobs and do their best in the light of common sense and of what they might learn from other supervisors in the neighbourhood.

The trustees committees operated over areas of different magnitudes. Some controlled a single club, others a group of clubs in a town or in a county. There were many advantages in operating over a large area. Some of the larger bodies, such as the Durham Community Council, had instructors in music, in drama, in physical training, in handicrafts, and in other subjects. The National Council of Social Service had also its own staff of specialists and peripatetic instructors. It was also within the competence of local education authorities to supply instructors, and in a few cases they did so, but usually they pointed to provision made in their own institutes.

The National Council of Social Service exercised a general leadership in all this movement, stimulating the formation of clubs, advising on methods, giving help in a variety of ways. It supplied, for instance, pamphlets giving advice on such technical matters as the building of clubs and the keeping of club accounts. It arranged for the insurance of third party risks on very generous terms ; an important matter since these risks were very real. It also negotiated with the Ministry of Labour on such matters as the effect on the right to unemployment benefit of voluntary work on amenities schemes, or of absence at holiday camp. There were many similar questions. It was useful both to the Ministry and to the unemployed, and to the trustees of clubs, that there was a central organisation which could conduct such negotiations.

Another enterprise of the National Council of Social Service was the establishment of three central training places for leaders in unemployed welfare work. All three were country mansions ; King's Standing, near Burton-on-Trent ; Hardwick Hall, in County Durham ; Wincham Hall, Lancashire. Wardens were installed, and instructors of various kinds. Unemployed men who had shown initiative and some capacity for leadership were sent to these for periods which ranged from a week up to six weeks. They received intensive training in such matters as handicrafts, dramatic work, horticulture, and in the technique of club management. The centres were also used for the training of supervisors. They were of special value to isolated clubs, of less value to clubs in areas where the work was strongly organised on regional lines.

The finance of unemployed welfare work was interesting. Funds were derived from a number of sources. The members of the clubs in nearly all cases paid subscriptions, usually a penny a week. These subscriptions usually covered the smaller running expenses and made a contribution to the cost of lighting and heating. A good deal of money was raised locally by committees responsible for the general upkeep of the work, and there were often gifts in kind. Money raised locally was supplemented, usually on a pound-for-pound basis, out of funds supplied by the National Council of Social Service. The National Council of Social Service itself got its funds partly by appeal to the public and partly from Government grant, the latter also on a pound-for-pound basis. After 1934 the Commissioner for Special Areas made grants in those areas over which he operated, and these grants were made on more liberal terms than those operating elsewhere.

Of the funds supplied by the philanthropic public, a substantial part was provided by " adoptions." At the close of 1914–18 war a number of English towns adopted French or Belgian towns, raising funds which were sent to aid in their reconstruction. The same device was now adopted to help the areas of this country devastated by industrial depression. Thus, the county of Surrey adopted Jarrow, Bath adopted Redruth, Ruislip adopted South Hylton. There were ninety-six of these schemes known to the National Council of Social Service, most of them having been negotiated through it. Similarly the staffs of a number of organisations adopted pieces of work. Thus the staff of the B.B.C. contributed regularly and generously to support a club in Gateshead. In 1937 there were 5,500 members of the staff of the National Provincial Bank who were subscribing regularly to a Staff Fund for the Distressed Areas, and there were many other cases. In all a very large income was derived from these adoptions, and it was a steady income ; it eased the burdens resting on the shoulders of organisers of unemployed welfare work, it contributed a good deal to its extension and to improvement of its quality, and it was a notable piece of generosity on the part of those who were in the main men and women earning very modest salaries. The adopters naturally required to be assured that the money was well spent ; sometimes they contented themselves with receiving reports, sometimes they sent down some of their own number to see for themselves. They did not as a rule expect any direct participation in management, though there were one or two instances where staffs subsidising work in their own locality also directed it in whole or in part.

Much was done for men ; very naturally, women prominent in social service inquired what was being done for women. The number of unemployed women was not great except in the textile areas and in a few large towns. But unemployed men had wives and daughters, and these had their share of hardship. Work among women was accordingly started. In Lancashire and Yorkshire clubs were opened for unemployed women. In other parts of the country clubs were started for the wives and daughters of the unemployed. This work amongst women was to grow immensely and to be very successful. It was, however, successful mainly because it met a general need of working-class women rather than because it met a special need of unemployed women. In the early stages it usually took the form of keep-fit classes, cooking classes, dressmaking classes ; holidays were arranged ; women were admitted to the music and dramatic sections of men's clubs. Whilst women's clubs usually remained separate organisations from men's clubs, they often used the same premises, and there was a growth of co-operation between men and women, especially in the cultural activities. In the early days there was considerable ungraciousness on the part of the men in some areas, and a good deal of friction.

There were also formed a certain number of clubs for special classes of men and women, e.g. for black-coated workers and for typists.

Unemployed welfare work was much attacked. Some of the attack came from members of the Labour Party, who held that this kind of work was merely palliative and that it was made an excuse for omission to deal drastically with the problem. The request from the Government that the National Council of Social Service should undertake the promotion of such welfare work came soon after the collapse of the Labour Government and the coming into power of a Coalition Government in circumstances which provoked great bitterness. The Government had recently cut unemployment benefit by 10%. It now assigned a paltry sum of £20,000 to be used to keep the unemployed quiet and to soothe the conscience of the public. So at least it appeared to many Labour men, and they attacked the National Council of Social Service as being the catspaw of an inefficient and reactionary government. There was, in addition, the deep-seated dislike which many Labour men feel in any case for philanthropy.

Trade unionists were usually members of the Labour Party and shared its objections, and they had also objections of their own. They objected to men working without pay, and on that ground they disliked the amenity schemes and they disliked much of the work which men put into making their clubs more serviceable. In some districts a good deal of pressure was put on unemployed trade unionists not to join the unemployed clubs. Some shopkeepers also had objections ; it was said that the cobbling and the furniture-making done in the clubs took away custom from the shops.

Lastly, there was the hostility of some social service organisations. The National Council of Social Service had been growing in prestige since 1920, but its claim to be a national body had been assumed, and it was not accorded by the whole body of social service organisations. Some of these bodies had pioneered in this sphere of unemployed welfare work, and they were disappointed that supervision should be entrusted by the Government to the National Council of Social Service.

Altogether there was a quite unusual amount of hostility, some of it very bitter, directed against this particular enterprise in voluntary social service ; and councils of social service, and especially the National Council, were to a number of persons anathema.

This opposition is not to be dismissed as entirely factious and stupid. It is difficult to think that successive governments handled the problem of unemployment well. Its main outlines were clear by 1925, and diagnosis was not lacking. Much that was done by the Commissioner for Special Areas in 1933 and thereabouts, could and should have been set in hand six or seven years earlier. The refusal to launch public works schemes on a big scale seemed to many a mistake. The provision made for the unemployed was certainly meagre. Many at the time, and many more in retrospect, considered that the Government handled the problem badly.

But in view of the fact that the Government was the government of this country, and that it had decided in its wisdom or its folly, that no more could be done for the unemployed, it is difficult to see how the voluntary organisations could have acted otherwise than they did. They could not stand by and see the unemployed rot. It was inevitable that voluntary effort should be applied to the mitigation of their hardships ; and that being so, it was best that the voluntary effort should be as vigorous and efficient and wisely directed as possible. It is difficult to see how the National Council of Social Service could have refused the task which the Government asked it to undertake. Nor did the undertaking of it express approval or disapproval of the Government policy. It was sometimes contended that the unemployed were doped by the clubs ; that in the absence of them they would have agitated more strongly for better treatment. It seems unlikely. Membership of an unemployed club did not prevent any man from taking part in any protests. There is no reason to think that if the clubs had not existed there would have been more active political opposition. It is more likely that more men would have sunk into deep lethargy, as indeed many of them had done before the clubs were started.

Much of the opposition of trade unionists to the work done in the clubs was entirely unjustified. It was work for which payment could not have been obtained. There is not a shred of evidence to support the contention that these nursery schools, recreation grounds and so on, would have been made by paid labour if they had not been made by free labour. They would not have been made. Nor was there ever any serious charges that the men who learned carpentry would compete with fully trained men. When some trade unionists demanded that men should not lift a finger to help themselves and their fellows they made an unreasonable demand. Even if there had been a small percentage of men getting into industry by such back doors, or a small percentage of work done gratis which might possibly have been done for wages, the risk and harm would have been small as against the harm of men rotting in idleness. To do the trade unions justice, it was seldom the big leaders who objected ; it was the small fry.

The shopkeepers' objections had even less justification. It is impossible to prove, but it is highly likely that the amount of trade they lost was infinitesimal. The men could not afford to send their shoes to be mended, could not afford to buy furniture. In any case home repair of shoes is an old widespread practice. And with regard to furniture, one might as well argue that a man should not grow vegetables in his garden or allotment because it injured the local greengrocer.

As to the aggrieved social service organisations, they had not much case. The Government wanted to have one body to deal with, and the National Council of Social Service commanded wider confidence than any other body. Actually the National Council of Social Service offered representation to all the societies concerned upon the special committee which it set up, and that committee was virtually autonomous.

No one who had any close contact with the unemployed

during the great depression, can think of that period and of their plight as being other than a catastrophe of the first magnitude. Those years of acute unemployment were years of deep tragedy, of unspeakable suffering, of much wreckage of human lives. Nothing can undo the mischief which was done. They would have been much worse years, if it had not been for the work of the National Council of Social Service, and of the other bodies which organised and directed a vast deal of help from outside and of self help within the areas worst hit. They gave men an interest and a status and a function which saved them from the worst mental effects of idleness. And it is in considerable measure due to them that there were some real and considerable gains to set against the losses, that it was precisely in this bad period that there was in more than one drab town a veritable renaissance, a new interest in and access to things of beauty and the pleasures of the mind.

Chapter V

VOLUNTARY CASE-WORK SOCIETIES

by

HILDA JENNINGS

THE universal perception of the innate relationship between man and man has resulted in every age and place in an attempt to find the unifying principle in society. During the present century in this country the growth of the social services has been the characteristic expression of this continuous urge. The main aim of these services has been to level out inequalities based on economic privilege by ensuring that provision for common needs is available to all. The assumption has been that when the members of society have been freed from the disrupting forces of social injustice and economic insecurity, they will go forward in unity. Case-work services have both contributed—although not always voluntarily—to the acceptance of this assumption and have borne witness to the need to find a deeper level of social integration.

Case-work is usually understood to be concerned with the welfare of the individual. At its inception it was recognised, however, that relationships within the family, because they were based on biological necessity, differed from all other relationships of a less universal and more ephemeral character. Hence, case-work agencies generally considered the individual in his family setting and the term " Family Case-work " came into use. Different human values and social functions are attached to the family in different phases of society. Nevertheless, its importance to the individual and to society continues to receive practical recognition from all types of caseworkers. As in the field of medicine, the word " Case " is used to indicate a pathological condition. The aim of social case-work is thought of as the restoration of ailing individuals and families to a full and healthy functioning in society. Organised case services are further distinguished from the activities of private philanthropists by the recognition that they serve a social purpose and by the consequent attempt to

c

mobilise all the resources of society in the service of its individual members.

The aim of this chapter is not to give a detailed survey of the
work and development of voluntary case-work services—to do
this would, indeed, afford scope for a separate book—it is
rather to discover what principles, if any, are embodied in them
which have a lasting validity, how far they have been able to
permeate other forms of social service with these principles, and
to what extent they are now fitted to play a part in the future
development of society.

Pioneer social services are necessarily characterized in some
degree by the outlook and conditions of the time in which they
have their origin. The fact that case-work services dated from
the formation of the London Charity Organisation Society in
1869, meant that the early case-workers could not wholly escape
from the current obsession with the economic functions of man.
In the second half of the nineteenth century the test of individual
welfare and good citizenship was commonly thought to be the
power to contribute to material progress. The successful father
of a family was the man who was able to cater for all the
economic needs of his dependants. If he succeeded by exceptional effort in sending forth his children better equipped to
play their part in the increase of wealth than their neighbours,
he was worthy of praise.

The Charity Organisation and its provincial counterparts,
even after the first brief phase when they were largely concerned
to prevent the misappropriation of wealth by those who would
not produce it, for a long time accepted this point of view.
They were, however, fortunate in the deep humanity of such
early adherents as Octavia Hill and Canon Barnett, who
believed firmly in the latent forces for good inherent in human
nature and in the remedial and positive effects of personal
contact and friendship. They thus brought to bear on the
doctrine of family responsibility a conviction of the innate
ability of the individual to rise above his environment and to
overcome misfortunes, if helped on the one hand by individual
friendship, and on the other by the planned use of all available
resources. They were often highly successful in awakening new
hope and determination in their clients and in restoring them
to the main stream of economic and social relationships.

It is, perhaps, worth while to quote one instance of case-work at this stage of its development which shows both its strength and its weaknesses. A father met with an accident. Inquiry revealed that he had a long history of industry and self-support. The case-worker was concerned to prevent the need for recourse to the Poor Law with its possibly demoralising effects on man and family. With infinite patience and thoroughness a plan for the family was worked out. Money was raised from the employer and from private donors to send the man to a Convalescent Home and subsequently to aid in the support of the family while he was trained for light employment. In the meantime it was assumed that it was the duty of wife and children to play their part in maintaining family independence. The baby and toddlers were put into a Day Nursery and the mother was sent out to daily work ; a boy was placed on a Training Ship, and a situation was found for an older girl in resident domestic service. Finally, when the man was ready to take employment, he was helped to move into another house near his new place of work. The family were once more self-supporting. In all this, tact, persistence and sympathy were needed in order to obtain sustained co-operation from all concerned. Nevertheless, no wider considerations were allowed to interfere with the clearly perceived economic aim. The twofold burden of house-work and paid employment imposed on the mother, and the possible effects on the children of this sudden uprooting from family and neighbourhood associations, were deemed of secondary importance. It is not surprising that some clients refused to co-operate, nor that this type of organised charity aroused some antagonism based on its apparent ruthlessness.

Case-work services, indeed, are often faced with the dilemma that effective help to their clients involves their re-adjustment to a society which is itself imperfect. The acceptance of current social standards may thus involve a conflict of values and prevent the self-integration of individuals and families at deeper levels. At a very early stage case-workers felt impelled to try to change the social structure. The impulse of philanthropy, even when controlled by the realisation of the social implications of its expression, overflowed beyond the narrow categories of the helpable and the unhelpable. Moreover, the very thoroughness with which the life-histories of individuals were investigated brought about the realisation that merit and de-merit did not necessarily coincide with success and failure. Case-workers were forced to try to analyse the causes of poverty and family failure. From the growing volume of case-records and the personal knowledge of social environment gained by the pioneer workers was built up the material for social research and for propaganda for social reform. Sir Charles Loch and other case-work experts played an important part in the work of the Poor Law Commission and were foremost among the members who urged the need for the kind of reform advocated in the Majority Report. They pressed for the provision of Labour Exchanges, for the de-casualisation of labour, and for some form of social insurance.

They undertook both research and pioneer experiment in other fields and anticipated in many respects the provision of specialised services later undertaken by the State. Indeed, the very success of some of their experiments, and the evidence which they afforded of the extent of the need and the numbers to be catered for, helped to bring about the assumption of public responsibility in various fields of social service. They were, however, deeply committed to the policy of dividing the field of material relief between organised and co-ordinated voluntary agencies and the Poor Law, both of which maintained the family as the unit. They were, therefore, violently at variance with advocates of the break-up of the Poor Law and the assumption of responsibilities in the field of relief by departmentalised services, such as Education and Public Health. Indeed, it appeared to some of their successors that it was their duty to oppose any extension of public responsibility for social services of the personal kind. The result of this quarrel was that for some years the direct influence of the family case-work services on the public services was diminished and their main development was through the extension of voluntary services to new fields.

The medico-social services were among the earliest and most important of these. The first Hospital Almoner was appointed from the ranks of London Charity Organisation Society workers in 1895, and the service spread first to other voluntary hospitals and later to a growing number of municipal hospitals. Sickness was known to be a common cause of the breakdown of family self-support. It is to the credit of the early case-workers that they also perceived the reverse side of this problem and succeeded in persuading some medical experts that social and economic conditions in the home had an important bearing on the success or otherwise of medical treatment. Here then was a first acknowledgment of the value of co-operation between the practitioners of two different sciences. Here too, an application of case-work methods and principles to a field of work where the first approach was not from the angle of failure of economic function, but was due to an appreciation of the interaction of different aspects of the individual's make-up on his welfare as a person.

Other specialised societies, such as those providing for the care and after-care of physically disabled persons, crippled and invalid children, disabled adults, the blind, the deaf, and the epileptic and tubercular, also maintained some degree of continuous contact with the appropriate medical services, and adopted to a varying extent the principles and technique of the case-work services. They shared with the Hospital Almoners the characteristic approach from the side of the physical aspect of their client's need, and the consequent tendency to refrain from allowing themselves to be obsessed with his economic function, important though this was recognised to be in any plan for his total rehabilitation.

In many of these societies experienced workers were mainly drawn from the family case-work agencies or obtained their initial training there. It followed, therefore, that the importance of the family unit, the belief in a constructive effort to restore individuals and families to full social functioning as far as their disabilities allowed, and the belief in the value of personal relationships, permeated the specialised voluntary societies. The family case-work agency, on its side, made use of the medico-social services, by referring special needs to them and co-operating with them to promote the welfare of families in which they were mutually interested.

Three other factors contributed to the recognition of the work of case-work agencies beyond their own boundaries. One was the obvious utility of the case-paper method of keeping records which they developed. As long as philanthropy found expression mainly in individual help to another individual in immediate need, records were felt to be unnecessary and were, indeed, repugnant to the donors. Immediately organised case-work societies began to evaluate the problems of their clients in the light of their personal history and to attempt long-term remedial work in which they used all available resources, records became necessary tools. A technique was evolved and passed on from one worker to another in the case-work offices. Gradually it was adopted as a matter of convenience by other voluntary agencies and by Poor Law officials and some other public social servants. The records thus kept were not always very adequate nor illuminating, and occasionally case-paper work was confused with case-work itself. Nevertheless, the adoption of the system did sometimes help to bring about a recognition of the value of constructive work and of the importance of the family unit.

Linked with the recognition of the need for careful records was the system of Mutual Registration of Assistance. This embodied a principle which had been given official recognition as early as 1869—the year when the London Charity Organisation was founded—by Mr. Goschen in his Poor Law Minute. It was again strongly advocated in the Majority Report of the Poor Law Commission in 1909, but was only applied partially and in certain localities. Where the system was put into operation it was usually at the instance of the family case-work agency. Through it, the latter not only prevented overlapping and waste of resources in relief, but spread some understanding of its own aims and principles among the other agencies, whose co-operation was sought.

More important as a cause of continued influence throughout the whole field of social service is the part played by the case-work agencies in the training of professional social workers. The London Charity Organisation, together with some of the Residential Settlements, shared the initiative in promoting training courses, which included the study of the social sciences together with guidance in practical work and field observation. Early in the present century certain Universities began to provide basic courses in social science, but continued to make use of the voluntary social agencies for the practical part of the training. Training in case-work is still regarded as an essential part of the equipment of a social worker. Consequently, professional social workers with a social service diploma have carried a knowledge of its principles and technique into branches of social service outside the main case-work field. It cannot be claimed, however, that in the University courses the theoretical and practical sides of training have yet been satisfactorily integrated. Nor has a synthesis of the social sciences been achieved, so that the students may always see the various " subjects " of study as part of a concerted attempt to understand society as a whole. One method of helping to ensure this is obviously by guidance in the application of all branches of social science to the individual and the family. Here, therefore, it appears that case-work has still an important further contribution to make.

The break-up of the Poor-Law on the lines advocated in the Minority Report of the Royal Commission was a natural result of the odium attached to the system of deterrence. Organised charity had attempted to co-operate so closely with the Poor Law that it was bound to share in its unpopularity to some extent. When, therefore, the relief of distress became associated with the various public social services outside the Poor Law, the influence of the case-work agencies was not sufficient to prevent the evils inherent in the attempt to deal with individuals in categories and the consequent failure to appreciate their intimate dependence on family welfare.

Nor could the public social services wholly escape the current obsession with material values and economic inequalities. As in the voluntary field, it tended to be assumed that the main function of social service was to cater for the under-privileged. Departmental administration and divided responsibility meant that even the attempt made by the Poor Law to cater for the economic needs of the family as a whole was abandoned. With all the multiplicity of sources of relief in money or kind and the growth of insurance benefits, the family was still too often left below the poverty line. Family welfare, as apart from family relief, was hardly considered.

In London, however, where the voluntary case-work services were most influential, the London County Council undertook in the sphere of child welfare, an experiment which showed that public responsibility could be combined with case-work principles and the use of voluntary service. The principal organiser of the L.C.C. Children's Care service, like the first Hospital Almoner, was drawn from the ranks of the C.O.S. secretaries, and, as far as possible, trained social workers with some knowledge of case-work were appointed as her local assistants throughout London. Through the instrumentality of this organising staff some thousands of volunteers were recruited, and to some extent trained, and were appointed to form School Care Committees. The Committees were officially recognised as concerned with the whole welfare of the child in his family setting. Instead of the homes being invaded by an ever-increasing army of officials concerned severally with child neglect, the following up of medical treatment, free meals, and the after-care of the adolescent, the school visitors were responsible for dealing with all types of problems and could consider their interaction and the needs of the family as a whole. Some of the failures and unintentional cruelties, due to ignorance of the determining factors in individual children's lives, were thus avoided.

There were attempts on similar lines in certain other areas, but, in the main, case-work failed to permeate the typical public services, and there was little attempt to do more than meet an immediate limited need. Where a good Care Committee in London was asked to consider an application for school dinners or to deal with persistent failure to provide medical treatment or with a problem child, it usually tried to find out what other home and family difficulties—an ailing mother, an over-crowded home, the failure of family relationships—were at the root of the difficulty. It then spared no time or trouble in an attempt to ensure a lasting improvement through personal interest and social work. The departmental official, even if he or she happened to have social interests and experience, was limited in time and energy by the demands of a service, whose staffing was based on a conception of category needs, and by the tyranny of numbers.

The main exception to this point of view was in the Probation service, where the adoption of curative and educational aims instead of the old penal ideas, meant that the individual had to be considered and helped as a person and with due consideration of his personal relationships, and of the varied influences on his development.

While, with a few significant exceptions, the family case-work agencies were compelled by mutual antagonism and suspicion to function outside the sphere of public social services, the specialised case-work societies of the medico-social type were more successful in achieving recognition and co-operation. One of the reasons for this was the fact that such services were often closely connected with institutionalised provision. The Hospital Clinic or Tuberculosis Dispensary might be the starting point of their work or, alternatively, they themselves might be forced to promote auxiliary group services. Examples of these are to be found in Convalescent Homes for the use of ex-hospital patients, in the sheltered workshops for tubercular persons, in the Residential Homes for the Blind, and in the training institutions for crippled persons. A more recent development has been the Rehabilitation Centres sometimes promoted by Voluntary Councils for the Disabled Adult, side by side with officially approved training centres, or serving as a preliminary to admittance to these. The provision of such facilities may originate with the voluntary agency or with the public authority. The significant fact is that, whether publicly or voluntarily organised, they are usually associated with personal work of the case-work type. Wherever a specific disability has prevented an individual from functioning normally in society, group or category provision has been recognised to be insufficient. John Smith and Tom Brown may both have lost a leg and been trained as tailors or watchmakers, but they are not equally suited to a particular employer or vacancy. Both have different family problems and re-act differently in apparently similar emergencies.

Similarly in the field of mental deficiency and later in that of mental health, services involving knowledge of personal and home differences and the ability to adjust treatment to these, have grown up, and are more or less closely in touch with institutional and group services. Moral Welfare Associations also follow case-work lines but maintain links with Homes, Shelters and other services. A newer, but probably a growing field for combined services of this type, is that of old age. Here, too, societies, attempting in the first place friendly visitation, may find themselves impelled to provide Homes for some of their clients, and such services as social clubs, Home Helps or circulating canteens for others.

The important factor in all this work from the point of view of case-work is not whether the provision is made from public or voluntary funds, but the fact that the individual is given his due place in the provision for the category or group. Personal need is the determining factor in treatment, and not equality through uniformity.

G*

By 1918, the voluntary social services were beginning to recognise that disproportionate attention to the economic needs and functions of man resulted in a distortion of outlook and a limitation of service. The development of the science of psychology and the production of a literature of case-work, mainly by American social workers and students, were among the most important agents in bringing about a change of attitude. The case-work societies in this country had early discovered methods of investigation and recording by which they had attempted both to assess needs and to discover all the available resources for treatment. In America a more systematic analysis of the case-work technique and function was attempted. In 1917, Mary Richmond published *Social Diagnosis* and this came to be recognised as a text-book for case-workers. The case-paper method provided an enormous reservoir from which illustrative and comparative material could be drawn. It was possible with its help to analyse and classify causes of social maladjustment. A study of this material, together with the growing knowledge of individual psychology, suggested that such causes lay deeper than the interaction of character and economic or social conditions. The extraordinary differences in personal reactions to apparently similar situations were noted and it was recognized that these individual variations provided the clue to individual treatment. People began to think in terms of personality rather than of character alone and to recognise the importance of emotional attitudes and habitual modes of reaction and types of social relationship.

Whereas the early case-work societies had devoted their efforts to mobilising agencies in the service of the individual, the new psychiatric social workers of the inter-war period strove to mobilise the sciences in the attempt at team-work between doctors, psychologists, psychiatrists and social workers. Both the essential unity and the many-sided nature of man were recognised. Here again, American example and influence were important. The Commonwealth Fellowships awarded to social workers in this country enabled them to study field work in America. They came back full of enthusiasm and soon exerted a considerable influence on their colleagues in various branches of professional social work.

The concern caused by Juvenile delinquency during and after the 1914–18 war and the general acknowledgment of the importance of promoting child welfare which was characteristic of the twentieth century, as well as the stress laid by the psychologists on the importance of child development on lines which would lead on to healthy adulthood, facilitated the establishment of Child Guidance Clinics. The Children's Courts began to use these as a guide to understanding treatment, and in some cases they were provided as part of the public education service. In the general sphere of mental health also great strides in knowledge and technique were made. The psychiatric social worker, and the method of team-work were adopted in many Mental Hospitals.

The work was necessarily experimental. Miss Cormack in her chapter on case-work services in *Voluntary Social Services*[1] has set forth some of the stages of development, as the aims, limits and methods of psychiatric social work were clarified and tried out in the field. In any new service there is a natural tendency to be dazzled by fresh discoveries and to make claims which can only be justified after a process of trial and error. The reaction may also go too far, but, in the long run, if the discovery is a genuine one, a more just appreciation of possibilities and limits is reached. The more important the discovery and the wider its field of application, the longer the process is likely to take. Psychiatric social workers would probably not claim that their functions and the methods appropriate to them have yet been fully determined. They have, however, rendered a great service to case-work generally. They have re-affirmed the importance and vitality of the will to growth and the need for conscious co-operation in any attempt at change. By showing character and environment as only part of the factors affecting the whole self and its powers of social adjustment, they have provided a corrective both to the individualist attitude of the early voluntary agencies and to the over-specialised outlook which has been characteristic of the public social services of the last forty years. As these principles gain wider recognition, it becomes increasingly clear that the integration of the individual and of society cannot be achieved merely by mitigating or abolishing differences due to economic privilege.

Even before the recent war, there were signs that public

[1] " Nuffield College Social Reconstruction Survey ", *Voluntary Social Services*, pp. 104–6.

authorities and the informed public were beginning to realise
that comprehensive public provision of social services was likely
to be wasted in part, unless action were taken to enable
individuals to benefit by it. Some Housing Authorities had
rent-collectors working on the lines advocated by Octavia
Hill ; welfare workers were appointed to deal with family
problems on new estates. Many teachers realised that it was
not enough to blame the parents for the children's sins and
were ready to welcome the suggestion of appointing visiting
teachers on school staffs or to co-operate, as in London, with
voluntary case-workers ;   parent-teacher associations were
formed ; health visitors found themselves obliged to go beyond
their specialised province and often gave some of their own
time to family problems of a social nature.

Wartime conditions, and perhaps especially evacuation,
brought a healthy realisation of individual differences and the
need for individual study and treatment. With this came new
services of the case-work type. The Ministry of Health made
it possible for Local Authorities to appoint trained welfare
workers, and there are signs that their penetration into areas
where professional social work had received little previous
recognition may have lasting effects. Air raids and the need
to organise information services both of an emergency type and
in the more permanent organisation of Citizens' Advice
Bureaux meant that personal service of a new kind had to be
provided for citizens as such, irrespective of class or income.

The pioneer London Marriage Council has been the fore-
runner of provincial services on allied lines, the need for which
was only too clearly demonstrated by the family problems
arising out of prolonged separation and new conditions of life.
In these services the newly discovered method of team work was
adopted. Doctors, whether general practitioners or specialists
in appropriate branches of medicine, lawyers, psychiatrists,
psychologists, clergy, and social workers were enrolled on panels,
to be called on as required in individual cases. The unique
importance of the family and of right relationships within it was
reaffirmed. Mental Health and Child Guidance social workers
also were called on to accept new duties during the war.
Special Homes for children, who could not adapt themselves
to new conditions and relationships when evacuated, often had
a psychiatric social worker attached to them or acting as con-

sultant. The National Council for Mental Health was asked to undertake responsibility for the after-care of ex-members of the Forces suffering from personality disorders.

The older forms of family case-work which sought to promote rehabilitation in the economic sphere and help in material problems also continued to meet a real need even in the war-time years of full employment, and despite special Government provision to meet the emergencies of service men and their families. They, too, were called on to deal with difficulties arising from faulty relationships and broken homes, and in the case of the Soldiers', Sailors' and Airmen's Families Association often acted as the home agents for the Service Welfare officers.

It may be said, then, that the voluntary case-work services have evolved in such a way that they have still a function to fulfil in a society very different from that in which they originated. For a long time their influence was restricted by their cleavage from the main stream of social thought and provision. They have been able to shed that part of their gospel which was merely an attempt to rationalise the imperfect social assumptions of the post, and have discovered a new and more unifying conception of individual and family function. They have lived through an era when, on the one hand, the prevalent desire for the swift provision of equalising and comprehensive services led to the haphazard and piece-meal growth of the public services, and, on the other, the voluntary social services pinned their faith to co-ordination. It now appears that the State is about to attempt unification and planned development of its services. Yet neither co-ordination nor planning can prove a substitute for integration. The case-work adherents have still need to bear faithful witness to their lasting principles. They will probably do this both by voluntary initiation of new services and developments of existing ones, and by penetration into public social services. It is fortunate that they have reached a stage where they once more have a clearly defined faith. They stand for the unique value of each individual, for belief in his self-integrating powers, and for the importance of the work of assisting him to build up social relationships, first in the family in which he is nurtured, and then, through the habits built up there, in an ever-widening series of circles of association. If they can bring these principles to bear on the society which is now being shaped, they may help to secure the general recognition that an integrated society can only be achieved if it consists of integrated individuals.

Whether there are unique and permanently valuable functions which only voluntary services can perform in the field of case-work, depends on their own ability to develop further. The early case-workers, often deeply imbued with religion, achieved a release and up-springing of the self in many of those who came to them for help, despite their limiting conception of social function. They did this because, consciously or unconsciously, they acknowledged a super-social bond. In substituting a scientific for an ethical approach, there is a danger that present-day case-workers may tend to think exclusively in terms of social relationships, and be afraid of what they cannot understand. It will be equally dangerous if, while seeking to avoid passing moral judgments on their clients, they throw overboard the conception of absolute values and of a characteristic perfection of the human, as of other, species. In this way they can only be lost and confused in uncharted seas.

Both social relationships and the conception of the social functions of groups and institutions change. The society, which, on a functional basis only, at one time approaches integration, is liable either to become fossilised or to fall apart. The State can only embody the desires of contemporary society. The voluntary association is not thus cabined and confined. Its proper task is always to give expression to the questing spirit of mankind. Through case-work, individuals can be helped to free their whole personality, provided that the tie which binds them together in society, is recognised to be more than social in its origin and scope. It is only by the perception of the existence and nature of the animating principle which enables the many members to function as one body, that a society of self-determining individuals can grow adventurously.

Chapter VI

COMMUNITY CENTRES AND COMMUNITY ASSOCIATIONS

by

HENRY A. MESS *and* HAROLD KING

THE first world war awoke in Britain an acute sense of the need for rehousing. The legacy of pre-war years, coupled with the almost complete cessation of building and maintenance work during the war, caused a problem of acute complexity. The responsibility for meeting it was placed on the local authorities, stimulated, subsidised and supervised by the Ministry of Health. Under a series of Housing Acts, large numbers of houses were built. By 1938 there were to be found on the outskirts of almost every town one or more council estates. Some were very big : at Becontree the London County Council built 4,000 houses within a few years. Large populations were brought rapidly on to sites where a few years previously there had only been a few scattered houses. Many of the new estates were in fact towns in their own right, much bigger than many of the old historic towns of the country. One of the Liverpool estates, for instance, was larger than Chester.

These new estates differed from old towns, however, in more respects than that of size. Sir Ernest Barker has pointed out some of their peculiar features. They did not develop gradually but came into being " by an act of immediate total creation." Generally almost the whole population belonged to one social class and was very nearly on one economic level, the wages of adult males usually falling between £3 and £4 a week. As a result of these facts there was a considerable difference in age structure from the general population. From the point of view of organisation the most serious factor was that the new estates did not constitute a unit of local government, and sometimes were divided between the areas of several authorities. A further complication occurred when, as often in the case of the London County Council, the houses were owned by a local authority other than that responsible for providing statutory services. These factors would have been enough to make the development of a satisfactory social life difficult in the extreme. There was an added and equally great difficulty in the fact that those who planned and built the new estates and moved tenants to them do not seem for the most part to have had any realisation that to build houses was only the first step towards creating an organic urban society. Little was done to provide facilities for recreation or for cultural purposes. There were no public buildings, often no sites on which to erect them, and no organisation to use them had they been there. Even provision for more obvious social needs was poor. When the first tenants arrived at Watling in 1927 the nearest shops were half an hour's journey distant. There were no public halls, no public houses, only one church inconveniently sited. The first permanent school was not opened till the end of 1928 ; for a considerable time after that there were children not attending school for lack of accommodation. The park was not opened till 1931. The story is typical. The first settlers on new estates everywhere found them bleak and comfortless, lacking most facilities for social life.

A beginning of social organisation came fairly quickly on most estates, however, and, significantly enough, tended to originate spontaneously among the tenants themselves. Often it took the form of Tenants' Associations concerned in the first place with questions of rent, repairs and similar matters arising from their common tenancy of the local authority. There were often also beginnings of clubs and societies, greatly handicapped for lack of meeting-places. Out of these elements came the beginnings of associations whose objects were to represent the general interests of tenants and promote the social development of the estate. Sometimes the new residents were stung into activity by the hostility of the older inhabitants of adjacent areas. This seems to have been the case at Watling which again can be considered as fairly typical. A Watling Residents' Association was founded in 1928 which was stated to exist for :

(a) promotion of the interests of residents on the estate ; and
(b) for their well-being in such social and other activities as may be found necessary.

In the early days " The Association had no house of its own, not even a cottage, not even a hut. Its early activities

had to take place off the estate."[1] Later it borrowed or hired
church halls. In 1931 it was able to rent a cottage ; in 1933
it acquired a centre with a hall capable of holding 264 persons,
a common room for 80 persons and a small adjacent hut and
billiards room. Three years earlier the Association had
acquired the full-time services of an organising secretary. The
struggles and difficulties of some new estates were abridged
because they were able to profit from earlier experience and
because there had come to be some realisation in influential
quarters of what was happening. In 1929 the National Council
of Social Service formed a New Estates Community Committee
and obtained a grant from the Carnegie United Kingdom
Trust for the development of social work on new estates and
for the necessary central administration. It also received
assurances of assistance from local authorities. In the next
ten years much was done to foster social life, not only on the
new estates, but elsewhere ; for it was found that similar
problems existed, perhaps not so acutely, in other areas. They
existed in privately built estates, large blocks of flats, indeed
almost everywhere in the large towns. In the new estates the
work had to begin from the beginning and the need was more
glaring. The scope of the Committee's work was widened and
it became the Community Centre and Associations Committee.
Immediately before the second world war there were some 220
Community Associations in existence.

The second world war gave a tremendous impetus to the
movement. Its circumstances caused a great development of
neighbourhood activities through the necessities of Civil
Defence, particularly the organisation of social activities for
Units as a measure to maintain morale during the long " stand-
by " periods. As a result neighbours came to organise themselves for common purposes and in the process to learn to
know one another and to participate in common social and
cultural activities in a way that had seldom happened before.
Parallel developments took place in the Home Guard and in
the educational schemes of the fighting services. The result
was a widespread realisation of the possibilities inherent in
community organisation and a recognition by the Government of the even greater possibilities which lay behind these
beginnings. Such developments received careful consideration

[1] Ruth Durant, *Watling*, p. 41.

when reconstruction plans were being formulated with the result that the Education Act of 1944 imposed on local education authorities a duty to provide facilities for " further education," the intention being made very clear by the Ministry's publication of the pamphlet *Community Centres* shortly after the passing of the Act. The National Council of Social Service for its part attempted to meet the new situation by encouraging the Consultative Council of Community Associations to become a Federation of Community Associations, an autonomous body associated with the Council and provided by it with secretariat and services.

The end of the war, therefore, saw much enthusiasm for Community Centres, even though many of the enthusiasts were perhaps not quite clear what a Community Centre was and had never heard of a Community Association. It was shared by the elected authorities of the country, local and national. Nevertheless the promise of early and sweeping development was soon qualified by shortages of materials and manpower which made it clear that new building for community work was likely to be considerably postponed. In these circumstances a short-term policy was developed, both by the Ministry of Education and by the National Federation of Community Associations, the main point of which was the desirability of maintaining enthusiasm by the use of temporary or makeshift premises in which interest could be kept alive and new activities developed. In the meantime more ideal plans for the future were to be elaborated. It also became clear that the need for trained personnel to act as wardens, organisers and so forth was likely very greatly to exceed the supply. Short- and long- term training schemes were therefore developed but results are by no means clear yet. Perhaps on the whole these brakes on enthusiasm were no bad thing. The Community Centres movement is still very young ; many of the pre-1939 conceptions are already obsolete ; and there is a great deal of exploration and experiment necessary before firm common conceptions can be realised.

One other interesting post-1944 development may be noted. The Community Centres movement has now spread, not merely to the areas of large towns indicated above, but also to the market and small country towns where the complicating factor of a strongly developed traditional cultural life frequently exists. The adjustment of this older and often more exclusive type of activity to the new needs and the new conceptions raises some interesting problems.

It has been observed that many older ideas are already obsolete. It is not true, however, to suggest that the fundamental conceptions have altered. Very early in the development of the movement the National Council of Social Service propounded definitions of " Community Centre " and " Community Association " which are still sound :

> A Community Centre may be defined as a building which (1) serves a community organised in an association which is responsible for the management of the building ; and (2) provides facilities for the development of the recreational, cultural and personal welfare of members of that community ; and (3) constitutes a meeting-place for voluntary organisations or other groups in the community which need accommodation.
> A Community Association may be defined as a voluntary association of neighbours democratically organised within a geographical area which constitutes a natural community, who have come together either as members of existing organisations, or as individuals, or in both capacities, to provide for themselves and their community the services which the neighbourhood requires.[1]

It has also been suggested that local authorities have considerable powers with regard to the provision of Community Centres. Since these powers relate largely to the question of finance their existence is important and their interpretation may prove to be even more so. The most important of the relevant Acts is the Education Act of 1944. Section 41 makes it a duty " of every local education authority to secure the provision for their area of adequate facilities for further education, that is to say . . . (b) leisure time occupation in such organised cultural training and recreative activities as are suited to their requirements for any persons over compulsory school age who are able and willing to profit by facilities. . . ." Section 42 requires local education authorities to prepare and submit schemes of further education and to consult with interested bodies in their area in preparing their schemes. Section 53 gives power to local education authorities to " establish, maintain and manage, or assist the establishment, maintenance and management " of a considerable variety of

[1] New Estates and Community Councils, Paper No. 1.

recreative buildings in which Community Centres would be included. It further provides that in making arrangements for the provision of these facilities and the organisation of activities, they shall " have regard to the expediency of co-operating with any voluntary societies " with similar objects.

Clearly these powers are very wide indeed. They impose the duty of seeing that the area is adequately provided, among other things, with Community Centre provision and of building, managing and staffing whatever structures may be thought necessary for the purpose. In other words it is now within the power of a local education authority to do the whole work of erecting and managing Community Centres; and within its duty to see that the work is done by other agencies if not by itself.

The question arises as to whether it is desirable for the local education authority to take so large a part. The Act clearly envisages the possibility of co-operating with, among others, voluntary bodies at various stages; the Ministry's *Community Centres* urges the importance of such voluntary co-operation in every scheme. The National Council of Social Service and the National Federation of Community Associations would clearly, from the definition quoted above, go further still. They would regard it as essential that the management of the Centre should be in the hands of a representative group composed of residents of the neighbourhood concerned. Nevertheless it is obvious that if Community Centres are to be erected in anything like the required numbers, it can only be done if financial assistance amounting to a very large proportion of the capital cost is obtained from statutory sources; and they can only be effectively managed if the authorities contribute a substantial proportion of the necessary cost. The working out of the possibilities here indicated obviously offers interesting (and dangerous) possibilities for the future of the movement.

So real is the sense of these dangers among those who have been long and intimately connected with the voluntary Community Centres movement (Sir Ernest Barker, for instance) that they have sometimes advised procedure by the other two Acts bearing upon the provision of Community Centres; where the implied dangers of statutory control are thought to be not so great.

The first of these Acts is the Housing Act of 1936 which states that " the powers of a local authority . . . shall include a power to provide and maintain . . . any recreation grounds or other buildings or land which in the opinion of the Minister will serve a beneficial purpose in connection with the requirements of the persons for whom the housing accommodation is provided."

The second is the Physical Training and Recreation Act of 1937 which was renewed after its wartime suspension by the Education Act of 1944 and amended to the extent of making the Ministry of Education rather than the specially constituted National Fitness Council the main grant-aiding body. Section 3 of the Act permits the Ministry of Education to make grants " towards the expenses of a . . . local voluntary organisation in respect of the training and supply of teachers and leaders " and " to the funds of any national voluntary organisation . . . either in aid of its work as a whole or . . . of any specified branch." Section 4 of the Act provides that " a local authority may acquire, lay out, provide with suitable buildings and otherwise equip and maintain lands whether situate within or without their area for the purpose of gymnasiums, playing fields, holiday camps or camping sites or for the purpose of centres for the use of clubs, societies or organisations having athletic, social or educational objects and may manage those lands and buildings themselves either with or without a charge for the use thereof on an admission thereto or may let them or any portion thereof at a nominal or other rent to any person, club, society or organisation for use for any of the purposes aforesaid." Authority is also given for " the training of wardens, teachers, and leaders . . . for securing that effective use is made of the facilities." It is further provided that " a local authority may for the purposes of the Act contribute towards expenses incurred by another local authority or by a voluntary organisation."

It is clear that the joint effect of these two Acts is to offer some alternative to procedure under the Education Act. In particular the possibility of direct grant from the Ministry is of considerable importance and has already been used in certain instances where local difficulties were experienced. It is perhaps necessary also to add that the emphasis in the Acts is on further education ; although the tendency is for that term to bear an ever-widening interpretation particularly now " informal " methods of education are brought within its scope. The provision in the case of the Housing Act must be in connection with housing accommodation provided by the local authority. Finally, these two latter Acts are permissive only and are thus very sharply distinct from the Education Act which imposes duties.

There has been considerable discussion of the type and design of building required. It is in this direction perhaps that greatest progress is being made and some schemes that were considered good often as recently as 1939 would now be regarded as somewhat out of date. The need for buildings is great and urgent ; it is necessary, however, not only that there should be buildings but that they should be good buildings. One of the lessons of the last twenty years has been how much good social life is dependent upon good buildings. Clearly also the size and layout of a Community Centre will depend upon many considerations—the size of the population to be served, the potentialities of the site. Nevertheless there are certain common factors : a large hall suitable for meetings and theatrical performances with a good stage is obvious ; and in large centres of population an additional smaller hall would be desirable. Common room, canteen, games facilities and adequate provision of small rooms for committee meetings and classes are also important.

After buildings perhaps the most important consideration is leadership. In a movement with such a great possible future it is no longer practical to depend upon the voluntary part-time leadership of enthusiasts as was so often done in the early days. The organisation of a Community Association and of a Community Centre is a skilled and difficult job needing men and women who not only have natural gifts but considerable experience and training. The need to find and train these people is, as was indicated above, one of the bottle-necks of the moment. The organising leader must be able to discover latent talent to provide the sectional leadership in the Centre and to enlist the help of technical experience of various kinds. He must be able to supply information and contacts and a good deal of secretarial administration is required.

Group organisation is perhaps worth a separate word. With the tremendous growth of the movement it is found necessary not merely for paid leadership in the Centres themselves but for the services of Secretaries of Federations of Community Associations covering, for example, the area of a County

Borough ; and for promoters, organisers and specialists working on even broader areas. The Education Act clearly envisages that there is a place for Community Centres in the educational system of the country and its staffing is another of the problems that await solution in the future.

The management of Centres requires consideration. The National Federation thinks it necessary that the management should be in the hands of a Community Association, but here again the actual relationships with local authorities who may have contributed a large amount of the funds is being worked out, as it must, in practice. There is no inherent difficulty here. The ownership of the building and the interests of the ratepayers can be supported by a Holding Committee as a form of trusteeship while the day-to-day management and maintenance can be placed squarely on the Association which invariably includes representation of the local authorities.

The interest of local authorities in this field is leading, on an increasing scale, to the relation of other statutory activities to the work of Community Centres. In some cases they are housed in the Centres, e.g. public library, maternity and child welfare clinic, estate office. Here again and particularly with the development of such national bodies as the Arts Councils and the Council for Industrial Design, there is a wide field for possible co-operation in informal education which we have hardly begun to explore.

Another question of importance is the extent to which a Community Centre can serve all ages. It is now generally accepted that it should provide for all types and groups of adults, e.g. some very interesting experiments have been made with clubs for old people included in Community Centres. The inclusion of youth activities is a further and separate consideration. It appears clear that they need their own premises and probably their own paid leadership. There is nevertheless a potential relationship here which again has not yet been defined. Since, however, to-day's members of youth organisations will be to-morrow's members of Community Associations and Centres, some kind of liaison would appear important.

Community Associations are not only important phenomena in themselves but have also thrown new light on more general social problems, especially upon the problems of neighbourhood living. With the growth of great towns the sense of community arising out of neighbourhood has been very much weakened, how much perhaps many of us hardly realised until the war compelled a neighbourhood organisation and we got to know for the first time people who had been living next door to us for many years. The ward means little as a political unit, the town is too great, too impersonal to be a satisfactory political or social unit. The new estates raised these problems in an acute form. Physical neighbourhood was there; real community was non-existent. In some of the new estates a community spirit has been born and has grown too ; in some cases also it has dwindled. It is also possible to see some of the conditions of growth or failure to grow and of decline.

In the first place, there is the important phrase in the definition of a Community Association. It consists of " neighbours democratically organised within a geographical area which constitutes a natural community." The area must be such that its inhabitants meet frequently in a variety of relations. It is a face-to-face group. The roads and distances and facilities are such that it is easier for them to have social intercourse with one another than with persons outside the area. It is important to notice, however, that physical contiguity is not the only point ; it has already been clearly demonstrated that a main traffic highway or a railway embankment can be boundaries which the community spirit will never cross. The area and population should not be too big. There are other organs—Councils of Social Service, Community Councils—more appropriate for larger areas or secondary groups. From 500 to 2,000 families would appear to be the best size of population and the area should not be of much more than one mile radius and should not be traversed by any main natural or artificial features. If the area and population are smaller than the 500 families it is probably better that social organisation should be part of a larger area and population. When the small town builds a small new housing estate there is much to be said against developing a separatist conscience. On the other hand some huge estates and *a fortiori* all large cities are too big for the neighbourhood spirit and it is already clear that they will require to be served, not by a Community Association, but by many Community Associations each one having its own centre, although there may still be a Civic Centre, a Federation of Community Associations and some activity in common.

Another point which has emerged is that it is of immense help to the development of community sense if the borders of the area are clearly demarcated. The Watling sense of its own identity, as is brought out very clearly in Mrs. Durant's study, was well defined so long as Watling was separated by fields from its neighbours, Edgeware and Hendon. When the fields were built over the sense of identity was weakened. In the sprawling new estates of the inter-war years, the lack of distinction in boundaries is frequently a major fault. The recognition of this fact has been responsible for the emphasis in modern town-planning schemes on the clear definition of neighbourhoods by main highways and the limitation of towns by the preservation of an open green belt ; together with, of course, the use in both cases of natural features of division.

There is probably an advantage in an arrangement which makes neighbourhoods also political units.

In the consideration of these questions the Community Association movement is obviously coming into close contact with town planning. Indeed the projected building of new towns and the development of a planned community raises in an ever more acute form the social questions raised by new housing estates a quarter of a century ago. Much was learnt from the mistakes made in the building of those housing estates. But there is still much to be learnt, much on which indeed we are ignorant, and there is a consequent need for a wide and rich variety of experiment. Social organisation is a necessary function of social life. It is only one aspect of that life of which economic life is another aspect. Our concern must be with a full and many-sided life offering potentialities for every individual. It will have been noticed how many times in the above the uncertainties of the future have been indicated. These uncertainties, however, must not be taken to involve major considerations. The social organisation of the future is something on which none of us can afford to be indifferent. It is already clear that Community Centres will have a large part to play in it. The exact details of their structure, management and relationships with other bodies and authorities still have to be worked out. Nevertheless it is already apparent that they have a major part to play if " the century of the ordinary man " is to be realised in the full sense of the phrase.

Chapter VII

THE NATIONAL COUNCIL OF SOCIAL SERVICE WITH APPENDIX ON WORK IN RURAL AREAS

by

JOHN MORGAN

The National Council of Social Service stands for co-operation as the " rule " of social service. The old-fashioned conception of social work as an effort to help other people must give place to a new conception of social service as the common effort to achieve social well-being.[1]

THIS quotation summarises, if summary is possible, the essential core of the purpose which underlay the foundation of the National Council of Social Service in 1919, and which has remained its primary purpose ever since.

To write the history of this organisation (a task which should be undertaken before those in whose memories it is largely enshrined are gone) would take more space than is available here. To trace its roots further back in the Minority Report of the Poor Law Commission, in the Guilds of Help movement, or in the British Institute of Social Service founded in 1904, to mention only three of the main sources of its inspiration, would be a fascinating study in the history of social institutions of this country, but must await the probe of the social historian of this century. This chapter is an attempt to show, by examples, how a powerful and extensive organisation has been created and how it has maintained its basic purpose, so well summarised in the quotation with which the chapter begins ; to relate some of the main themes in its development to its place in the structure of social institutions ; and to assess in some measure its machinery and its function in the tasks of reconstruction which now lie ahead.

It is important to keep the Council's primary functions clearly in mind, for a study of its annual reports over the years 1919–44 shows a bewildering variety of activities, a list of which covers

[1] Vol. I, No. 11. *Social Service Review*, the Journal of the National Council of Social Service.

such widely diverse activities as the promotion of rural industries, the development of community life in towns and villages, the encouragement of Parish Councils, the foundation of the National Association of Boys' Clubs, the recruitment and training of social workers, the promotion of study and research in social service, or the foundation of the Citizens' Advice Bureau service. These and many other activities are the practical results of a fairly consistent policy, and the aim of this chapter must be to trace the development of that policy rather than to catalogue its visible results.

At the same time it is desirable to have some measure of the Council's growth. Perhaps the simplest way of doing that is to study its annual expenditure.

	£		£
1919–20 (21 months)	2,207	1933	19,953
1921	1,269	1934–5 (15 months)	28,064
1922	1,310	1935–6	32,182
1923	1,878	1936–7	37,210
1924	2,010	1937–8	37,149
1925	2,457	1938–9	41,287
1926	3,323	1939–40	40,492
1927	3,935	1940–1	36,940
1928	4,830	1941–2	37,960
1929	5,608	1942–3	42,942
1930	6,912	1943–4	45,644
1931	6,898		
1932	8,101		

The figures offer an interesting footnote to the study of the finance of voluntary organisations, which is discussed more fully in another chapter. It should, however, be noted that the great increase which began in 1933 and went on until 1944 was met very largely from voluntary sources, although in the period from 1935 onwards there were substantial contributions from statutory funds in respect of specific services undertaken by the Council. Reference will be made later to this financial aid from statutory sources. The figures are given now to illustrate in a simple and graphic way the extent of the Council's growth.

A conference on War Relief and Personal Service held in London in July 1915 set up a joint committee to prepare a plan for a national consultative council of social agencies. This was the origin of the National Council of Social Service, which was formally inaugurated in 1919 and incorporated 13th May 1924.

It is not without significance that the first conference promoted by the new Council was held in Oxford in 1920 on " Reconstruction for Peace."

There emerged from these early discussions two clearly marked policies, which can be seen throughout the whole history of the Council's work. The first was a deep concern with the need to improve and enrich the quality of life in rural areas. The second was the recognition of the need for a real measure of common action in social work in urban areas.

The structure of the Council at its inception has been maintained throughout its history, though the emphasis placed on the different forms of representation has changed considerably from time to time. The National Council of Social Service is a representative body; it is made up of representatives of Government departments and local government organisations, national voluntary organisations in every field of social endeavour, and local co-operative social service agencies such as Councils of Social Service, Community Associations, and Rural Community Councils.

This structure in itself serves a special purpose since it brings together on neutral ground, as it were, three very different groups of interests, all of them closely engaged in the administration of social policies, each one of whom would find it difficult to meet the others on its own ground without its being over-cautious about its commitments. Meeting as members of a Committee of the National Council of Social Service all can contribute to a common policy and can exchange information and ideas, without the same ties which unavoidably restrict discussions which are held under the auspices of one or other of the interested parties.

In bringing together in this way the varied interests in social administration to consider particular problems, the National Council of Social Service also performs another useful function. In modern society there is a real need to bridge the gap between administration and the intentions of the administrators, and those whom the administration is attempting to serve. This gap is partly due to the difficulty of interpretation, and it should be an increasing part of the Council's work to serve its members and the general public by explaining simply the purposes and methods of those who are working the machinery of social service—whether it is statutory or voluntary. It is also a necessary part of the Council's function to provide an effective means to interpret the problems and difficulties of the beneficiaries of the social services to those whose task it is to administer those services.

The use of this pattern of co-operation as part of the essential function of the Council can be illustrated in a number of ways.

From the policy of the early 1920's to improve and enrich the quality of life in rural areas, there emerged a clear recognition of the need for representative Village Committees with a concern for the social life in the village, and for physical facilities in the nature of a village hall within which the village social life could develop. A more detailed account of this will be found in the Appendix to this chapter. What is important here is to notice that these two needs came together in the village halls policy of the Council—which was to promote and encourage the building of village halls, which would be managed by representative Village Committees. In doing this work the Council brought together the Carnegie United Kingdom Trust, the Development Commission, representatives of the local authority organisations, and the major voluntary organisations whose activities were related to the countryside —of which perhaps the most outstanding are the Women's Institutes. The success of that policy has never been in doubt, and throughout its history all three partners—the Village Committee, the voluntary organisations, and the statutory authorities—have worked together with a smoothness which is a tribute to the British instinct for co-operative action.

The same pattern can be seen in the emergence of the Community Centres and Associations movement. The social needs of the inhabitants of new housing estates which were erected by the public authorities between the wars came to notice in 1925 and were tackled in a practical way in 1928. The first new estates Community Committees consisted of representatives of the two national voluntary organisations with the longest experience of social work of a community kind in urban areas, namely the British Association of Residential Settlements, and the Educational Settlements Association. This joint committee was assisted from the first by representatives of the Ministry of Health and the Board[1] of Education, and it very soon came to have on it representatives of local community

1 Now the Ministry of Education.

associations themselves. By 1938 a Community Centres and Associations Committee had emerged which was widely representative of all the statutory and voluntary agencies whose interests engaged closely on this problem. The emphasis throughout in this movement has been on the importance of the autonomous local group providing the energy and initiative which the local committee must have if it is to make a success of its own community life. This emphasis has now resulted in the formation of an autonomous National Federation of Community Associations. This is the counterpart of the equally clear need for a representative Village Committee, which has been one of the main threads of the Council's rural policy. It is in the recognition and organisation of self-acting local groups that the National Council has done some of its most fruitful social work.

In the case of village halls, the Carnegie United Kingdom Trust, in association with the Development Commission, announced[1] a post-war allocation of funds for the continuation and development of this policy in the years following the war of 1939-45. The Ministry of Education, by publishing a report on the subject of Community Centres and by urging local educational authorities to accept their responsibility in this matter under the new Education Act, has accorded official recognition and a place in the broad framework of the nation's educational system, to the conception of a community which needs, in addition to its physical environment, an active neighbourhood life. Thus the pattern of consultation and co-operation which is implicit in the structure of the National Council has produced in these two fields (as in others) an effective practical policy, which shows its results in the local neighbourhood.

This pattern also has an important part to play in the close integration of the voluntary social services themselves. As the community moves into a period when close and integrated planning is essential for its economic life, so it is clear that economic planning must be matched by social planning. This, though it may not yet be fully recognised, is a challenge to the voluntary social services. They have grown up, each beginning with a job to do and a particular contribution to make to a specific social problem. Thus it is that most voluntary social services are what Henry Mess would have described

[1] In August 1945.

as " functional " in character ; their aim and purpose is to serve the needs of a particular section of the community—for example, adolescent boys—by a particular method—as, for example, scouting. The need to-day, which has been emphasised during the course of this last war, is for a much closer integration of all these " functional " agencies in a general plan of co-ordinated service. If a plan of this kind is to be real, it cannot be a paper scheme thought out and imposed from the top, even though there is general agreement on its necessity. It must be an organic growth, coming naturally from the work of the several organisations, and it must take place in relation to the enlarging functions of the statutory authorities in the field of social affairs. There is a great deal of evidence to suggest that the National Council of Social Service has something to contribute in this process of organic growth. Part of its method throughout its history has been the holding of conferences at which particular social problems were explored and discussed by all those who had an interest or experience in the particular social problem ; conferences of this kind, indeed, contributed as much as any other single factor to the rapid and successful development of the Community Centres and Associations movement to which reference has already been made. It is, therefore, of importance to trace how, beginning in 1936, the Council has used the method of conferences to achieve a real measure of co-ordinated voluntary social service, not by imposing administrative schemes—it would in fact be impossible for the N.C.S.S. to impose any schemes since it can apply no sanctions—but by providing the means for free discussion.

In 1936 there was established a Standing Conference of National Youth Organisations. Here the principal youth organisations met in regular conference to discuss problems of common interest ; the National Council's function was to provide it with a home and a secretariat. The early years of the Conference were tentative. It did not bind any of its members without reference to their own responsible Committees or Councils ; each member organisation retained its independence, but all contributed something to the development of a common purpose. During the war the service of youth was recognised as an essential part of the educational structure of this country, and it is written into the Education Act of 1944.

As the Ministry of Education and the local authorities take up more generally the service of youth, they have found in the Standing Conference of National Youth Organisations (as it has now become) a single coherent group which concentrates the experience of long years of successful experimental and institutional work in this field. The machinery is ready there for an effective partnership in the service of youth, and from the tentative discussions of its early days there now emerges a more self-confident and more closely integrated piece of social machinery.

This reference to the Standing Conference of National Youth Organisations is given in some detail because this technique has proved so successful that it has been applied in other fields of social service. To meet the evident needs of co-ordinate action in war-time there was set up in 1938 a Standing Conference of National Organisations, which has served throughout the war as a means by which the resources of the voluntary agencies could be quickly and easily tapped by any of the statutory authorities which might have need of their services. The history of co-ordinated action by voluntary social services in the blitz and in evacuation, to mention only two of war's emergencies, is both fascinating and exciting in its complexity and its human interest.

Other consultative conferences of this kind have brought together the various voluntary organisations in groups which relate to their own experience and functions. Thus there are to-day the Women's Group on Public Welfare, representative of all the major women's organisations, and the National Old People's Welfare Committee, to mention only two more groups of the same character which have emerged during the course of the war.

The same tendency to co-ordinated action can be seen in other fields with which the N.C.S.S. has not itself been associated. For example, all the voluntary societies serving the Armed Forces in the provision of comforts and canteens in the field have been most closely integrated in the Council for Voluntary War Work.

This search for means of co-ordinated social action is one of the most important parts of the National Council's work and yet perhaps it is the least well known. Of it might be said what the Council's Annual Report said in 1922—

" Much of the everyday work carried on at Stapeley House (then the Headquarters of the N.C.S.S.) cannot be recorded in this Report, consisting as it does of quietly helping forward co-operation among different groups, of consultation with national agencies or public departments in regard to difficulties encountered by local Councils, or of bringing different groups of representatives into conference on particular subjects."

So far this pattern of consultation has been discussed in relation to the broad aspect of national administration. Like any other form of social service, if it is to be effective, it must have its reflection nearer the ground. The National Council of Social Service itself grew out of the work of a number of local Councils of Social Service and local Guilds of Help before the war of 1914–18, and it has always had as one of its primary aims the development of local organisations of the same representative character as itself, and of the same purposes in relation to local voluntary social service as itself. It has always given every assistance it could to the local Councils of Social Service in urban areas, and to Rural Community Councils in rural areas. Although these bodies can be stimulated by the provision of efficient services of advice and information and by the provision of conference machinery for consultation on a national scale, these local organisations must be firmly rooted in local initiative, if they are to have any meaning, and must retain their autonomy.

There is now a tendency to erase the distinction between town and country and to think in terms of Community Councils which represent the interests of both. It is also of some importance to record that the scheme of Regional Officers of the N.C.S.S., originally established in direct relation to the Government's plans for the dispersal of the central organs of the State in time of war, provided a new link between the National Council of Social Service and the local voluntary social services. Like the Regional Commissioners for Civil Defence, there were only a comparatively few occasions when the Regional Officers of the N.C.S.S. were called upon to perform their function, as originally conceived, of providing a focus for voluntary service to meet the needs of a direct attack. But the presence throughout Great Britain of accredited representatives of the National Council has been of great value as an additional channel by which the National Council's information and policy could be

D

more closely related to the facts of the social situation in the field.

This increasing dependence on local action may have an increasing importance if voluntary social service is to achieve that integration without compulsion which may well be its major contribution to the new community which it is hoped will emerge from the years of transition now immediately ahead. It is a practical comment on this feature of the Council's war-time machinery that from it has sprung, among other things, an autonomous Scottish Council of Social Service which is already firmly rooted in the social framework of that country.

In addition to its function of providing the machinery of co-operation in the realm of voluntary service, the National Council has always been sensitive to the need to improve the quality of social life in the local community. Reference has already been made to the work which was done in connection with village halls and Community Centres. It is not always recognised that this was the prime motive which lay behind the Council's active participation in social work for the unemployed. This has been the biggest single piece of practical social work which the Council has undertaken, and at the same time has been by the general public perhaps the most misunderstood of all its activities. Dealing with this work, the Council's Fourteenth Annual Report says that :

> The need to give everyone who desires it opportunity to develop tastes and talent that find little outlet in their daily work is there, whether or not work (in the sense of industrial employment) is available.

The Council and its officers were only too well aware of the devastating economic effects of unemployment. But they also recognised that, in addition, the very fact of unemployment excluded its victims from the normal social groups of their neighbourhoods. There was a crying need for some new social grouping in which the unemployed could participate as members, and for facilities by which they could express themselves as human beings with tastes and talents of their own. That new social grouping and those facilities were to be found in the Community Service Clubs.

The extent to which these members of the community responded to the recognition of their human needs can be seen in the history of the Community Service Club Movement.[1] It is not without significance that in all these clubs the members themselves made substantial financial contributions through their membership fees of a penny or twopence a week. The funds which were made available through the N.C.S.S. from the Ministry of Labour, and later also from the Special Areas Commissioners (responsibilities later taken over by the Assistance Board), were administered in such a way as to encourage rather than destroy the development of local autonomy, democratic management of the clubs, and a firm reliance on local initiative. Unemployment was the outstanding social problem of the late 1920's and early 1930's, and it would have been wrong if no attempt had been made to meet these deep social needs. It is not surprising, but most unfortunate, that the size of the problem and of the contribution which the National Council of Social Service was impelled to make has tended to obscure the other work of the Council.

This Community Service Club movement has shown how well rooted it was in the community by the persistence of the club movement throughout the war years when unemployment was a factor of relative unimportance. It is only one example of the way in which a representative body, with its contacts in every field of social service, can be used to make practical experiments to meet new types of social need. The National Council has performed a similar function in other ways, as for example in promoting and fostering new organisations. To mention only three, it played a major part in the founding of the National Association of Boys' Clubs, the National Federation of Young Farmers' Clubs, and the Youth Hostels' Association.

The existence of a representative machinery in the National Council of Social Service shows practical results in all kinds of ways. The creation of the Rural Industries Equipment Fund during the war is a good illustration of yet another type of need being met by joint action. It was clear that increased food production would depend on a great increase in mechanical equipment in agriculture. Agricultural machinery needs skilled mechanical maintenance. A scheme was evolved by which the Rural Industries Bureau trained village blacksmiths to use modern machinery in their shops for the repair and

[1] See *Out of Adversity*, published by the National Council of Social Service, 1939.

maintenance of the new machines. The National Council of Social Service, with a revolving war fund supplied through the Development Commission, supplied these smiths, when trained, with essential equipment to bring their shops up to date, and recovered the cost from the smiths, treating the cost of the equipment as an interest-free loan. In this way the statutory Department and the appropriate voluntary organisations were able, by co-operative effort, to make a substantial contribution to the nation's food production.

Perhaps the best known and the best example of co-ordinated action in the creation of a new service is the Citizens' Advice Bureau service. It was clear in 1938 when war became almost certain that the social upheaval which would be the immediate consequence would create many and varied personal problems —particularly for those who were moved from their own neighbourhoods or bereft of the member of the family upon whom they had relied for the management of the family affairs. While not itself a body undertaking case-work, the N.C.S.S. was, of its nature, aware of and in contact with all those voluntary societies which undertook case-work. It was with the organisations and individuals who had experience of dealing with individual personal problems that the Council took counsel on the ways in which this need for information and advice could most effectively be met. This need, however, is not simply a war-time need, though the fact of war threw it into such prominent relief that immediate action was necessary. The Council's interest in this problem can be traced back as far as 1923, when it gave evidence to the Inter-Departmental Committee on Public Assistance, which in its Report[1] said :

> We think it would be advisable that there should be in every large centre of population some officer conversant with the members and methods of Assistance Authorities generally, not identified with any particular public service, but in close touch with persons engaged on public administration, who would be in a position to give reliable information and assistance both to individual applicants and to officers of the several services. . . .

There could be no more accurate description of the main purpose of the Citizens' Advice Bureaux.

This service, like all those with which the National Council has been associated, was firmly rooted in local responsible and

[1] Para. 147.

independent committees ; indeed, the recognition of a Citizens' Advice Bureau by the National Council of Social Service as part of the movement was made contingent upon the existence of a responsible and independent Committee of this kind. There grew up throughout the country very rapidly a network of about 1,000 individual Citizens' Advice Bureaux, staffed very largely by unpaid volunteers, who provided the goodwill and counsel of a neighbour for those to whom the war had brought personal difficulties, and who needed guidance on the meaning to them of the war-time regulations and restrictions. Behind these unpaid volunteers there was an efficient and skilled service of accurate information and administration. The Citizens' Advice Bureau service is provided by the National Council of Social Service with a steady flow of accurate information, based on official sources, but set out in simple and non-technical language and carefully broken down and indexed for easy reference. The basis of this service is the publication of *Citizens' Advice Notes*, which have now become a standard work of reference on the legislative and administrative documents in so far as they affect the ordinary civilian.

The administrative framework of the Citizens' Advice Bureau service is interesting in that it shows how a central machinery can provide adequate links throughout a nation-wide organisation, without impairing the autonomy of the local organisation. Each Bureau (or each group of Bureaux in a local government area) is a self-governing unit, and is responsible for its own affairs. From a comparatively small sum made available by the central government during the war years (£25,000 a year for the whole country) individual Bureaux could receive grant-in-aid up to a maximum of half their total expenditure, and these grants were made through a Grants Committee by the National Council of Social Service.[1]

The local Bureaux are represented on Regional Advisory Committees, and on a Central Committee, to which the National Council has delegated responsibility for the service and to which, therefore, the staff of the Council engaged on the C.A.B. work are responsible. The administrative framework is held together and its staff at the centre are kept closely informed by Travelling Officers, who are employed by the

---

[1] See *Citizens' Advice Bureau in Great Britain and Advice Centres in Liberated Europe.* Published by the National Council of Social Service, price 2s. post free.

National Council and whose services in advising and guiding the work of the Bureaux are available wherever they are needed.

This service is important, not only because it shows something of the method and the pattern of voluntary service, but also because it has led the way to new official services. One of the problems of government in a complex democratic society is to ensure that the governed know their rights, and know how to obtain them. As legislation and administration become more complicated, so the need for adequate information and advice becomes more apparent. The fact that some means of interpretation is now an essential part of public service has been recognised in the establishment by the Ministry of Labour of a Resettlement Advice Service, and by the encouragement of local authorities to provide adequate information services about their own activities and services.

It will be seen that the National Council of Social Service must depend on the character and quality of its staff work a great deal more than an organisation which has a simpler and more direct objective. Its primary duties lie in the sphere of relationships ; the relationship of men with their neighbours in the village, in the new housing areas, in the districts of the great urban populations ; the relationship of one voluntary society with another ; the relationships between statutory agencies and non-statutory (or voluntary) agencies ; the relationships which will achieve true local autonomy with nation-wide efficiency ; and the relationships which will ensure that there is genuine control of policy by the many and varied constituent parts which make up the whole. In so far as its staff work, both in its central committee and conference work and in its field officers, is successful it will remain unnoticed because the relationships are smooth. In so far as the right balance is not achieved in any of these manifold relationships, it will be apparent, as any form of ill-balance is apparent, in the form of tensions and disagreements.

In addition to skilled and practical staff-work, certain other instruments are available and they require consideration. One of these has already been mentioned. In the last twenty years the National Council of Social Service has distributed somewhere between £5,000,000 and £6,000,000, of which about £3,000,000 was distributed to charitable organisations nominated by the donors through the Council's Benevolent Fund, and about

£2,000,000 was distributed to other, mainly local, voluntary organisations from funds made available through Government departments for specific purposes. Certain valuable results follow from the distribution of funds in this way. Individuals who make use of the Benevolent Fund, while ensuring that their subscriptions over a period of years remain constant, since they are made under general seven-year covenants with the Fund, at the same time are able to vary the amounts and assign their gifts each year according to needs of the times. The Benevolent Fund can only make payments for genuine and recognised charitable objects, and thus it not only ensures for the donors a means of flexible, and for that reason more discriminating, almsgiving, but it also encourages reputable organisations.

The use of Government funds is even more interesting. A general policy is laid down ; within the terms of that policy and subject, of course, to the supervision and audit which must accompany any use of public funds, the break-down from bulk sums to the small but essential grants for social purposes or social experiment is administered by representative committees of the National Council of Social Service. In this way it is possible for public funds to reach local voluntary effort with a maximum of benefit and a minimum of inessential administrative control. From relatively small sums of public money can come great stimulus to genuine self-help. For example, it is noteworthy that of the very large sums—by far the largest of the sums distributed in this way—administered in grant-aid to the Community Service Clubs—or as they were originally called the Occupational Clubs—every pound of Government money was matched, and more than matched, by money raised from non-Government sources. It is even more important that a substantial proportion of the funds from non-Goverment sources came in pennies and twopences from the club members themselves.

Another social return which has been reaped from this technique of using public funds has been in the possibilities it offers for experiment. It is not easy for a State department to finance an experiment or to provide facilities for a small section of the population, unless it is prepared to extend those facilities very widely to the whole of the relevant section of the population. Note should be made of the successful camp schools, initiated by the National Council of Social Service from funds made available by the Special Areas Commissioners, or the many and varied experiments in adult education, including residential education, which were conducted in the 1930's as part of the Community Service Club movement, or the promotion and advisory work on community life, which was grant-aided under the National Fitness Act, 1937. All these testify to the usefulness of the voluntary organisation as a means of encouraging social experiment from public funds. It is a technique which may have great possibilities in future, when the social consequences of a great war bring in their wake new and difficult social problems requiring community action. The voluntary organisations can make a substantial contribution to social progress if they are ready to make new experiments without necessarily waiting for support from public funds, but winning it and then seeking support from the State to improve and apply the results on a wider scale. But they must at the same time be ready both to acknowledge failure and to relinquish to the statutory authorities successful experiments as soon as they are ripe for more universal application. Only thus will the voluntary organisations justify their value as pioneers or their case for support from statutory sources.

Another instrument which the National Council of Social Service has developed, particularly during the last few years, is the promotion of social study and the dissemination of accurate information. The publication of the book *Our Towns —A Close-up*, is a significant milestone in the Council's history. That book, which has been acknowledged as a classic of its kind and quoted in the Government's White Paper on Education which preceded the Butler Act of 1944, was the product of group research conducted under the auspices of the Women's Group on Public Welfare. Incidentally the collection of evidence and publication of this book is a justification in yet another form of the Council's technique, to which reference has already been made, of promoting and staffing consultative conferences of this kind. There have followed a number of studies[1] in each of which a single issue of social importance has been isolated and studied.

---

[1] *Dispersal*—a study of the social consequences of removing office staffs from London and other large cities.

Holidays—a study of the problems which will arise when holidays with pay legislation becomes effective.

British Restaurants—a study of the lessons to be drawn for peace from the wartime developments in communal feeding.

The need for adequate social research is now being acknow-ledged. Organisations with a closely defined function tend always to concentrate their resources in energy and staff on the immediate objective. They become rapidly immersed in the day-to-day problems which require solution, almost invariably by empirical methods, if the task they have set themselves is to be performed. This creates two possible dangers. In making decisions they may be led to pass by some essential social problem because it is not, at that moment, a matter of immediate concern and then fail to come back to it as new practical issues arise. The other danger is that, even if they can spare time and staff to undertake study and research work, their studies will almost certainly be limited in their scope by the immediate objectives of the organisation. The result is that social ques-tions which do not fall clearly within the purview of existing organisations, will tend to be ignored, and social questions which are, as it were, adjacent to a number of different organisa-tions will tend to be left alone by each one of them.

There is, therefore, a real need for some organisation which will maintain a more general survey of the whole range of social service, bringing to public attention social issues wherever they appear. It is also necessary to know what is already being done. There are a number of organisations whose sole object is study and research in particular spheres of social need. Sometimes a need will be revealed in the general survey which can be met by the extension or adaptation of some existing piece of research. Sometimes a social issue has only to be brought into focus for some existing body to recognise it as peculiarly their own and to take steps to investigate it. At other times, especially in considering future developments in social service, it may be necessary to promote studies which will result in the formation of new organisations and the encouragement of new policies.

There are rich possibilities for the future in study and research, not only in co-ordination of what already exists, but in exploring new social needs, not for the sake of the study, but for what the study will produce in social action.

The National Council, with its widespread contacts through-out the country and over the whole field of social administra-tion, statutory as well as voluntary, has a great contribution to make to social progress in this country. Its studies are not in-

D*

tended to be exhaustive sociological examinations ; that is more properly the function of academic foundations. They serve to point the issues and raise the questions of immediate practical social affairs on which evidence is needed and dispassionate analysis is essential if suitable action or further and deeper study is to be provoked.

Henry Mess in the early drafts which he prepared for his study of the National Council of Social Service laid particular stress on the shortage of really good literature on social service. It is not without significance that there are many of the great pioneers of social progress, for example Sir Joseph Morant, or Edwin Chadwick, of whom there are as yet no adequate biographical studies ; or that there is little adequate published material on the techniques of social service, as those who try to train social workers will readily agree ; or that there are very few adequate studies of British social institutions, though Britain is rich in societies, organisations and statutory machinery of social administration. There is a task of the greatest importance waiting to be done in the interpretation of social service, or, as Henry Mess once wrote, in the " restatement of the philosophy of social service and the illumination of its methods." This is a task which the National Council of Social Service has attempted, but which needs to be done on a much more thorough scale. A useful start is recorded in the Council's recent Annual Reports in the establishment of a specialist Library, and by the systematic collection of current information. A great deal more should be done by the developing of all the modern techniques of interpretation—visual, through exhibitions, films and illustrated books and papers ; aural, through public meetings, and above all by means of the radio ; and written, through a sustained publications programme.

A new side of the Council's work, which has only shown itself in the most recent of the Council's Annual Reports, is the growing extent of the Council's international and overseas relations. Members of its staff have recently been to the United States of America, Canada, and to several countries in liberated Europe. In the coming years much may depend on the relations of the British people with the people of other nations. It may be a matter of the gravest significance that these relationships should be improved not only as between governments, not only as between traders, but also as between communities which have a rich and varied pattern of social life beyond, and in addition to, the political and commercial patterns which have hitherto largely predominated in international relationships.

A start has been made by establishing close contacts with international organisations, particularly the bodies responsible for the economic and social policies of the United Nations, and with the United Nations Educational, Social and Cultural Organisation. Proposals for the interchange of social workers and administrators between Great Britain and other countries are beginning to ripen and should prove a valuable means of international co-operation.

The Council has played its part in the formation of the Council of British Societies for Relief Abroad, an organisation which integrates the work and programmes of voluntary agencies in Britain which have each their distinctive contributions to make to the bewildering variety of relief problems in liberated Europe. It is an interesting side-light on the Council's work in the industrial areas in the pre-war years that the distinctive craft-work techniques developed in the Community Service Club movement have been found to have a practical application to the programmes of camps for displaced persons in Europe ; and the National Council of Social Service in 1945 provided a small team of craft specialists to advise on this matter. Another promising move has been the establishment in London of an International Common Room for Social Workers, where information can be exchanged with visitors from overseas.

Many voluntary organisations, for example the Boy Scout movement, or the Y.M.C.A., already have a long tradition of international work: many others have a notable record of relief and educational work in great international crises, such as for example the social problems left after the war of 1914–18. The full contribution of the National Council of Social Service in this, as in other fields, will probably be worked out empirically, for that is the British way, and policy will grow rather than be formulated.

It is clear already that substantial values will accrue to international relationships if non-governmental agencies can bring their rich and varied experience to the common fund.

The National Council of Social Service, then, is a complex. Social service has many interpretations : the one feature which is common to all its definitions is a primary interest in the rights, duties and opportunities of men and women as citizens and as members of the community. The chief purpose of the National Council of Social Service is to provide the machinery which enables the agencies, statutory and voluntary, engaged in social administration to be aware of and to operate in relationship to other agencies engaged in similar or relevant spheres of work. In conjunction with and as part of its approach to this purpose, the Council has a fundamental concern for the principles of local responsibility, and of autonomy of individual organisations ; and an abiding concern for the quality of community life. The Council thus represents a balance of social forces, and its immediate policies must always be the resultants of the forces predominant at any given time. To maintain sound and effective relationships with the statutory authorities, and yet remain independent ; to develop genuine co-operative relationships with the many and varied voluntary societies and yet to fulfil the responsibility of action when action is necessary : these demand a sensitive and flexible instrument. Nor must it be forgotten that a state of balance, while difficult to achieve, and still more difficult to maintain, also produces sometimes a deceptive appearance of inactivity. It would be inhuman perfection if the true balance were always achieved, but the attempt has been made over a very wide range of social policies, and much has been learned of the techniques and the instruments of co-operation without compulsion.

APPENDIX TO CHAPTER VII

Note. *Henry Mess published an essay on " Social Service in Rural Areas "
in the* Political Quarterly *(January-March 1943), Volume XIV. No. 1.
It was to have been the basis for a revised study as part of this book. As
it was first written, this essay dealt almost wholly with the developments in
rural areas for which the National Council of Social Service was responsible, and it has been thought more suitable to use it as the basis of an
appendix to the general study of the National Council of Social Service.
So far as possible Dr. Mess's own text has been retained, but it has been
brought up to date to cover the main features of the rural work of the Council.
A broad account over a wide range of rural social services will be found in
Part III Chapter 12 of* Voluntary Social Services, *published for the
Nuffield College Social Reconstruction Survey by Messrs. Methuen.*

In 1917 a recently formed Rural Organisations Council, to which
were affiliated sixteen societies, called a couple of conferences. The
conferences were concerned mainly with such matters as rural
housing after the war, the establishment of small holdings for
returned soldiers, and the possibilities of attracting industries to
rural areas. But time was also given to considering the needs of
rural education and questions of social amenities. The members of
the Council realised the need of village halls ; but they took a
gloomy view of the prospects of getting them, still more of maintaining them. Reference was made to the value of the performance of
plays by villagers, and examples were quoted from the Cotswolds
and from Grasmere. A paper was read on " Rural Disfigurement
and Its Remedies." A good deal was said about the defects of
rural education. There was an adumbration of what are now known
as Village Colleges. Indeed, many of the schemes which were to
be fruitful in the post-war years were adumbrated ; quite a number
of them existed *in petto.*

These conferences marked a growing interest in the problems of
rural life and a growing desire to do something about them. The
conferences were held in Oxford, and it was in and around Oxford
that action of a new kind was first taken. In 1919 the Oxfordshire
Rural Community Council. It was no mere coincidence
that its birth was within a few months of that of the National Council
of Social Service ; the same kind of ideas, and some of the same
group of men, were behind both. At the same time the Carnegie
United Kingdom Trust was getting into its stride ; the Trustees
had formulated a policy in which rural enterprises occupied a
prominent place. And statutory authorities, both central and local,
were becoming more active with regard to rural needs, especially
cultural needs. As a result of all this there was in the years following the war a great deal of fruitful experiment in which there was
elaborate and intricate collaboration between voluntary and

statutory bodies of various kinds, more particularly between the National Council of Social Service, the Rural Community Councils, the Carnegie United Kingdom Trust, the Development Commission, the Board of Education and the Ministries of Agriculture and of Health, County Councils and Rural District Councils and Parish Councils, and a large number of voluntary societies.

Very important was the development of Rural Community Councils. The Oxfordshire body was so obviously useful that an attempt was soon made to apply its method to other areas. In 1922 the Carnegie United Kingdom Trust made a grant to the National Council of £1,000 a year for three years to enable it to promote the formation of Rural Community Councils in other areas. In 1923 the Kent Rural Community Council was formed. Within the next decade thirty Rural Community Councils were started. Further grants were made by the Carnegie United Kingdom Trust until 1926, when in pursuance of its settled general policy it withdrew its help from that field of effort and turned its attention elsewhere. A few of the Rural Community Councils had become well established, but it was not so in the majority of cases, and a crisis was only averted and further advance was only made possible by the Development Commissioners stepping into the gap left by the Carnegie United Kingdom Trust's withdrawal. The finance of Rural Community Councils has continued to be a great difficulty, and some of them have collapsed, mainly on that account, though financial weakness is obviously a reflection, in part at least, of want of local interest. At the outbreak of the second World War there were twenty-two Rural Community Councils in existence.

During the early part of the war it seemed that some Rural Community Councils might find it even more difficult to keep going. In its later stages, it became clear that the war had brought new tasks and new opportunities to the Rural Community Councils which have led to much vigorous development, including the creation of new R.C.C.'s in Hereford and Worcestershire and the development of a most interesting three-county Community Council for Cambridgeshire, Huntingdonshire and the Island of Ely. There are now twenty-six Rural Community Councils covering twenty-four administrative counties in England and twenty-five in Wales.

Rural Community Councils are very similar in general structure to the National Council of Social Service and to the urban Councils of Social Service ; they are composed of representatives of the chief voluntary social service organisations within their area together with representatives of the statutory authorities, who may be full members or who may be sent merely as assessors and observers ; there are also a few co-opted persons, representing no particular body but valuable for their general interest or for their special knowledge. The aim is also comparable : it is to secure co-operation as fully as possible, to review steadily the social needs and the social provision of the area, and to enhance the welfare of the inhabitants. A Rural Community Council, like an urban Council of Social Service and like the National Council of Social Service, is not primarily an executive body : its business is not so much to carry on social services itself as to see that they are carried on. But in practice a Rural Community Council, like the other bodies named, does usually find itself involved in a certain amount of executive action.

It has been one of the marked differences between the Rural Community Councils and the urban Councils of Social Service that the former have been mainly concerned with the enrichment of normal life, whilst the latter have been much pre-occupied with the relief of distress. Both Rural Community Councils and the urban Councils of Social Service have come into existence to remedy bad conditions : but, whilst the latter may be said to have been concerned with specific diseases and crises of urban life, the former have been concerned not with particular positive evils but rather with the general condition of low vitality.

The area over which a Rural Community Council has operated has usually been an administrative county. There are obvious advantages in a coincidence of area of operations of the chief voluntary body and of the chief statutory body. It has sometimes, however, its inconveniences. In a number of cases the county is too small to be able to afford the machinery of a Rural Community Council, and in particular to raise the salary of a really competent chief officer. (It may be doubted in many of these cases whether the area is not also too small for efficient local government, but a discussion of that is outside our theme.) In such cases there are advantages in taking a larger area of operations, two, or perhaps three, adjoining counties. It is interesting to note that the Rural Community Council in five instances covers a wider area than one administrative county.[1]

One of the unsettled questions of Rural Community Council policy is their relation to the towns, especially to the larger towns and the industrial towns, within their area. Social work in towns, as we have said, tends to have another emphasis ; it is more concerned with the relief of distress and the meeting of particular crises. In any case it is concerned with populations with different outlook and different interests. Some Rural Community Councils have confined their attention to the strictly rural areas and to rural problems, as distinct from urban problems. Others have taken the towns into consideration. Especially in the years following 1931 there was some attention given to helping the unemployed in the towns ; and there was concern expressed by some supporters of Rural Community Councils lest they should be diverted from their original purpose. Other Rural Community Councils have considered it to be part of their normal work to deal with the towns within their area ; this appears to have been the policy in Notting-

---

[1] Cambridgeshire, Huntingdonshire, and the Island of Ely. Lincolnshire (parts of Lindsey and parts of Holland). Suffolk (East and West Suffolk). Sussex (East and West Sussex).

hamshire.   In Kent there was particularly striking action ; in 1930 the Kent Rural Community Council was converted into a Kent Council of Social Service, covering the whole geographical county, including such typically industrial areas as the Medway towns.   The Kent Council of Social Service is a strong body, well staffed ; it has offices in Folkestone, Maidstone and Sidcup ; and it seems to be fairly successful in dealing with both urban and rural problems.   But opinions differ sharply as to the wisdom of combining rural and urban work in the same organisation.

The Rural Community Council is the co-ordinating body in each county : its responsibility is to see that services are provided ; but the actual provision is, as we have indicated before, made by a number of organisations, often in an intricate collaboration.   We shall now consider some of the fields of social work which have been entered.

In the first place, there has been the provision of libraries.   This has been due in the main to the initiative of the Carnegie United Kingdom Trust, whose partners in the enterprise have been the local education authorities.   In the second place, there has been the field of formal adult education.   Here there has been a good deal of co-operation between the Rural Community Councils, the Workers Educational Association, the local education authorities, and the Carnegie United Kingdom Trust.   In the earlier years especially, the officers of the Rural Community Councils did a good deal of pioneering and undertook duties which in later years have usually, but not always, passed to the extra-mural boards of universities.   In some cases the Rural Community Councils have continued throughout to employ tutors and organisers for a wide range of cultural and educational work under the regulations for Further Education.

The Carnegie United Kingdom Trust has played a considerable part in this work also, notably by its grant to the Sawston Village College and by its grants to the Workers Educational Association to maintain resident tutors in country districts.   The Rural Community Councils have continued to do a good deal of work in connection with informal education ; they have, for instance, in a number of counties arranged series of health lectures in collaboration with the Red Cross.   In 1935 the National Council of Social Service negotiated with the British Broadcasting Corporation for a special series of talks to villagers, and the Rural Community Councils did their best to stimulate interest in those talks and to see that they were discussed.

With regard to music and drama a great deal has been accomplished.   In this sphere also the great Trusts have been very helpful. In most counties there have been formed music and drama committees of the Rural Community Councils.   In many counties there have been arranged schools for producers of plays and schools for conductors of choirs and of orchestras.   Usually there are yearly festivals at which dramatic societies and choirs compete.   The

Rural Community Councils have also been closely associated with the development of the Rural Music Schools. The plays chosen and the music rendered are usually of good quality; the performances sometimes reach a very high level. In addition to this evocation of local talent, there has been the arrangement of tours by professionals, notably the Village, Country Town and School concert parties which toured the country between 1920 and 1935. All this work in the field provided a firm foundation upon which the Carnegie United Kingdom Trust, after the most careful inquiry by the "Hichens Committee," based its policy for large grants in aid of musical activities, which came into operation in 1940. There are now 50 county music committees, and the Carnegie United Kingdom Trust has set up its own machinery for assisting the development of musical activities. The effect of the black-out and other war-time difficulties was, over the course of the war, one of the factors which led to a great increase in the demand for local music and drama, which in its turn was greatly stimulated by the activities of C.E.M.A. (now the Arts Council of Great Britain), an organisation for whose conception and early years the Pilgrim Trust was mainly responsible, and which is now an independent body financed by the Treasury. The National Council of Social Service has remained throughout the convener of a Joint Committee for Drama, bringing together the organisations, particularly the British Drama League, which has its local counterparts in county drama committees.

As activities were multiplied in the rural areas, the need for meeting places became more apparent. In 1924 the Development Commissioners placed in the hands of the National Council of Social Service a sum of £5,000 out of which loans could be made for the building of Village Halls. The loans service proved very popular and very successful. The National Council of Social Service placed on record in its annual report for 1933–4 that in respect of 265 loans to villages to build halls there had been no single case in which a village hall committee had failed to keep its promise to re-pay. Grants were also made by the Carnegie United Kingdom Trust towards the cost of new buildings. And after 1927 grants could be obtained also from the National Fitness Council. And also in a few cases grants were made by the Land Settlement Association in areas where it was operating. With this financial help some 800 village halls were built between 1918 and 1939. They have been of many kinds, sometimes converted cottages or barns, sometimes adapted houses, sometimes entirely new buildings. In the construction of many of them there was a good deal of voluntary labour given. Most of them are pleasant buildings; quite a number are of considerable æsthetic merit. It has always been an essential point of policy that grant-in-aid should be made available only for buildings which were architecturally sound and related to their surroundings. The war, of course, put a stop to building operations, and many village halls were requisitioned for military and other defence purposes, though strenuous and often successful efforts were made by the National Council of Social Service to prevent villages being unnecessarily deprived of their only means of social and cultural life. Since the war ended the Carnegie United Kingdom Trust have resumed their support and have set aside £100,000 over five years to grant-aid village hall building and extension schemes, and the Development Commission have renewed the loan funds. The creation and improvement of village halls in all parts of the country is likely to be one of the significant features of village life in the future, as building restrictions are gradually relaxed.

The work of Rural Community Councils in the encouragement and improvement of rural industries is another feature of their work which has made a substantial contribution to the well-being of the countryside. The Rural Industries Bureau was set up in 1921 on the initiative of and with financial assistance from the Development Commission. The purpose of the Bureau was " to maintain trades ancillary to agriculture in that state of efficiency which the needs of the farmer demanded."[1] The Bureau provided a technical advisory service which helped the rural craftsman to meet the changing needs of the times, especially those which resulted from greatly increased mechanisation. This service was carried on largely by the provision of technical officers who could advise and instruct, and it was aided by means of a library service, the provision of designs, the preparation of exhibitions and the promotion of trade organisations. While its major effort before the war was directed to the modernisation of methods and the protection and education of the rural blacksmith, it also made its mark in the woodworking, saddlery, basketmaking, pottery, textile, and quilting trades. The contribution of the Rural Community Councils was to provide the administrative framework through which these services could be made known to and used by the rural worker. Most Rural Community Councils had on their staffs a Rural Industries Organiser, whose mission was to enlist the support of the rural craftsman in the task of preserving and improving these industries which form a vital part of a healthy rural economy.

The value of this work has been amply demonstrated in war-time. The call for increased food production has led in its turn to a great extension of the use of agricultural machinery. This machinery, if it is not to lie idle, needs skilled repair and maintenance work, and the nearer the source of maintenance to the farm, the less waiting-time there is between the withdrawal of the machine and its return to productive work. The Rural Industries Bureau, therefore, undertook the task of training rural blacksmiths to maintain agricultural machinery. In order to help him to equip his shop with the necessary modern machine tools and equipment, the National Council of Social Service operated a Rural Industries

[1] *Report on the Work of the Rural Industries Bureau, 1929–36.*

Equipment Loan Fund, which enabled the craftsman, when trained, to obtain the tools he needed.

It has been noted that one of the primary objects of the National Council of Social Service is to bring together the statutory and voluntary agencies engaged in social service. In rural areas, the Council's contribution has been somewhat different. It has from the first laboured to show that the Parish Council, the smallest and the oldest unit of local government in this country, has an essential part to play in the social life of rural areas. In this it has been successful, especially in the later years of the war. An advisory service was organised in 1935 which gave Parish Councils accurate information on their powers, and encouraged them to use those powers, which are by no means as limited or as unimportant as at one time they were thought to be. Conferences have been held in all parts of the country which have roused local government authorities to recognise the way in which the Parish Council can serve its community. Proposals have been framed for the reform of local government so as to ensure that the Parish Council is better able to play its part. The war has brought Parish Councils many opportunities to show their capacity and they have taken their chances. In the result there is now a flourishing National Association of Parish Councils, and it seems probable that in the future there will be a steady increase in the number of vigorous well-organised Parish Councils, making their contribution to the social life of the rural areas.

Chapter VIII

THE WORK OF VOLUNTARY SOCIAL SERVICES AMONG CHILDREN BEFORE SCHOOL-LEAVING AGE

by

VIOLET CREECH-JONES

IN modern times there has been little difficulty in awakening public sympathy for the helpless and the weak, and for none less than for children. Ignorance, ill-health and poverty among children cannot be attributed to their own stupidity, rash conduct or wilful improvidence. Society, through the generations, has slowly reversed the view that the sins of the fathers should be visited upon the children. There has, however, even to the present day been a conflict in men's minds between the positive desire to do what is right for the child and the negative aim to do nothing which might lessen the sense of duty and the feeling of responsibility in parenthood. Social work, therefore, for children began among the orphaned and deserted where the criticism of undermining parental responsibility could hardly be made. It was not until the present century and the economic expansion which had preceded it that the idea of the child as a person in Society distinct from being a possession of its parents, was recognised by common assent and by law.

Much of the work, therefore, of the voluntary associations on behalf of children between the two world wars has had the double purpose of doing what is best for the child and educating and training the parents that they become better equipped to fulfil the duties of parenthood. Probably the most effective work of voluntary associations has been where the parents have been persuaded to co-operate in the improvement of conditions for their children.

Our purpose in this chapter must be first to give some account of various voluntary associations for normal children living at home with parents and enjoying a normal family life. We shall deal with the infant and toddler to five years of age, and therefore shall consider the work in maternity and child welfare, children's nurseries and the Nursery Schools. This must include a reference to the efforts that have been made by the voluntary organisations in teaching of parent-craft and the need for the building up of sound bodies and minds of the children. We must also include the work done for children of school age, including the work of Care Committees and those efforts for the better employment of leisure time as, for example, the Play Centre Movement and Children's Country Holiday Fund.

We shall then pass to a consideration of the work done for children deprived of a normal home life—the orphaned, the illegitimate, and the neglected child.

Consideration must finally be given to the work done for the delinquent and maladjusted child. This will include some reference to the co-operation of voluntary associations with the work of the Children's Courts and the Children's Branch of the Home Office.

The work among children physically and mentally handicapped is described in another chapter.

I. THE NORMAL CHILD UNDER FIVE

Until 1919, when the Ministry of Health was established, practically all of the work for the under-fives was carried out by voluntary associations from charitable and public-spirited motives. In 1906 the National Association for the Prevention of Infant Mortality and for the Welfare of Infancy was established to co-ordinate the work already done on behalf of mothers and children. Earlier organisations existed, e.g. " Association of Infant Consultations " and " Schools for Mothers." At the beginning of the century " Milk Depots " were opened in industrial areas such as Huddersfield and Battersea where sterilised milk was sold daily for infants and where mothers could bring the infants to be weighed and inspected by a doctor. This was largely municipal effort, but in many of the schemes there was a combination of municipal and voluntary effort. Outstanding among these was the St. Pancras School for Mothers, founded in 1907, which co-ordinated the municipal work of notification of births, advice cards to mothers, and health visiting, with the philanthropic work of " The Babies'

Welcome " and " School for Mothers ", where the mothers and babies were given medical attention—classes were held in cookery and in the making of babies' clothes and Provident Maternity Clubs and Fathers' Evening Conferences were also arranged.

In 1911 the Kensington Baby Clinic was opened as a memorial to Mary Middleton and Margaret Macdonald. That was not only an infant consultation centre, but also a medical treatment centre for children. Eight years later an in-patient department was also opened. The organisation which later was to be known as the " Association of Maternity and Child Welfare Centres " was formed in 1911, its object being the establishment of centres where expectant and nursing mothers and toddlers could have advice on diet and clothing, receive medical attention, and be taught the rudiments of mothercraft. At that time there were already in England and Wales 100 such infant welfare centres. The founders of this movement were prompted to action by the high mortality of infants and mothers in childbirth. The figures in England and Wales in 1900 showed the infant death rate as 154 per 1,000 registered live births. In 1904 it fell to 145, in 1910 to 106, in 1919 to 89, and by 1939 it was reduced to 50. The inquiries of the Ministry of Health in its early days in 1919 showed that no less than 45 per cent of the 5,000 deaths of mothers during childbirth were considered to be preventable. The maternal mortality rate remained fairly constant between 1900 and 1933 at 4 per 1,000 births, and this in spite of the work in maternity and child welfare in the ante-natal clinics. Since 1935, however, this rate has fallen to a little over half of this —a reduction attributed by Dr. F. Grundy[1] to the introduction of new drugs of the sulphonamide group to combat sepsis. " Whereas in 1935 a serious case of infection had only a fifty-fifty chance of recovery, by 1940 almost every case treated with the new drugs recovered." These discoveries in medical treatment do not diminish the value of the work done by the Maternity and Child Welfare Services, which for more than forty years have been pegging away at improving the environment and developing ante-natal clinics for spreading knowledge in hygiene and nutrition.

[1] Medical Officer of Health, Luton, in an article in *Todd's Directory of Health and Social Welfare* (1945-6).

Many of the centres created were housed in makeshift buildings such as church halls, and in rooms in social and educational settlements, where much devoted work was done under difficult conditions by professional people and lay women concerned with the welfare of the child. It was soon found that the mere holding of a clinic was insufficient. Gradually the work extended to the care of the mother. Provision was made for dental treatment and so on. Classes were held in the proper feeding and care of the child, in needlework and knitting and in general subjects such as hygiene, keep-fit, etc. In the very poor neighbourhoods a Day Nursery was sometimes opened so that the babies of mothers who were obliged to go out to work could be minded.

Much of this work was entirely supported by voluntary contributions, but after the first world war the State itself began to assume some responsibility for this social service, and from 1919 grants were made by the Ministry of Health direct to the voluntary committees and were generally based on 50 per cent of the approved expenditure.

In 1929 some of this maternity and child welfare work was taken over entirely by the local authorities, though a considerable part still remained in the hands of voluntary associations. From that time onwards the Committees controlling the voluntary maternity and child welfare centres received a very high percentage grant (between 80 per cent and 90 per cent) from the rates and the allocation made to them in the block grant by the Ministry of Health.[1]

It is of interest to note that many organisations sprang up to further this work immediately prior to and during the first world war. They often tapped the same charitable sources for their funds, and were sometimes overlapping in their aims. To find an outlet for Red Cross activities in peace-time, an effort was made in 1919 to co-ordinate the welfare work on behalf of children by the formation of the Central Council for

[1] MATERNITY AND CHILD WELFARE CENTRES

	Owned, controlled, and financed entirely by local authorities	Governed by voluntary committees
1935	2490	813
1941	2832	796
1942	2893	819
1943	2994	831

(From *Todd's Directory of Health and Social Welfare*, 1945–6.)

Infant and Child Welfare. (This Council in 1927 became known as the National Council for Maternity and Child Welfare.) This body consisted at first of twelve affiliated organisations including the Association of Infant Welfare and Maternity Centres ; the Invalid Children's Aid Association ; National League for Health, Maternity and Child Welfare ; National Association for the Prevention of Infantile Mortality ; National Society of Day Nurseries; and National Baby Week (later Welfare) Council. Its primary object was " to promote the development of the welfare of mothers and children ; to provide a central bureau of information on subjects connected with maternal and child welfare, and to maintain a library for the use of students and other workers concerned ; to organise popular instruction through exhibitions, museums, lectures, demonstrations and loan of teaching appliances ; to arrange conferences and congresses of authorities and organisations concerned with maternal and child welfare, to establish in foreign countries and British dominions overseas, local councils or committees to further any of all of the above objects." The Council sought to co-ordinate services as they found them and to organise the supply and distribution of funds and workers. In 1922 Carnegie House, the centre for this work, was opened, and year after year societies such as the Child Guidance Council and the Save the Children Fund (1930), the Nursery School Association (1933), and the Association of Nursery Training Colleges (1936) became associated with its work, and by 1945 there were nineteen constituent societies.

It was at the end of the last century that the *Day Nursery* movement began and a little later, in 1906, the National Society of Day Nurseries was founded purely as a voluntary movement. At this time there were about thirty nurseries. The object of the Society was to set a standard ; to bring together matrons and others interested for mutual discussion on the problem of the nurseries—to act as an information bureau and to encourage the setting up of more nurseries. In the first great war the Board of Education officially recognised eighty nurseries and gave to the voluntary associations grants towards their cost of fourpence per child attendance. 1918 saw the passing of the Maternity and Child Welfare Act, and that gave permissive powers to local authorities themselves to open Day Nurseries. Comparatively little was done in this respect, however, except by the most progressive of the authorities, and much of the work continued to remain in the hands of voluntary associations.   Later, in the schemes made by the Ministry of Health under the Local Government Act, 1929, there were included in the London area alone 35 Day Nurseries, run by voluntary associations, to which the Metropolitan Borough Councils of London were instructed to pay, in the aggregate, £18,890 per annum. By 1933 there were throughout the country 100 Day Nurseries, 18 run by local authorities, 82 by voluntary associations. By 1938 the figures were 102 Day Nurseries, plus 59 homes, affiliated to the National Society, making a total of 161, accommodating 5,709 children.

Much of the pioneer work in this development was done by the National Society of Day Nurseries, recently renamed National Society of Children's Nurseries. This Association has been concerned not only with the provision of suitable accommodation for this service, but also with the personnel for the running of the nurseries. It has organised over the years a course of training for Nursery Nurses and awarded a diploma to students after a training of two years. This course will now be arranged[1] by a Joint Examining Board, constituted by representatives of the Royal Sanitary Institute, Nursery School Association, National Society of Children's Nurseries, Association of Nursery Training Colleges, and Associated Council of Children's Homes, together with nominees of the two Ministries. During the recent war years there has been an enormous increase in wartime nurseries, due to the fact that the Ministry of Health paid the total capital and maintenance costs, less 1s. per day charged to the parent of the child attending. Local authorities were allowed to affiliate to the National Society of Children's Nurseries, which affiliation fees, together with gifts from the United States, relieved the Society from financial worries. But the work of the Society in advising on equipment and staffing, in training Nursery Nurses, and awarding its diploma has increased greatly during these years of war. This work must continue even when the Nursery Service becomes statutory and part of the national health scheme. The Day Nursery Service has been provided in the past mainly for those children whose mothers have been in full-time employment either because of

[1] Under a joint Circular of the Ministry of Health (126/45), and Ministry of Education (59).

economic necessity or, during the war, because of taking part in the national effort. During recent discussions on the future of Day Nurseries the point of view has been put publicly that such nursery provision should be available for all whose parents desire the service. A case has been made for them to be used occasionally when parents desire to go out together or when the temporary illness or death of the mother makes it necessary for the small child to be cared for outside the home. In the early nurseries, financed entirely by voluntary subscriptions and often partially staffed by voluntary workers, the aim was to come to the aid of the necessitous family, but now that the provision is considered for general application it would obviously need to become statutory.

The development of the *Nursery School* movement in this country owes also a great deal to the work of the voluntary associations. It began early in the present century when (in 1911) Rachel McMillan and her sister Margaret opened at Deptford the first nursery school for children under the compulsory school attendance age. The idea behind this experiment was to train the small child in self-reliance and social conduct, by giving him healthy surroundings, interesting occupation and teaching how to live in a community. The emphasis throughout was on the importance of the child, although the Nursery School movement has always emphasised the need for the closest co-operation between the school and the home and the teacher and the parent. The Nursery School movement was not confined to poor children ; indeed, much of its work has been encouraged by those parents who recognised its value to the child and could afford to pay for the service.

A good deal of prejudice had to be broken down in the early days because current opinion was that a child of two and a half was best left with its mother and within the circle of the home. It is true that children were frequently accepted in the elementary schools from the age of three, but until recent years no special provision was made for them either in equipment or in the methods of teaching. One of the advantages of the nursery school was that the small child found itself in the environment devised to fit it—for instance, hooks for its clothes which it could reach, and tables and chairs of correct height.

Gradually a few local educational authorities opened nursery schools and paid attention to the equipping of nursery classes in the elementary schools. This they were enabled to do by the permissive powers given to them by the Fisher Act of 1918, when the local education authorities were permitted to supply or aid the supply of nursery schools and nursery classes " for children over two and under five years of age or such later age as may be approved by the Board of Education, whose attendance at such a school is necessary or desirable for their healthy physical and mental development." During the slump of 1931, instructions were issued limiting nursery schools to " children who by reason of unsuitable environment require careful attention to their physical welfare." The setback following these instructions is revealed in the figures recorded in the Annual Reports of the Nursery School Association. They state that in 1934, there were 62 recognised nursery schools accommodating 4,933 children out of a child population (two-to-fives) of 1,700,000—34 of them run by local authorities and 28 by voluntary committees. Next year there were 72 nursery schools, and in addition 19 sanctioned, giving 5,440 places. By 1937 the schools numbered 96 (10 established by the Save the Children Fund in special distressed areas) and a year later 107, accommodating 8,300 children. Of the 115 nursery schools in this country just before the outbreak of the recent war half were provided by the local education authorities. The total accommodation was for 9,500 children only and there was little prospect at that time of any improvement in that position. Most of the war-time nurseries made provision for children of nursery-school age. Unqualified wardens and some fully trained nursery-school teachers were engaged to teach them, but the enthusiasts of nursery schools have felt that owing to the long hours during which these war-time nurseries were open, in spite of good effort, they fell far short of nursery-school standards.

The Nursery School Association, since its establishment in 1923, has worked hard to encourage the establishment of these schools. It sought to advise on the design of the schools and the making of the right kind of educational equipment for them and to assist in educating public opinion on all matters relating to nursery-school education. Its membership consists mainly of teachers, doctors, parents, administrators, and public representatives on local authorities.

It is largely to the credit of this Association that the recognition of the nursery school as an essential part of a complete educational system, in the Education Act, 1944, has been won. The Act declares that " A local education authority shall have regard to the need for securing that provision is made for pupils who have not attained the age of five years by the provision of Nursery Schools, or where the authority consider the provision of such schools to be inexpedient, by the provision of nursery classes in other schools."

The work of the Association, however, does not end with the acceptance of this principle. Its work in advising the local education authorities on design, equipment, and the training of nursery-school staffs is still imperative.

II. THE NORMAL CHILD OF SCHOOL AGE

We turn now to the work done for the *normal child of school age*. Social work for such children has frequently been done with the school as centre. The local education authorities have encouraged the work of many associations which supplement their own work for the child under fourteen. Although in this country school medical inspection has been developed since 1904 (in 1905, forty-nine education authorities had appointed school doctors; by 1907, school medical inspection had become compulsory). But it is not too much to say that the success of the school medical inspection depended in the early days almost entirely on the voluntary work of the School Care Committees—committees approved by the School Managers and concerned with the welfare of the children. There was the initial resentment on the part of many parents to any interference in their control of their children. Often through ignorance and stubbornness they refused to carry out the instructions of the doctor or dentist and it was largely due to the powers of persuasion of the Care Committee secretary that the opposition of the parents was gradually broken down. In the early days of school medical inspection many mothers refused to attend while their children were being examined and ignored the advice given by the doctor. Then also much of the treatment recommended had not, until recent years, been provided. Treatment centres, dental clinics for school children, were slowly set up, and School Care Committees have done great work in the last forty years in following up cases after medical inspection. Medical treatment has been arranged, cards procured for treatment in voluntary hospitals, financial aid given or easy payments arranged for spectacles, surgical instruments, etc.

Care Committees were appointed by the School Managers to the majority of the elementary schools following the Education (Provision of Meals) Act, 1906. In 1909 it is a matter of interest that twelve paid assistants were appointed to each of the twelve districts of London, but much of the work of investigation still remained in the hands of the voluntary committees. This partnership of the paid social investigator and the voluntary worker concerned itself with all matters connected with the health and well-being of the school child.

The School Care Committees throughout the country have helped in many other ways in providing boots and clothing for necessitous children and in investigating and assessing the need for free or cheap milk and meals. Before the coming of the present close co-operation of the Juvenile Employment Exchanges with the school authorities, the School Care Committee generally interviewed the school leavers and tried to find them jobs best suited to their ability. These social workers were the " go-betweens " between the schools and the homes and consequently in this respect made an invaluable contribution to the welfare of the child.

Attention has also been given to the schoolchild in its leisure hours. In many districts in our large towns where public open spaces are few and the houses are overcrowded and without gardens the children have only the streets to play in and their homes afford no space where homework can be done or some hobby pursued in peaceful surroundings. To minimise those disabilities Play Centres, organised by voluntary workers, have been created on school premises or at social or educational centres (maintained by voluntary subscriptions) to amuse and to teach hobbies to children of school age so that they utilise their leisure to advantage. The children have been able at many of these play centres to buy their tea for a few pence. This has meant, in recent years, that children of school age whose parents are at work can be supervised from 9 a.m. to 6.30 p.m. first at school where they remain for dinner and then for tea and play at the play centre. The play centre movement was established as far back as 1897 by Mrs. Humphrey Ward in St. Pancras at what is now called the Mary Ward Settlement. In 1904–5 the Children's Play Centre Fund was opened to establish play centres in elementary schools, and within a year the first seven centres were opened. The Treasury in 1917 agreed to allow a grant to be given to the Fund towards the provision of such centres and two years later the L.C.C. made a grant also to the centres in its administrative area. With this financial backing the movement expanded its influence in London and also to 46 other local education authority areas. By 1932–3 there were 41 centres open in London in the evenings, with an annual attendance of 1,500,000 children, and by 1938 there were 58 evening play centres and 34 holiday play centres. During the early days of the war these play centres were opened in settlements, church halls, and air-raid shelters, and on the 1st April 1941 the L.C.C. took over the organisation and maintenance of all the London play centres from the Children's Play Centre Fund.

The Save the Children Fund has also opened several of these play centres. In 1918 the Hop Scotch Inn, St. Pancras, was opened as a Junior Club for boys and girls, and has recently been opened during the day as a play centre for the under-fives. Some very interesting play-centre work has always been done by the residential settlements. The particular advantage of the settlement centres has been that there is some continuity for the child when it leaves the play centre at the age of fourteen since there is generally a club to which the child can be transferred. Another development for the school child was the provision for as many children as possible of an annual holiday in the country. The largest and best known of these organisations was the *Children's Country Holiday Fund*. This Society goes back to 1884, and was founded to arrange suitable accommodation for children in the country and to assess and collect according to the family income, by easy payments over a period of weeks, the cost of the holiday, and to provide escorts to conduct the children between their own homes and the place of holiday. In its first year 4,600 boys and girls had a holiday ; by 1912, 46,602. The number in 1936 was 33,919, and the total from 1884 to 1939, 1,563,128 children.

In any account of voluntary work among children the *Save the Children Fund*, mentioned already, must not be omitted.

Founded in 1919 and incorporated in 1921, it is " an association whose aim it is, irrespective of race, country or creed, to
preserve child life wherever menaced by conditions of hardship
and distress and to raise the standards of child care and protection throughout the world." The scope of its work is international, consisting of forty national organisations in thirty-six
countries.

It has helped in our own country to organise and finance
residential nurseries and nursery schools, junior clubs and play
centres, both for British children and refugees and coloured
children, and was particularly active in the distressed areas
during the years of the trade depression.

The School Journey Association is another society concerned with
school holidays. It was founded in 1911 to co-ordinate the
work built up in the previous twenty years in the schools for
making arrangements for groups of children to travel in their
school holidays. The aim was to act as an advice bureau as
regards travelling arrangements and suitable accommodation
for parties of school children. The work of the Association
expanded so that in the years immediately preceding the
second world war the Association was advising and making
arrangements for large parties of children to travel to Europe
and distant parts of the Empire. It worked in closest co-operation with the school organisation. The holiday leaders were
the teachers, and, although the journeys were recreational, the
preparation for them in lesson time and the arrangement
during holiday time of the curriculum on school lines made them
primarily educational.

III. The Orphaned Child

So far we have described the voluntary work concerned with
the normal child enjoying a home. We turn now to the work
for children who have not had normal conditions, the first
obvious group of which is the orphan. The care of the
orphaned child has always been the recognised concern of
charitable groups of men as also of all great religious organisations. Since the Middle Ages when the Guilds undertook to
support the orphans of their members, trade and professional
organisations have frequently established as part of their benevolent work homes for orphan children, e.g. the Teachers, Com-

mercial Travellers, Railwaymen, the Masons, etc., all have such homes. Certain religious communities, as for example the Jewish Board of Guardians and the Catholic Welfare Council, care for the orphans born into their own faith. But by far the majority of orphaned children are cared for by philanthropic bodies such as Dr. Barnardo's, and by such societies as the Church of England Waifs and Strays, the National Children's Home and Orphanage, etc., which although, in the case of some, were founded by a particular religious denomination, have long made an appeal for funds to the general public and have admitted any orphaned child.

The attitude of most organisations concerned with the work towards the children in their care has undergone a significant change with the growth of social ideas within the present century. In their early days some of the societies showed a conscious effort to keep the children in " their proper stations." The girls were seldom trained for anything but domestic work and the boys rarely taught a trade, but left to swell the numbers of the unskilled casual labourers while many were encouraged to emigrate. Between the wars this approach to employment and settlement has almost completely broken down and it is generally true that great pains are now taken to find out the abilities of the child and to make provision for the most suitable training. Thus children from the National Children's Home and Dr. Barnardo's may, if suitable, be trained to earn their living in a great variety of callings, not excluding such posts as scientific workers, librarians, teachers, dispensers, veterinary surgeons, etc.

The best of these orphanages are concerned with ways and means of making up to the child the loss of a normal family life. Efforts are commonly made by means of the cottage-home system to break down the institutionalism which in the past exposed these societies to much criticism. Both Dr. Barnardo's Home and the National Children's Home have training centres for the men and women engaged in the work of running their Homes.

Dr. Barnardo's Home is probably the most famous and was founded as far back as 1865 by " the father of nobody's children." It is to-day governed by a voluntary council of twenty. Since its foundation 132,683 children have been received and trained in these Homes. These children have been cared for in various ways, sometimes in large institutions, subdivided into cottage homes, and sometimes boarded out in private families. At the close of 1944 more than 37 per cent of the children, i.e. 2,979 out of 7,961, were boarded out.

The Church of England Waifs and Strays, founded in 1881, provided for over 56,000 children. By the end of 1944 there were 6,073 children in the care of the organisation ; 4,889 in homes and war nurseries, 1,263 boarded out, and 112 in other Church Homes.

The Methodist Church also felt its concern for the homeless children, and in 1869 formed the National Children's Home. It undertakes to train and supervise the children in its care up to the age of sixteen years. After the children leave the Home they are still supervised. The Home is able to admit between 800 and 900 boys and girls a year.

The other bodies working in this field are the Catholic Child Welfare Council, the Jewish Board of Guardians, and the Shaftesbury Homes and *Arethusa* Training Ship.

The six large organisations form the Associated Council of Children's Homes, and between them, in 1944, were responsible[1] for 35,182 children, of whom 30,300 were resident in Homes, 3,880 were boarded out, and 1,002 had been adopted.

In 1945 the Home Secretary appointed a Committee under the Chairmanship of Miss Myra Curtis, to investigate the subject of all children's homes run by voluntary associations and public authorities, e.g. public assistance committees of local authorities. The recommendations of the Committee are now being studied and an announcement as to what action will follow will be awaited with interest by all concerned with the welfare of the orphaned and deserted child.

IV. THE ILLEGITIMATE CHILD

The next group concerns children who have not had the advantage of normal home conditions and are illegitimate.

It is rare, and usually only in the case of the most exclusive type of orphanage, that help is denied to a child merely on the ground that it is illegitimate. The large organisations providing for orphan children stress the fact that they are willing to receive any child in need of a home. The majority of aban-

---

[1] Figures (approx.) supplied by Rev. John H. Witten, Principal of the National Children's Homes and Orphanages, Highbury Park, London.

E

doned and deserted children are illegitimate and usually have been abandoned by mothers not necessarily callous and wanton, but for whom the struggle for existence with the child is too difficult to face.

The voluntary associations working on behalf of the illegitimate child have been formed either to make possible that the mother remains with her child or to arrange for the proper adoption of the infant. *The National Council for the Unmarried Mother and her Child* was formed in 1918 with the threefold object (1) to obtain reform of the existing Bastardy and Affiliation Acts, (2) to secure the provision of adequate accommodation to meet the special aim of keeping mother and child together, and (3) to deal with individual inquiries on behalf of the unmarried mother.

The National Council is linked with the National Council of Social Service, and is one of the earliest constituent societies of the National Council for Maternity and Child Welfare.

The primary object of the National Council for the Unmarried Mother is to keep mother and child together, and the twenty-fifth annual report (1943-4) asserts that " our experience makes us believe that only when it is really impossible that the mother should care adequately for her child ought it to be adopted and, moreover, that such adoption should be arranged only by trained and experienced persons." The work of the Association has grown. In 1919 the number of cases registered was 452. In recent years the numbers have shown a remarkable increase—in 1941-2 they were 1,882—by 1943-4 they had reached 4,113.

The work of the Council has been many-sided. It has sought to remove the stigma of illegitimacy from the child, and under the Legitimacy Act, 1936, 30,000 children have been re-registered. In recent years it has represented the interests of the unmarried mother in deputations to Government departments on such matters as maternity benefit and children's allowances, and it has acted as a centre of information about homes and hostels for unmarried mothers and helped in providing suitable employment for the mothers.

The association has been run entirely by voluntary effort, but in the autumn of 1943 its financial position became so critical that an appeal had to be made to the Ministry of Health for aid. A grant of £500 was made towards the cost of the work.

The *National Children's Adoption Association* had its origin in the desire of its founder (the late Miss Clara Andrew) that it should assist children orphaned or rendered destitute by the 1914-18 war and help the victims of desertion or cruelty. The purpose of the N.C.A.A. has been to agitate for the reform of the laws governing the adoption of infants and to arrange for adoptions " on the principle that in all adoption it is the welfare and happiness of the child that must be considered first and foremost." A number of hostels have been opened by the Association where adopters and babies can meet.

In 1943, 265 children were placed with adopters and 188 adoptions were legalised. The following year 306 children were placed with adopters and 246 adoptions were legalised. It was not until 1926 that the Adoption of Children Act was passed providing for legal adoption, and then only after many years of agitation. In 1939 the Adoption of Children (Regulations) Act was placed on the Statute Book. This measure provided that all adoptions arranged by bodies of persons should take place through registered adoption societies or local authorities and partly did away with the commercialisation of adoption which had hitherto prevailed. It prohibited payments of any kind in respect of adoptions. But war-time conditions have afforded many opportunities for haphazard and privately arranged adoptions and the law still needs tightening up in certain respects.

The National Adoption Society is concerned with the legal adoption of infants mostly under twelve months old. Occasionally toddlers under two are dealt with but never children of school age. It was registered in May 1943 by the L.C.C. under the Adoption of Children (Regulations) Act, 1939, and during its first year it arranged 749 adoptions.

V. The Neglected Child

The last group of children without normal home conditions is the neglected child. The best-known organisation concerned with such children and the cruelly treated child is the National Society for the Prevention of Cruelty to Children. This was founded in 1884 by Benjamin Waugh for the purpose shown in its title, but it has assumed the positive function of giving " the kind of advice and assistance to erring parents which will help them to give their children the life to which they are entitled." At first the Society operated only in London, but it soon extended its activities to the whole of the British Isles.

The growth of the work of the Society can be seen from the following figures :

Date	Cases handled	Children affected	No. of prosecutions
1884	95	175	9
1912	54,118	156,637	2,356
1918	38,422	112,024	1,421
1925	38,559	95,512	882
1938	48,523	120,995	819
1944	41,050	107,312	1,452

The prestige of the Society has grown. In the year 1944, 93% of the cases were taken up and satisfactorily dealt with by warning and advice. This makes a significant contrast with 1889–90, when only 54·1% of cases taken up were satisfactorily dealt with by warning and advice. In the year 1944–5, of the cases handled only in 1·5% of them were prosecutions necessary. This again makes a significant contrast with the year 1889–90, when 12·6% of cases were prosecuted.

The work of the Society is organised on a regional basis, each with its own officer and inspector, and group of voluntary workers, who raise locally most of the funds for running the Society. The inspectors receive and investigate complaints, give advice to neglectful and cruel parents in their homes— and try as much as possible to avoid prosecutions. When all other methods have failed they supply facts to Counsel who prosecute on behalf of the N.S.P.C.C., and act as witnesses for the prosecution. In 1889 there were only ten inspectors. The number in 1912 was 250 ; in 1938, 271 ; and in 1945 there were 227 inspectors. At the present moment the aim of the Society is to have 300 inspectors at work, and to have 3,000 centres from which to spread knowledge of the purposes for which the Society stands. Rightly, it claims that the most important part of its work is done without any need of prosecution. " Parental instinct," it says, " is being cultivated and strengthened." The Society " is as anxious to preserve the rights of parents as to redress the wrongs of children. . . . The inspectors do all they can to avoid prosecuting parents."

Much valuable work has been done by the Society in using

the Children and Young Persons Act of 1933, not only for the prosecution of parents who have neglected their children, but also in bringing before the Juvenile Court children in need of care and protection. This widening of the scope of the Society in conjunction with the Juvenile Courts has assisted largely in the improved protection now afforded to children.

VI. The Maladjusted and Delinquent Child

Before considering the work of voluntary associations on behalf of children in this category, reference should be made to the work of two voluntary societies which have been concerned with the emotional and psychological aspects of child welfare, namely, the State Children's Association and the Child Guidance Council.

The State Children's Association was founded in 1897 and for many years was under the Chairmanship of the late Lovat Fraser. As its title suggests, it was concerned primarily with children who had come under the protection of the State because of (1) destitution (e.g. in the hands of the Boards of Guardians, later called the Public Assistance Committees, of the local authority (County Council or County Borough)), or (2) recommendation by the Courts.

This Association was primarily a propagandist organisation, pointing out the advantages of the boarding-out system with foster-parents in private homes, rather than the grouping of children in large institutions. It emphasised the drawbacks of institutionalism and pressed for the extension of the probation system, whereby the child who had broken the law could remain in his home and be befriended by the Probation Officer. The 1928 report of the State Children's Association compares the percentage of children put on probation in 1924 and 1927. Thus, in 1924, of the 25,804 children brought before the Courts, 5,972 or 23·14% were put on probation, and in 1927, out of 22,448 children 6,302 or 28·07% were put on probation.[1]

---

[1] The use of probation for juveniles brought before the Courts for indictable offences has also grown since the last war.

1918—25·4%.
1925—47·6%.
1931—55·2%.
1934—54·1%.
1939—61·3%.
1942 and 1944—each 44·6%.

The 1930 report of the Association restates its purposes as (1) the furtherance of boarding-out, (2) the advancement of probation, (3) the appointment of clinics for the examination of child offenders. The 1932 report expresses regret that no observation centres for the treatment of young offenders were provided under the Children's and Young Persons Act of that year, but in 1935, as a result of a joint deputation with the Child Guidance Council to the Home Office, the Association claims that a scheme for the training of staffs for children's Homes was initiated.

The Association disappeared in 1937 on the death of its Chairman, who was a Member of Parliament and therefore able to promote the ideas of the Association, both in Parliament and outside. It was accordingly able to focus public attention on the need for children to have a natural home life, during the period when the care of public assistance children was passing from the hands of the Guardians to the County Councils (in 1930), and when the Children's and Young Persons Act of 1933 was being framed.

The second body mentioned above was the *Child Guidance Council* (now incorporated with the Central Association for Mental Welfare and the National Council for Mental Hygiene to form the National Council for Mental Health). It was founded in 1928, as the result of a generous grant from the Commonwealth Fund of America, and joined the National Council for Maternity and Child Welfare in 1930. Its objects were to advise and assist in the setting up of Child Guidance Clinics—to train social workers for child guidance work, to supply workers to be lent to newly formed clinics from the London Child Guidance Clinic, to award fellowships to students of psychology to continue child guidance work (in 1931 four fellowships were awarded by the Council in psychiatry and two in psychology), and to act as a centre of information for all interested in child guidance work. In 1935 there were 18 clinics and by 1937 they had increased to 46, 11 of them wholly and 12 of them partly maintained by the local authority. Twenty-three were entirely supported by voluntary contributions. In the following year there were 54—16 wholly maintained by local authorities receiving 50% grant from the Board of Education as part of the School Medical Service, 10 partially maintained and 20 voluntary clinics. By 1942 there were 62 and by the next year they had increased to 68. In 1945 they numbered 84, 53 of which are maintained by the local authority as part of the School Medical Service.

The importance of the work of the clinics has slowly gained public recognition, although the problems of evacuation and the blitzed towns during the war have made the need of them more pressing. They are being increasingly used both for diagnosis and treatment by education authorities, by magistrates of Juvenile Courts and by anxious parents. The earliest purpose served was one of vocational guidance and much prejudice had to be broken down, but now the team composed of psychiatrist, psychologist, and psychiatric social workers, who form the staff of the clinics, is frequently called upon, not only to try to detect the causes of emotional disturbances from which difficult children suffer, but to furnish intelligence and psychological reports to the education authorities and to the magistrates of the Juvenile Court. Sometimes a Juvenile Court, in cases of child delinquency, will make a probation order with a condition that the child attends a Child Guidance Clinic for treatment, where, by methods of play therapy, careful observation, and attention to the child's physical and mental weaknesses and to its home conditions, the child can be helped to develop those qualities necessary for life in society which he previously lacked.

Frequently, however, the magistrates feel that the child before them needs something more than a probation order with condition of residence or attendance at a child guidance clinic, and they commit the child to an *Approved School*. Again the provision of such schools was first made by voluntary associations, and it is only within recent years that some of the enthusiastic local education authorities have made similar provision. The earlier schools were provided by (a) large orphanage institutions, e.g. Barnardo's National Children's Home, which provided Approved Schools in addition to their schools for orphans and deserted children, or (b) by religious organisations, e.g. the Salvation Army, the Church Army, the Crusade of Rescue (Senior Schools for Catholic children only), the Society of Friends, Jewish Board of Guardians, and the Police Court Mission. All such schools, whether controlled by local education authorities or by voluntary associations, are approved and inspected by the Home Office, which makes a 50% grant towards the cost of maintenance.

In the Home Office Directory of Approved Schools, etc. 1941–2, of the 30 Approved Schools for Junior Boys, 20 are managed by voluntary associations and 10 by local education authorities, and of the 15 Approved Schools for Junior Girls, only 1 (Gisburne House) is managed by the local education authority (the L.C.C.).   In 1934 there were 57 Junior Approved Schools, 44 managed by voluntary associations, 13 by local education authorities.   During the war 1939–45, 19 new Approve Schools (Junior Intermediate and Senior) have been established by 8 voluntary associations.

The schools vary widely in type, classified for boys, junior intermediate, and senior, and for girls into junior and senior. The only co-educational school approved by the Home Office is the Caldecott Community, which was founded as a nursery school in St. Pancras in 1911, and became in 1917 a country boarding house for London children.   In 1930 the Council of the school decided to provide refuge and education for the child with abnormal home conditions.   Since 1940 about 20% of the children under the age of eleven admitted have been charged under the Children's and Young Persons Act, 1933, and sent by the local education authorities through the Children's Courts.   Preference is given " to the sensitive intelligent child who in the opinion of the Committee is best able to benefit by the kind of education offered at the Community." Caldecott Community is therefore unique in certain respects.

Much discussion is at present taking place as to whether the normal and the delinquent should be educated together, and also whether the local education authorities ought to be responsible for the education of all the children in their areas.   The latter suggestion would mean that the local education authorities would take over all the Approved Schools.   Opinions differ as to the respective functions of local education authorities and of voluntary associations in education, but all agree that there is still great need for experimentation in this field of work.   It may be that the voluntary association (generously aided from public funds) is one of the means by which experiment can be best achieved, but there is no reason that the control exercised in the administration of the schools of the local education authorities should be so rigid as to cramp initiative and experimentation.

Much of the social work among children that has been described has passed, or will be passing, from the hands of the
voluntary associations as their functions are made statutory
and become part of the compulsory functions shared between
local authorities and Government departments. Will then the
need for these voluntary associations cease to exist? Their
pioneering zeal, beneficial influences, and practical vision have
rendered great service to our national life. Is their usefulness
drawing to a close?

There has been, as we have noted, a great change in the
attitude of the voluntary associations themselves towards the
people they are trying to help. They have been influenced in
turn by the growth of social ideas, a better understanding of
society itself, and a more scientific approach to the problems
within their care. It is true to say that those which previously
showed patronage or were merely concerned with being kind
and good to the poor have banished such ideas from the
administrative work of their voluntary service. A great change
of approach and method has evolved during the period under
review and the voluntary social worker goes now into the service
properly trained to play his part in mitigating the injustice
and inequalities that our social and economic system have
allowed to arise.

It may be that the voluntary associations will experience
great difficulty in raising voluntary subscriptions on which they
have hitherto relied. With the increase in taxation necessary
for the financing of the social services provided by the community it may be that the less spectacular voluntary services
may find themselves in straitened circumstances.

During these war years society after society has found it impossible to raise its funds. Voluntary maternity and child
welfare societies have been obliged to hand over their centres
to the local authority, and as the report on the National Council
for the Unmarried Mother says, " in London to-day it is quite
impossible to raise funds through the usual peace-time means
such as dinners, dances, garden parties, sales and the like."

It would be unfortunate if this spirit of social endeavour and
voluntary service disappeared from the services of our social
life and the experience built up over the years were lost. One
of the great problems for democracy will be how to retain
within the ever-widening sphere of State action the initiative

E*

and pioneering ardour, the goodwill and discreet helpfulness and public spiritedness which are such marked features of these modern voluntary associations.

The need for such interest and activity surely ought not to cease when the pioneer stage of their work is passed : when, for example, day nurseries, nursery schools, maternity and child welfare centres have become accepted parts of the work of local government, what more can the voluntary associations do ? They can become advisory ; but can the virility of an organisation remain when the only task left for it is to talk and advise and not to create ? These are some of the questions that suggest themselves at the present time. We take the view that in a dynamic society a place must always be found for experimentation and pioneering effort, and this can often best be done by associations of people bound together by enthusiasm for a particular cause, and working, with some regard to social analysis and knowledge, in a milieu untrammelled by the limitations imposed by an administrative machine serving a more limited ideal. For those who care greatly for the ever-changing needs of children in a developing society a way must be found for them to demonstrate the further stage ahead. Society cannot afford to restrain by formality and undue regulation the visionaries and practical spirits who would forge ahead, and somehow its machinery and institutions must be flexible enough to reconcile them within its progressive purposes.

The relationship of voluntary associations with services run by the State was admirably expressed by Sir Thomas Barlow, M.D., in a speech delivered for the National Association for the Prevention of Infantile Mortality and the Promotion of the Welfare of Children Under School Age—as long ago as 1912 : " The great pioneers in all good citizenship are the voluntaries. From them the initial impulse and the tentative experiments come. They educate the public conscience and they widen and deepen the demands on the municipality and the Government for higher standards of health and education. But the best results are gained when they go on working side by side. The cordial co-operation of voluntary effort gives enthusiasm and warmth and sympathy to the official side and the official side gives compulsion when it is necessary, and continuity, permanence, and authority which voluntary work needs for its completion."

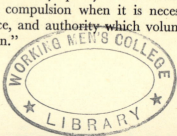

Chapter IX

WORK AMONG BOYS AND GIRLS

by

PEARL JEPHCOTT

I

THE twenty-year period between the two wars saw no great change in the types of organisations dealing with boys and girls. Most of the familiar types, clubs, Y.M.C.A. and Y.W.C.A., the Life Brigades, Boy Scouts and Girl Guides, Girls' Friendly Society, were in existence betore 1914. Five at least date back to the nineteenth century. There was no new invention of the importance of scouting, though several new and popular organisations were founded after the end of the war. These included the Youth Hostels Association, the Young Farmers' Clubs, and the Welsh League of Youth. The works' club, too, was largely a post-war growth. On the whole, however, the advances made were in scale, technique, and organisation rather than in any entirely new approach to the training of young people through their voluntary membership of a social group of their contemporaries.

No reliable comparable figures are obtainable, but there is no doubt that a far larger part of the country was provided with organisations for boys and girls in 1939 than in 1919, and that by 1939 the boys and girls attached to any such organisation had appreciably increased. Dr. A. E. Morgan estimated that in 1938 one in three young people was attached to a youth organisation or was receiving some form of continued education. Many of these attachments were very ephemeral. Many, too, were to organisations that met for no more than a couple of hours a week and that only during the winter months. Moreover, many of the organisations, though theoretically for adolescents, in actual fact had a considerable membership of school children and of people over twenty. Despite all the advances the fact remained that even by 1939 the voluntary organisations, in finance, personnel, and set-up, were quite inadequate to meet the leisure-time needs of an adolescent population of 2,750,000, 80% of whom had left school at fourteen, with a yearly influx of nearly 500,000 boys and girls.[1]

Of the juvenile organisations, some—Scouts, Guides, Boys' Brigade, Y.M.C.A.—were built up from the centre outwards, so that local units came into existence already federated. With clubs the position was different. They had been started in the past mainly by local efforts, and only later developed regional and national federations to meet the needs of the local units. Diversity of structure and the independence of the local unit, even when affiliated to a national body, were marked features of the voluntary youth organisations. Most of those concerned with the direction of the organisations fought strongly to maintain these two characteristics. The creation of effective machinery of co-operation between the different national voluntary bodies dealing with juveniles came later in the day. It was not until 1936 that the informal meetings of the voluntary youth organisations, first called by the National Council of Social Service in 1931 to discuss the allocation of Physical Training grants for camping, were replaced by the formation of a Standing Conference of thirteen of the leading voluntary youth organisations. Membership was confined to organisations with an adolescent membership of over 10,000.

The first piece of Government intervention in the recreational welfare of adolescents which touched the work of the voluntary youth organisations occurred in 1916 when the Home Office, to combat juvenile delinquency, asked local education authorities to form juvenile organisations committees and federated these in a Central Juvenile Organisations Committee. The effectiveness of these bodies varied greatly. In many areas they were never set up. In others their work was confined to such things as the provision of games leagues. Their influence on the voluntary organisations was relatively small, though they were the medium through which, under the 1921 Education Act, grants were first made to the voluntary organisations.

Within the circle of juvenile organisations there were a number of cleavages of opinion and of practice, sometimes resulting in tensions. Some organisations had a permanent religious basis. Others omitted specific religious teaching,

[1] A. E. Morgan, *The Needs of Youth*, Oxford University Press, 1939.

though most of the organisations contained some reference in their constitution to their function of meeting spiritual needs. There was further the denominational basis. The Girls' Friendly Society, for example, was Anglican and organised on a diocesan basis ; the Girls' Life Brigade mainly a Free Church body with strong attachments to the local church. The Churches as a whole had no uniform policy about their provision for juveniles. Some local churches maintained organisations open to all, irrespective of their religious affiliations, whilst others demanded a church loyalty. Some generously helped un-attached groups, whilst others regarded them as rivals, distracting young people from their own religious body and duties.

There was also very considerable rivalry between the further education provided by the local authorities in evening schools and institutes, some of which came to be run very much on club lines, and the provision made by the voluntary organisations. The former on the whole considered that the voluntary organisations were inefficient and were diverting, by their attractions, the attention of young people who should be doing serious study if they wanted to get on in the world. The voluntary organisations retorted that, though informal, they knew the real needs of the boy and girl better than did the local education authorities and were making provision for at least a few of that great bulk of adolescents who had no use for any kind of formal education once they had left school. These divergent aims and methods and the resulting competition were perhaps to be expected when we remember that both local authority and voluntary organisation were dealing with material so unknown in character, though in many cases so patently malleable, as the working-class adolescent.

During the inter-war period there was one marked trend. The early provision of the youth organisations was primarily social ambulance work. The organisations existed to keep boys and girls from the dangers and futilities of the streets and the undesirable older companions met there ; they were needed to counteract the effect of an inadequate home life and of a working life that took little particular account of the immaturity and special needs of the adolescent. For the girls in particular they were regarded as a safeguard of morals. It was repeatedly pointed out, though how much truth lies in the assertion has since been questioned,[1] that juvenile delinquency was kept down by the youth organisations. At the same time the youth organisations as a whole were not expected and took little action to draw attention to the unsatisfactory social conditions under which many of their members lived. They relied rather on attempting to strengthen the moral character of their members, as is shown by the frequency with which the words " self-respect," " discipline," " obedience," " fellowship " occur in their aims. These ameliorative functions of the youth organisations were highly desirable, and still are. But they are no longer regarded as the primary purpose for which the organisations exist. Youth organisations are thought of to-day as providing something valuable for the normal young person, in normal circumstances, and drawn from any social class. They are expected to provide an experience that helps to develop personality, a form of education that is a complement to the school, and a small society in which some knowledge of the duties of the citizen of a democratic state may be acquired.

Two other changes in the character of the organisations developed between the wars. The first, a reflection of the twentieth century's protest against modern urban life, led these youth groups to take an increasing interest in the country. Day outings to the country grew in number and were supplemented by a week's " camp "—the only type of holiday that was cheap enough to be practicable for many young workers. Holiday houses, open throughout the summer, were set up in a number of places. Moreover, the organisations began to be asked to function in country areas, and here found themselves faced with problems which inevitably led them to reconsider their original purpose and methods.

" Boys only " and " girls only " organisations were the accepted pattern in 1918. By 1939, though the uniformed societies were still one-sex, many of the other societies had regular nights where boys and girls were encouraged to take part in activities together. Some units, particularly in the club organisations, were formally constituted as mixed groups. This change, which developed fairly rapidly after 1936, was due to pressure from young people themselves and was often ignored or feared by adults. Those who did respond to it thought,

[1] See *Young Offenders*, Carr-Saunders, Mannheim, Rhodes, University Press, Cambridge.

presumably, that the single-sex groups gave the majority of adolescents inadequate experience and training for a world in which they were likely to have more leisure than their parents, had known, to move in wider social circles, as well as to work alongside each other to an increasing extent, even after marriage.

In juvenile work, as elsewhere in the voluntary societies, there was a growth of paid leadership. This need for trained and salaried leaders was emphasised by most people who examined work among juveniles, though the attitude of many people, particularly those on committees who had to raise the money to pay salaries was coloured by the old notion that voluntary service was, *per se*, better than paid. The need for training excited less dissension. In this matter of trained and salaried leadership, the girls' organisations moved further and faster than the boys'. The lowness of salary and precariousness of the posts was a difficulty. Both the lowness of salaries and the slow improvement in these can be illustrated from a National Association of Boys' Clubs handbook of 1930 which states that a club of 200 or more boys usually required a full-time leader, and that he should receive a salary of not less than £200 per annum " and will, of course, have been trained for the work." In a handbook dated 1935, the salary suggested had risen to £250 or £300, though this amount was rarely paid, and even by 1939 a minimum of £250 had hardly become recognised. After six years of war the relative position of men club leaders was little better and the minimum salary at which the N.A.B.C., in 1946, recommends a post is still as low as £300. Comparable salaries for a woman leader were £150 in 1930 and £200 in 1935.

The training schemes of the youth organisations were at first frankly makeshift, a few months at most of experience in two or three clubs, interspersed with some lectures, in which far too much ground was covered very inadequately. In this matter the Boy Scout movement were pioneers. They began a regular training of scout-masters as far back as 1919, when Gilwell Park was presented to the Association to provide a training centre for the former as well as a camping ground for scouts.

For some years the London Diocesan Council for Youth had run a training in club work on denominational lines. By 1934 the number of applicants from members of all denominations was so large that they asked the National Council of Girls' Clubs to take over the scheme, which they did and started the first eighteen-months full-time course of professional training.

In juvenile work, as in other kinds of social service, the period between the wars was not only a time of increasing profession-alism, but also increasing specialisation. Annual inter-club competitions, displays, and festivals were a major feature of many youth organisations from their early days. The Girls' Friendly Society competitions, for example, date back to 1921. It was largely in connection with such competitions that the demand came for teachers—generally voluntary—and that the possibilities of informal education began to be explored. From 1930 onwards the staffs of the national organisations increased and became diversified as was essential if the growing demands of the units for advice and help with their more formal activities were to be met. This increasing demand for more classes, for more people who could undertake the teaching of specific subjects, and for a wider range of subjects, was, of course, a direct result of the rising standard of education in the elementary schools and the general improvement in the working conditions of juveniles. The first public recognition of the work of the voluntary youth organisations (from a non-statutory body) was made in 1926 when the Carnegie United Kingdom Trust recognised certain of the juvenile organisations as eligible for library grants. The Trust here, as in many other directions, helped the youth organisations when, in 1930, it enabled the National Council of Girls' Clubs to appoint two women physical training organisers. Pilgrim Trust grants, in 1933, enabled the National Association of Boys' Clubs and the National Council of Girls' Clubs to extend their work, the former to provide and equip workshops for training in handicrafts and hobbies, the latter to appoint their first field organisers. Later, in 1935, King George's Jubilee Trust was founded as a central fund to assist in the maintenance and development of the work of national juvenile organisations dealing with boys and girls from fourteen upwards. The permanent income of the Trust was in the region of £30,000 a year. In 1935, through grants made from the Commissioners for the Special Areas Fund via the N.C.S.S.,[1] youth organisations were among the other voluntary organisations which were asked to extend their work

[1] National Council of Social Service.

in the special areas, and various of them appointed staff for this purpose.

The Education Act of 1921 had empowered local education authorities to provide social and physical training in day and evening classes, which meant that the voluntary youth organisations could theoretically secure what specialist teachers they needed. In many areas, however, particularly outside London, the regulations as to numbers and ages, and the unstable character of many of the voluntary organisations themselves, prevented anything like full use being made of this provision. Local authorities were also legally empowered to subsidise clubs and could, if they so wished, make grants towards salaries from 1921 onwards, facts of which the majority of people connected with the voluntary organisations were quite unaware. The amount of financial help provided during the next fifteen years was negligible, though as stated above, provision in kind (i.e. in the supply of teachers) was available from a certain number of authorities. It was in London that most use was made of the help of the statutory bodies, as far as youth work was concerned. Between 1921 and 1937 the Board of Education was not asked by the youth organisations to approve more than a trivial amount of expenditure. Despite this, however, both the quantity and quality of the services which the youth organisations provided developed. One indication of this growth is the increase in the amount of literature published by the organisations in 1926 as compared with 1939, and also the extent to which certain of them, for example the Scouts and Guides, spread overseas.

From about 1931 onwards most of the chief girls' organisations had physical training staffs and increased these when more money was available from the Ministry of Labour. The Lancashire Keep Fit movement sponsored by the N.C.G.C. spread throughout the country, reaching a large number of girls and women who had previously received no kind of post-school education. Most organisations were willing and even eager to conduct experiments in any type of activity that looked as if it might catch the interest of their members. It was inadequate premises, lack of equipment, the precarious nature of the voluntary help, and the volunteers' lack of knowledge of the technique of teaching, together with members who were hostile to anything that savoured directly of school, that made educational " classes " so difficult. At the same time if many, though not all, the volunteers were unskilled, many of the L.E.A. teachers, with their lack of club technique, could only cope with the formal class.

Ever since their inception financial stringency was the most obvious difficulty with which the organisations had to contend, although certain of them, particularly the Scouts and the Guides, made it a feature of their training that the local unit should be self-supporting and do no begging, a feature which, while admirable in many ways, put definite bounds to the extent to which the needs of the bulk of the adolescent population could be met. On the whole financial difficulties put a perpetual brake on their expansion, diverted their energies, and provided a legitimate excuse for ineffectiveness. Lack of adequate finance and the hand-to-mouth nature of the income of the majority of the organisations were particularly crippling in regard to their premises. A condemned school or a very old and probably insanitary house with a nominal rent was the normal type of building that a club looked out for when it was so ambitious as to aspire to have the sole use of premises of its own. By far the greater number of organisations rented odd rooms, for various nights in the week, from such much used buildings as a British Legion Hut or a Church Hall. Here the accommodation was often most unsuitable, the group being liable to constant interruption and having few or no facilities even for such an elementary need as storing equipment.

By 1936 the general attitude towards the youth organisations had begun to change. The apparently highly efficient and successful youth movements in Germany and Italy were becoming known in England. The degradation and danger of British unemployed youth was beginning to disturb the public conscience, particularly as the difficulties of the Juvenile Instruction Centres began to be known. There was a growing fear that war was coming and that one of the nation's most valuable assets was being neglected. A National Fitness Campaign was launched in 1936, and was followed by the Physical Training and Recreation Act of 1937. Area Committees with paid staff were required to survey local needs of physical recreation. Local education authorities and voluntary organisations could apply to the Board of Education for grants for any projects concerned with physical welfare, including the

salaries of physical training staff. By March 1939 £1,500,000
had been approved for expenditure on buildings, sports
stadiums, swimming-baths, etc. The first outstanding grant
which affected the voluntary organisations was a grant of
£1,500 made by the Buckingham County Council in 1938
towards youth work at the Slough Social Centre. Despite the
many facilities which the National Fitness Council offered it
was regarded with considerable suspicion by the youth organisations, partly because of its emphasis on physical, presumably as
opposed to moral, fitness, and partly because the scale on which
it worked was over-grandiose for the modest needs and ambitions
of the majority of the organisations. Despite this, however, from
the time of the passing of the Physical Training Act the State
made grants towards the voluntary youth organisations to an
increasing extent. As a result the whole position of youth
work was changed. The issue was no longer a question of
whether youth work should be adequately financed, but was
rather whether youth organisations and their leaders should be
provided and conducted by the local authorities, or subsidised
out of public money though controlled by the voluntary
organisations, or whether both financial support and control
should be shared. The issue came to a head in 1939 at the
outbreak of war, when the Service of Youth was started, but
the seeds of the policy inaugurated then were sown in these
earlier experiments.

II

The war period 1939–45 brought great developments in the
scale, and certain changes in the character, of the work undertaken by the voluntary youth organisations. They no longer
worked alone or as inferior agents in providing for the recreation
and informal education of young people. They were called
upon to give their experience and to co-operate very fully with
the State in a drive to improve leisure-time facilities for young
people launched at the outbreak of war. Three factors were
behind this drive : the first and most obvious was the urgent
need to provide a stream of recruits of high quality for the
Services ; the second, the realisation that effective members of
a democratic society have to be taught the principles and
techniques of a democratic way of life ; the third, the knowledge that war-time conditions might tell adversely on the

welfare of adolescents. The years of adolescence, below the age of call up but beyond that of childhood, were the obvious ones for such training. Both were matters of too much urgency and concerned too large a number of people to be left any longer to the existing voluntary youth organisations.

In September 1939 the Board of Education began to set up its administrative machinery for the new drive, and appointed a National Youth Committee with representatives from the Board, the local authorities, and the national voluntary youth organisations. In November it issued a circular *The Service of Youth* which gave the name to the new drive and official recognition to the fact that adequate provision was to be made for the leisure-time well-being of adolescents. The 146 authorities for Higher Education were required to set up youth committees within the next few months, a step which was followed later by the smaller authorities. Full-time paid staff, secretaries to the youth committees, and Youth Service organisers began to be appointed. Some authorities made direct provision for youth work and set up, as in Manchester, their own youth centres, while practically all began to help the existing voluntary organisations to extend their work within the authorities' area. The amount of work to be done was so great that there was relatively little overlapping, and gradually the voluntary organisations began to adjust their administrative areas so that they conformed more closely with those of the local authorities. The Service of Youth was constructed within this setting of a network of local committees, formed by the statutory body but with strong representation from the voluntary bodies. The plan was elastic and the partnership of the statutory and voluntary bodies, faced by the urgency of the national situation, a co-operative and constructive one in the majority of areas. Although the partnership was strengthened the principle of voluntary membership of the organisations was rigidly adhered to. From December 1941 all boys and girls were required at sixteen to register, and at the registration interview were recommended and encouraged to join some youth organisation. No compulsion was imposed and registration in fact, though it provided for the first time invaluable statistical information about the leisure-time habits of all young people, probably did not in itself result in a very marked increase in membership. Among the reasons for the large increase in effective member-

ship between 1939 and 1945 was the attraction of new pre-
Service organisations and the encouragement given to existing
organisations to improve the quality and quantity of the services
they offered.

Finance, the rock on which so much of the work of the
voluntary organisations had split in the past, was the first subject
with which most of the youth committees concerned themselves. Under the Education Act of 1921, through which local
education authority expenditure on youth work was eligible
for a 50% grant from the Board of Education, grants were made
for salaries of organisers and leaders, for buildings, for equipment,
and for running expenses. In most cases the grants were made
quickly, were on a generous scale, and were made without unduly
niggling or restrictive conditions. Where a local authority took
a narrow view of an unusual type of request the applicant could
take advantage of a loophole whereby, in certain cases, application could be made direct to the Board. The Board itself also
made large grants directly to the headquarters of the voluntary
organisations. Practically every type of voluntary organisation,
including those attached to religious bodies but excluding those
with a political affiliation, was eligible for grant-aid. Help in
kind was made available for the voluntary organisations, particularly in the free use of school premises and playing-fields.
Extensive use was made of these, and in many cases this sharing
of premises formed the first link, and in some cases it must be
admitted the first battleground, between the schools and the
voluntary societies. Grant-aid did, of course, convey the right
of inspection, but this was of such an informal character, and
the co-operation between His Majesty's Inspectors and the
voluntary societies was generally so good, that the old bogy of
Government control was seldom raised by the voluntary
societies. Increased financial support meant that, in spite of
the obvious difficulties of war-time conditions, on the whole
youth organisations could at last give their members better
material provision, particularly in the case of the units in non-
blitzed areas of the country.

The first use to which the organisations put the new funds
available was to increase their personnel, both at the national
and county headquarters and in the appointment of full-time
leaders to individual clubs or groups of clubs. The shortage of
people to fill all these new posts was acute; the number of

professionally trained youth leaders available was negligible. Training courses were started by the Board, the local authorities, and the voluntary organisations, with part-time courses for people already in posts, short week-end courses and day training schools. The co-operation of certain of the universities was enlisted. In London, for example, the Social Science department of Bedford College and the London School of Economics worked with the National Association of Girls' Clubs in connection with the training of full-time youth leaders, for whom a Social Science certificate was accepted as a basic requirement.

The teaching profession was the chief recruiting ground for the new personnel for youth work, particularly when it became evident that the Service of Youth was to be regarded as an integral part of the national system of education. The McNair Report on the Supply of Teachers and Youth Leaders, published in 1944, suggested the possibility that teaching and youth leadership might in certain circumstances be interchangeable professions. The acceptance of youth leadership as a profession comparable in status with teaching has tended to raise the salaries of leaders, though the situation still leaves much to be desired.

Training and the influx of many new recruits into the Service of Youth made evident the crying need for literature on youth work. By the end of the war a number of books and pamphlets on education in general, and in some cases its relation to the work of the voluntary organisations, had been published. Research on the interests and day-to-day lives of the post-school adolescents was undertaken, and the beginning of a background of fact on which to base youth work was built up. *The Times Educational Supplement* included in its weekly comments on formal education information on the Service of Youth, and did a great service in this way to the voluntary organisations.

The societies which made an immediate appeal to young people during the war were the uniformed pre-Service ones, particularly the Army Cadet Force, the Sea Cadet Corps, and the new Air Training Corps formed in 1941. Enormous and very rapid expansion took place in these. By 1941, for example, it was estimated that one in every four boys aged 16 to 18 was in the A.T.C. alone. Membership would have been greater had it not been restricted in relation to the needs of the Services.

A new uniformed organisation for girls, the National Association of Training Corps for Girls, which did not, however, lead directly to the Services, was set up by the Board.

The Red Cross and St. John Ambulance Brigade Cadets attracted many young people, and various non-uniformed wartime service groups sprang up. The popularity of all the above was due to the specific demands that they made for an active contribution to the war effort, a contribution somewhat similar to that which the boys' and girls' elder brothers and sisters in the Forces were already making. The technical training that they gave was concrete, related to immediate needs and adult in character. The pre-Service organisation had definitely discovered one type of approach, though possibly a temporary one, to young people which the older organisations, less dramatically urgent in their appeal, could not present.

The Churches, to which so many of the voluntary youth organisations were attached, reflected the national concern for the well-being of young people. Headquarters organisations like the Methodist Youth Movement increased their personnel, their training schemes, and developed their publicity. By 1945 it was probable that the majority of individual churches throughout the country were making some kind of weekly provision for the social as well as spiritual welfare of their adolescent members.

The local authorities differed widely in the type of provision they made for the young people in their area. In some they set up their own youth centres ; in others they relied on the schools and school staff to make provision ; in others again they preferred to leave the actual provision to units of the national voluntary organisations. In most areas the need was so much greater than the personnel or buildings available that they encouraged the setting up of pretty well any type of youth society, so long as a few responsible adults were connected with it.

Federation of the units of the voluntary societies to their national headquarters continued as in pre-war days, though on a larger scale. By 1944 eighteen of the leading national organisations, with an adolescent (14–20) membership of 676,000, were affiliated to the Standing Conference of National Voluntary Youth Organisations, the body through which the societies made known their common aims and needs, particularly to the Ministry of Education.

The war and the impact of refugees and of troops from abroad made the boys and girls keen to learn about the young people of other countries. They welcomed in many foreign visitors, had an extensive range of " pen pals," and between 1939 and 1945 built up a considerable fund of knowledge about foreign youth organisations, particularly those in the U.S.A. and Canada. By 1945 requests were coming in, for example from Australia, for British youth leaders to go overseas, particularly to help with the social science departments of the Universities and the training of youth leaders.

Public interest in the welfare of young people was strengthened by such B.B.C. programmes as the *Under-Twenty Club* and the *To Start You Talking* series, which brought the ultimate aims and new spirit in youth work, as well as the particular problems of adolescents, to the notice of adults in general, and not only to those who had a professional interest in education. Such publicity helped to dispel the slightly dated character that youth organisations in general bore in the eyes of some boys and girls. It also helped them to see that discussion of serious subjects can be a relatively light-hearted affair and gave them an admirable demonstration in the techniques of informal discussion.

The public's interest in the aims, methods, and experiments of the old youth organisations was strengthened by the publicity and discussion which preceded the passing of the Education Act of 1944. Professional bodies like the National Union of Teachers and such societies as the Workers' Educational Association, published memoranda in which they stressed the point that education cannot be confined to the school, that opportunities for the creative use of their leisure must be provided for young workers, and that specific training in citizenship needs to be given to young people when they have sufficient experience of life to begin to understand what membership of a democratic society implies. The youth organisations had consistently experimented on these lines, and when the Bill was under discussion they pressed for the raising of the leaving age to 15 and later 16, for more equality of opportunity in education, and particularly for compulsory part-time education, in working hours, up to 18—the provision which the Fisher Act of 1918 had made, but which financial considerations so soon wrecked. The Ministry of Education, in its provisions for County Colleges in the 1944 Act, appears to have had in mind the techniques of informal education of the adolescent which the voluntary youth organisations had been almost unknowingly evolving during the last twenty years. It seems probable that as these provisions of the Act are implemented, the work of the voluntary organisations may change somewhat in character, though educationists generally seem to agree that the widely varying types of small recreational societies, with a voluntary basis of membership, are likely to continue to be needed by young people however improved may be their formal education. At the same time the quality of the provision made by the voluntary societies will obviously have to keep pace with that made by the schools, though the provision itself will be different in character.

The voluntary organisations, despite the far-reaching changes which took place between 1936 and 1945, maintained three characteristics which they regarded as all-important. They laid increasing emphasis on the practical training that they gave in the elements of self-government, and were prepared to sacrifice immediate efficiency and tidiness of organisation for this. Club committees, youth councils, youth parliaments, inter-organisation councils, discussion groups were encouraged as essentials in training boys and girls to be both informed and co-operative. Importance was attached to the principle of members themselves making a regular subscription to their organisation which encouraged boys and girls to feel that they had some financial responsibility for and a consequent right to control their own society. The organisations also stressed the principle that the club or brigade or guild was primarily a group of young people who had voluntarily entered into a friendly relationship and that the quality of this relationship was the test of the true effectiveness or otherwise of the group. Finally the societies maintained strongly that the all-round development of the personality of the individual boy or girl was their prime concern, and that for this development it was essential that young people should choose for themselves how they would spend their leisure and not be dragooned by their elders. The task of the youth organisations was to help individual boys and girls, infinitely varied in character and need, to reach maturity along not one but many different paths.

A broad survey of the period 1918–45 shows the following

features in the development of work among juveniles, through the voluntary organisations :

(1) The character of youth work changed from being mainly ameliorative of bad social conditions to being broadly educational, and laid particular stress on training young people for membership of a democratic society. The organisations grew in efficiency and in the range of their activities and on the whole had a stronger hold on the loyalty of their members. More thought was given to their ultimate aims, and more attention paid to the genuine needs and potentialities of young people. The quality and quantity of the actual teaching given improved.

(2) The proportion of the juvenile population, particularly of adolescents, attached to the organisations increased. Though by 1939 it was far from satisfactory, by 1945 effective membership had greatly increased, particularly among boys. The pre-Service organisations made a great appeal. Provision was made in rural as well as urban areas, and the growth of mixed activities proved very attractive to young people of both sexes.

(3) None of the major national organisations died and many expanded greatly both at headquarters and in the number, though not necessarily the size, of their individual units. Few entirely new types of organisation arose, and the organisations set up by the local authorities under the Service of Youth followed closely the old "club" pattern. By constantly modifying their form but consistently keeping to their original principles, the organisations survived two wars. They proved, too, that it did not need a war to bring them into being and that they were able to meet the needs of young people in time of peace or war.

(4) The number of professional youth workers increased slowly until about 1935, when it began to increase fairly rapidly. From 1939 the increase was very marked and provision for training became a major concern of the youth organisations and the Ministry of Education. On the whole the youth organisations failed to throw up their own leaders, nor did they indicate that they could exist without adult " leaders."

(5) Salaries of professional leaders increased to some extent, though irregularly, but up to 1939 were unsatisfactory, particularly in the case of men. No real change in status occurred until the Service of Youth was started, when, with statutory funds available and appointments being made to their staffs

by the local authorities, salary increases became more general, though even by 1945 it would not be true to say that teaching and youth work were far advanced on the way to being interchangeable professions.

(6) Organised co-operation between the national youth organisations was sporadic and was more in evidence among the girls' than among the boys' organisations. Considerably more interest in youth organisations was taken by other types of adult voluntary organisations.

(7) With the inauguration of the Service of Youth in 1939 the statutory authorities gave increasing recognition and financial assistance to the voluntary organisations, and the latter made an effort to consider more exactly their ultimate purpose, and to increase their efficiency while maintaining their individual characteristics. Co-operation between the statutory authorities and the voluntary societies increased at every level and strengthened rather than weakened the latter as it became recognised that the Youth Service should be considered an integral part of the national system of education. Increased finance made it possible for the voluntary organisations to make better material provision for their members, particularly in the way of buildings, playing-fields, and equipment.

(8) The statutory authorities recognised the value of the principle of voluntary membership of youth societies and maintained the principle in their own schemes for youth work.

(9) Legislation helped to bring about the co-operation between the statutory and voluntary bodies, in particular the Education Act, 1921, the Special Areas Act, 1932, the Housing Act, 1936, and the Physical Training and Recreation Act, 1937. By 1939 the choice between the direct provision and subsidisation of youth work became a matter of great importance to the statutory bodies and raised in the field of juvenile work issues which arose elsewhere also. Under the stress of war-time conditions both methods continued to be adopted. The Education Act of 1944 stimulated interest in the voluntary societies and on the whole strengthened their position. The club technique of informal education was accepted as the rough pattern which the compulsory part-time education of the new county colleges would probably follow.

Chapter X

ADULT EDUCATION

by

W. E. WILLIAMS

I

DURING the last twenty-five years the growth of adult education has been more evident in its outer circles than in its traditional forms. The first half the century had seen the foundation by Dr. Albert Mansbridge of the Workers' Educational Association, a venture in which the Universities, co-operating with spokesmen of the working class, provided new opportunities for ordinary people to make contact with high standards of teaching in a wide range of subjects. This, of course, was not the first contribution of its kind made by the Universities, for in the previous century the University Extension movement had taken firm hold in some parts of the country. But the W.E.A., in a sense, was more class-conscious in its effort to give the workers access to some kind of university teaching, and although this effort has still produced very modest results in terms of student membership, the purpose behind the original effort remains. That is to say, the W.E.A. is more interested in the hard centre of adult education than in the more popular forms which nowadays flourish on the periphery. The kind of provision on which it sets the highest store is the university tutorial class which takes students through a three-session course, on their weekly spare evening, and although a majority of the students who tackle these arduous courses fall by the wayside before the end of the third session, it is not reasonable to denigrate the persistent effort the W.E.A. has made to maintain a high standard in this kind of extra-mural work. The other main form of provision fostered by the W.E.A. is the short course of twelve or twenty-four lectures. It is customary on most occasions when the more popular forms of adult education are discussed for the spokesman of the W.E.A. to remind us that their standards of teaching are more exacting than anyone else's in the same field. This claim cannot be contested, but it is one which scarcely takes sufficient account of the fact that the majority of the population of this island have neither the time nor the capacity for systematic courses of formal adult education. The figures themselves prove this. During its forty-odd years of existence the W.E.A. has possessed immense advantages for extending its cause. It has been befriended by archbishops, the universities, a strong section of the trade unions, and an increasing number of local education authorities. As a voluntary body it has retained absolute control over its policy and organisation, while from the hands of a benevolent Ministry of Education it has received substantial grants in aid of its teaching work. Yet despite these happy auspices and these good friends the W.E.A. has at no time achieved a student membership, even on paper, of more than 80,000. From these facts it is a reasonable deduction that while the W.E.A. makes a strong appeal to a small section of the country it has not proved its case to the majority.

The hard centre of adult education does not, nowadays, consist exclusively of the W.E.A. There are some local education authorities, notably the L.C.C., which are also able to provide a formal and systematic course of an advanced kind for students who are able to make the grade. In this work the local education authorities no doubt have advantages over the W.E.A., the chief of which is their increasing ability to provide decent accommodation for serious study. Such premises as those of the L.C.C. City Literary Institute, off Drury Lane, suggest that there might be more demand for higher forms of adult education if they could be housed, as in this case they are, in attractive and comfortable premises, including that indispensable adjunct, the canteen. Recent evidence of the growth of local education authority facilities for adult education of the sterner kind suggests that one good reason for the W.E.A.'s limited advance during the last forty years is the persistence with which they have clung to the conception that adult education is something that must be taken the hard way, and that it requires accommodation no more comfortable than that provided by an upper room over the co-op. or a schoolroom in the church hall. The pioneers of adult education, sustained by a grim spirit of Calvinism, were doubtless able to ignore their surroundings in their concentration on learning. But a nation which has found that entertainment could be conducted in comfortable surroundings is liable to insist on similar standards in the rest of its leisure activities. It is possible that if the W.E.A. would institutionalise itself, in terms of buildings equivalent to those of Community Centres, it might substantially enlarge its membership without losing its high principles of learning.

In any effective system of adult education in this country it is desirable to find room for " serious " adult students who are impelled by more than a mere " interest " in subjects, who are determined to get as deep as they can into some substantial field of knowledge. The enlargement of that solid body of serious students should remain one of the objectives of all educational planners. But the extent to which that " hard centre " is enlarged depends in part on an equivalent growth in the outer circles. If the more advanced kinds of adult education are to prosper in this country they must draw their recruits from those who are engaged in what might be called the basic training of adult education. The outer circles which have been referred to above comprise a large and assorted group of activities. They include Women's Institutes, Towns-women's Guilds, Community Centres, Rural Music Schools, the Y.M.C.A., and Y.W.C.A., and during the war they have been reinforced, on a prodigious scale, by the educational activities of the Fighting Forces. When such post-war institutions get into their stride as Youth Colleges and local education authority Community Centres, these outer circles will become more extensive than ever before.

II

In general terms the attraction which most of these movements offers is one of community interest rather than educational study. They are founded as a rule on a sense of comradeship or neighbourhood, and sociability has a large element in their procedure. In a good Community Centre, more than anywhere else, one sees how this principle operates. Few members of such a centre, to begin with, have any urgent or pronounced educational concern. But it is equally true that a majority of them are ready to be coaxed into some line of interest beyond that of mere entertainment.

Their real predicament is that they do not know what they want until they begin to enjoy it. They are, moreover, diffident about their capacity to become interested in, say, music, discussion, drama, hobbies, etc., and the only hope of bringing them into activities of this kind is to prepare for them a kind of ambush. No locality is better situated for an ambush than a Community Centre—and this is a further argument for the imperative need of good premises for all adult education activities. It is relatively easy to persuade even the self-conscious and shy to pay a prospective visit to a Community Centre, for the range of amenities it provides is so large that the individual need not feel, at the outset, that he is being pinned down to any particular objective. The air of the place, again, has a beneficent effect upon him and one way or another, before he can realise what is happening, he is finding himself drawn at least into the fringe of interest of some activity or other. These, in fact, are the circumstances in which thousands of people have been coaxed to pay some attention to the more elementary forms of adult education, and it is on this basis of interest plus sociability that increasing numbers of men and women are finding their way towards some acquaintance with the arts and towards some participation in various kinds of elementary citizenship. To them the experiment probably seems much more like membership of a club than anything else, and this club spirit is achieving the desire for a new change in the hitherto rather stuffy atmosphere of adult education. Whether or not people are improving themselves by exercising this interest they are certainly enjoying themselves. It may be observed in parentheses that it is this element of enjoyment in adult education which arouses the wrath of the Calvinistic Old Guard in the movement, who still cling to the antique conviction that education is doing you no good unless it hurts.

Some not unsympathetic observers of these movements on the periphery point out that a great deal of the informal work being done is rather loosely organised. It lacks such requirements of a " system " as staff planning, coherent purpose, adequate and well-planned leaders, and so on. To such observers a great deal of the interest manifested in the newer movements is a dispersed interest that " seems to lead nowhere." There is much justice in the criticism, but it is fair to remember that these movements themselves are highly self-conscious, that they are, so to speak, more of a guerrilla element in Army Education than part of a regular army. On frequent occasions these movements have expressed the desire for guidance and co-ordination. An occasional conference to discuss common problems is not enough, and the existence of a G.H.Q. for Adult Education would include among its benefits that of providing both counsel and co-ordination for bodies which often reveal more ardour than sense of strategy. This is not to suggest that adult education, whether of the formal or informal kinds, should " come under " the Ministry of Education. The Ministry, indeed, would be the first to point out that that is the wrong way of going to work. What is required is an authoritative central body, representative of all these teeming interests, which could serve as a clearing house for policy and perhaps as a supply agency for the great quantity of materials and equipment which adult education requires.[1]

III

It would be wrong to suppose that the more informal varieties of adult education are the product of the last few years. Several of them came into existence during (or soon after) the war of 1914–18—and it is significant that a similar enlargement of this field began during the recent years of war. To describe all these movements would turn this paper into a seedsman's catalogue, but a short description of a few of the bigger movements will illustrate the general nature of the development between the wars.

1. THE WOMEN'S INSTITUTES

The Women's Institute movement began during World War I as an auxiliary service to the work of the Ministry of Agriculture, and its original purpose was the valuable but limited one of encouraging country women to produce and preserve food supplies during a time of acute national shortage. That temporary objective became transformed after the war into one of a more vital and more permanent value. What began as an incentive to the production of bigger and better marrows has become a progressive and systematic training in community life. The country housewife used to be the Cinderella of rural

---

[1] The newly-created National Foundation of Adult Education may prove to be such a boon.

society. She carried more than her share of the family burdens
and got few compensations for it. Least of all did she get a
fair share of that contact with her own kind which is itself one
of the most valuable if imponderable experiences of community
life. Her role in most of the organised activities of the country
was that of a spectator rather than a participant ; when she
got outside her home at all it was as a rule to take a back seat
in the activities of the church, the political association, or the
bar parlour.

To the casual observer it might seem that many of the occupations of the average Women's Institute are calculated simply to
make its members more useful Cinderellas—to make them
better cooks or dressmakers. If the Women's Institutes did no
more than make their members cleverer at cooking and more
nimble with the needle they would be rendering an important
social service. But the real virtue of their achievement is that
these accomplishments are incidental to the bigger job of
teaching women how to associate for social ends. Apart from
the opportunities which the Institutes provide for their members
to learn how to make pigs or poultry pay, how to market their
fruit and jam, how to design more attractive rugs and baskets
—apart from these opportunities, the Institutes give country
women something of a sense of corporate unity. It is difficult,
indeed, for the sophisticated to appreciate what is going on in
the mind of the woman who for the first time discovers affiliations outside those of the domestic circle. All the petty details
of the monthly meetings, all the business of agendas and reports
and resolutions and decisions, are in fact a process of identifica-
tion. It manifests a bigger unit of life, a wider circle of significance. It is the beginning of an understanding of what community means.

It is this side of the Women's Institute movement—a side
not easy to define in precise terms—which is achieving on a
growing scale a very real and very remarkable educational end.
And it is the development of this sense of communal identity
which is producing so great a variety of organised activities
within the Institutes. There has been no need to force the pace.
The spirit of association has inevitably produced its manifesta-
tions. Thus the growth of such activities as discussion groups,
drama, music, and dancing has been an organic one ; and in
recent years it has evolved further into a co-operation with

F

class-providing bodies for the provision of elementary courses in such subjects as local history and literature and international affairs.

2. THE TOWNSWOMEN'S GUILDS

The Townswomen's Guilds movement is another instance of the transformation of an original function into one which serves new social needs. It sprang from the National Union of Women's Suffrage Societies, which after the partial enfranchisement of women in 1918 had become the the National Union of Societies for Equal Citizenship ; and when in 1928 women were granted the vote on the same terms as men, this movement abandoned all political activity and adapted its purpose into that of educating the new citizens. Although its pedigree is thus different from that of the Women's Institutes, the Townswomen's Guilds movement is in every sense a sister body. In general terms it is doing for women in urban areas what the Institutes are doing in rural areas. Its object is " the education of women to enable them as citizens to make their best contributions towards the common good " ; and its interpretation of that object is realistic and liberal. Its predominant purpose is to give townswomen a civic identity ; to provide them, through the business of the Guild, with the experience of self-government and social responsibility. And this central motive is consolidated by a variety of corporate activities, ranging from homecrafts and handicrafts to group discussions of international affairs. It is one of the youngest recruits to adult education ; but in its short life it has already passed out of the experimental stage and must inevitably expand. It is making particularly good progress in the new housing estates where a civic consciousness has hardly had time to develop. Like the Women's Institute movement it needs and deserves the co-operation of those voluntary bodies which can assist it in the more formal parts of its educational work.

These two movements are the most typical of their kind ; and it is significant that both are concerned with the educational and civic welfare of women. An identical movement for men does not exist. That is not to say that there are not men's movements comparable to these. But the divergence of aim is soon discernible when we come to consider examples of the men's movements in this field.

3. COUNCILS OF SOCIAL SERVICE

One of the most ambitious movements of the twenties was that instigated by the National Council of Social Service. Its objective, like that of the two societies already mentioned, has been to develop a sense of social responsibility ; above all to encourage the sort of voluntary service which is not only a valuable training to the person who undertakes it, but is equally a contribution to the amenities of modern life. Its functions are those of encouragement and of co-ordination ; and wherever a seed of local community feeling has shown signs of spontaneous growth, the National Council has been ready to foster it. It controls a fluctuating income from donations and Government grants, and for many years enjoyed generous financial support from the Carnegie United Kingdom Trust in the development of its many-sided activities.

Councils of Social Service fulfil a variety of ends. Some of them are simply co-ordinating agencies which try to secure a most useful measure of co-operation between the voluntary agencies and the public authorities of their locality. Some of them are working out civic activities for the new estates. Some of them supplement the work of local authorities by organising after-care services or clubs for boys and girls ; and some have even carried out independent housing schemes in their area. One of the most notable developments has been the movement towards the creation of Community Centres or Community Associations. This movement, retarded by the recent war, is still checked by the hold-up in building, but the conception of Community Centres has made such progress that they are likely to become thicker on the ground before long.

The basic assumption of the Councils is that " in every community there are many of the things which need doing, but which will not be done in ordinary conditions." The National Council of Social Service has not escaped the accusation that by adopting this motive it is serving the ends of a government which is parsimonious in its dealings with the social services. By some of its more partisan critics it was regarded during the years of depression as a sort of special constabulary whose willingness to undertake certain social services enabled the Government (these critics say) to escape more lightly than it should the responsibility for these services. But whatever degree of justification there may be for the suggestion that the Councils are doing what should be done by a government or a local authority, they have undoubtedly stirred up an ardent and industrious kind of voluntary effort. Those who participate in the work of the Councils may well feel that the stimulus to their own social sense, and the realisation of the ends represented in the agencies and clubs they are creating, are more vital than questions of political responsibility.

The work of the Rural Community Councils is as varied as that of their urban counterparts. A good deal of it has been the co-ordination of the activities of all bodies engaged in social services of one kind or another and the promotion of amenities in village life. The realistic attitude of the Councils, which exist now in most English counties, is illustrated by their persistent efforts to get villages to build a hall to serve as the centre of their social life. And the Councils have been invaluable in this respect ; for the business of building a hall involves far more than the provision of a loan for the purpose. It is an opportunity for a corporate effort whose ramifications go far into the life of a village. It is an object lesson in civic responsibility.

4. THE YOUNG FARMERS' CLUBS

The Young Farmers' Clubs are one of the most enterprising of rural organisations. They are open to boys and girls between ten and twenty-one. Their general aim is to cultivate a rising generation in rural England who will have a concern for the development and preservation of the best features of rural industry and rural life. They want their members to become a movement rooted in the land and caring for the land. The methods of the Clubs consist of such activities as training the members in the processes of stock-raising and husbandry, by a system of loans which enables them to acquire their own stuff —but they go beyond these practical considerations. The Clubs, that is to say, since they are governed autonomously by their young members, are an experience in the training of social responsibility and in self-government ; and are as valuable in their social and educational aspects as they are from the technical and economic points of view.

In some ways the growth of the Clubs has resembled that of Women's Institutes. That is to say the primary interest of getting together for immediate and practical ends has become supplemented by broader interests. Thus many Young Farmers' Clubs are nowadays as keen on current affairs or discussion groups or dramatic activities as they are upon stock-raising and similar technical interests.

IV

During the recent war there has been an immense expansion of what may be called potential adult education. How far these new developments are a temporary manifestation remains to be seen. One need not be a confirmed optimist to expect that much of the war-time education experiment and achievement will be consolidated in the coming years.

(1) ABCA

The synthetic word ABCA has enjoyed a wide currency during the last few years. It is, of course, the trade-mark of the Army Bureau of Current Affairs, the military institution which so surprisingly came into being after Dunkirk and which has since served a useful turn in the mental training of the British Army. The spirit of ABCA is poles apart from Balaclava, for it lays down with the full authority of the Army Council that it is a positive duty upon troops to " reason why " and to work out for themselves the problems and conundrums of current affairs. At its outset ABCA was in fact one of those revolutionary innovations at which governments look askance in times of peace, but which they can be persuaded to risk in the emergencies of war. After Dunkirk the British Army was not exactly in high spirits and it was finally decided that one possible tonic for its morale would be the privilege of openly debating the war in all its aspects. It was believed that it would do the troops good if, as citizen-soldiers, they were encouraged (like Cromwell's squadrons) to inform themselves by discussion about the causes and the consequences of the war in which they were so desperately engaged.

The ABCA formula was very simple. Its chief element was the weekly discussion in which the military unit (the platoon or the troop) became a social unit and, with its officer in the chair, proceeded to explore by discussion some such topic as Lease-Lend, Social Insurance, Bretton Woods, Trade Unionism, or Plastics. In these deliberations they were fortified by objective discussion—briefs written by independent experts and an extensive service of visual aids, documentary films, and similar reinforcements. And far from assuming that every second-lieutenant could take the chair by the mere light of nature, the War Office established training centres at which thousands of officers (men and women) learned by instruction and demonstration the main tricks of the chairman's trade. In its simple pattern of purpose and method, ABCA was a system of basic adult education mobile enough to suit the requirements of an army at war.

Like everything else in the Army, ABCA was sometimes done well and sometimes done badly, the decisive factors as a rule being the leadership ability of the junior officer and the interest of the senior officer. But there can be no doubt that ABCA helped to rally the British Army and to train troops in the discipline of free discussion. Its main results can be summarised thus :

(1) It has substitued the habit of rational discussion for the anarchy of barrack-room argument.

(2) It has trained thousands of subalterns in the ticklish art of taking the chair. This experience in management, acquired in the hard school of trial and error, will stand these officers in good stead when they go into commerce or industry or politics. ABCA has done much, in this way, to train the group leaders of democracy.

(3) ABCA has done far more than promote and equip discussion groups. It has installed and " serviced " thousands of Information Rooms throughout the Army. It has been a publishing-concern, issuing some of the most effective visual aids ever seen in this country. For the last two years, it has developed documentary drama, and ABCA's celebrated plays on current affairs have been far more palatable to the troops than the average Ensa show.

(4) ABCA has brought home to thousands of women, for the first time, a realisation of their responsibilities as citizens and given them the experience of forming their own opinions instead of relying on those of their menfolk.

(5) But ABCA's most remarkable feat has slipped through unobserved. It has established in the Army the principle

of compulsory adult education. There, indeed, is a revolution, and one which immediately raises the question whether in post-war adult education there is room for, and justification for, discussion groups in the factory and the retail business house. If the Army includes these things in " the King's time," is there a case in the future for including them in " the employer's time " ? If we have made soldiers take current affairs seriously by including it in their working time-table, could we encompass a similar sense of responsibility by putting current affairs into office hours ?

Many who have observed at close quarters the extent to which ABCA has managed to induce in the average soldier a sense of responsibility about current affairs at home and abroad, have expressed concern lest demobilisation should cut him off from this habit of discussion. It is, of course, a delusion to suppose that because they have learned to enjoy adult education in the Services, soldiers will clamour for it when they come out. They will not. They will *look* for it—and if they see it attractively displayed in the educational shop-windows they will come inside and settle down as customers. But if it is not put in their way, they will seek out other activities.

It would be wrong to suggest that the Army is the only section of the community in which discussion-groups have been established during the war. ABCA, in due course, spread to the Royal Navy and to the R.A.F., but only on a very limited scale and never with that backing from the Service high-ups which it enjoyed in the Army. If during the Release Period morale was poorer in R.A.F. ground-staffs and on the lower deck than in the Army, one very good reason was that the other Services failed to ABCA-ise the demobilisation plans and thus left sailors and airmen in the dark about the principles and the progress of release. ABCA was adopted, on a modest scale, in some sections of Civil Defence and in a few aircraft factories and Ministry of Supply hostels, but its civilian counterparts never had the authority or the resources for their work which the Army could command. There were many war-time discussion groups fostered by various educational bodies, and there was also a boom in Brains Trusts—that light-hearted but effective mode of public enlightenment which the B.B.C. was the first to promote.

Yet on the whole it is true to say that the British public was less educated about current affairs during the war than was the British Army. The public, it is true, was bombarded with exhortations from a legion of Ministries and encouraged by the Press to take a robust view of our fortunes. But seldom did it have the opportunity or the time to examine by discussion the abundance of opinions and interpretations by which it was beset. The merits of discussion cannot be overvalued in a democracy. Unless citizens shoulder the responsibility of talking things over and thinking things out they are in danger of becoming a mass Hallelujah Chorus to the will of a dictator or an oligarchy. The death of Hitler has not eradicated this risk. Nations are still to be found which prefer to rush a decision than to hammer it out by the light of reason, and in our own land there are those who rail against the deliberation of issues and clamour for a strong man to lead us to prosperity. But it is a basic necessity to the health of a democracy that its citizens shall concern themselves with national policy and thus provide that mass assembly of public opinion which is the only reliable trusteeship of representative government. A famous soldier-administrator, writing in the February (1946) issue of the *Journal of Education*, sounds a timely warning on this matter. He is General Sir Ronald Adam, Adjutant-General to the Forces from 1941–6, and he says:

We lost the last peace for many reasons, but at the bottom of all those reasons was our neglect to cultivate a popular knowledge of and attentiveness to world affairs. We were too willing to " contract-out " from our collective responsibility for the state of the world. To safeguard us against that liability of a war-strained people we need, on a national scale, an organisation which will not only set before us—week in, week out—the reliable facts of the situation on all fronts of public interest, but which will also encourage us to unravel their significance by the processes of honest adult discussion. We have more to learn than ever before about frontiers, blocs, loans, economic expansion, racial grievances, rehabilitation, and knowledge of these things will not come to us merely by skimming the headlines in the morning paper or sitting quiescent in the presence of a news-reel or a wireless set. Citizenship is an active state of being, and one way to develop that activity is by the regular habit of hammering-out the issues with our comrades and fellow-workers.

It is on that thesis and those assumptions that a new drive is being made to create a deeper discussion-mindedness among

the public.   The prototype of this effort is ABCA and its
sponsors are the Carnegie United Kingdom Trust.   In creating
early in 1946 the Bureau of Current Affairs the Trustees
illustrated the belief, widely held among responsible observers,
that the population as a whole might benefit from discussions
of the kind which were promoted among the troops by ABCA.

The Bureau has announced its purpose in plain terms.   It
does not seek to be a providing body in adult education and
thus enters into no kind of competition with the voluntary
or statutory bodies within that field.   But it " services "
any organisation which decides to run discussion groups,
whether that organisation is an industrial factory, a local
government office, a holiday camp (on wet evenings), a retail
store, a women's institute, a church association, a cadet corps,
or any similar body.   The decision to form a discussion group
or groups must be taken by the prospective members—and
from that point onwards the group can look to the Bureau of
Current Affairs for assistance in a variety of ways.

The business of the Bureau, broadly speaking, is threefold.
First it issues, every fortnight, a discussion-brief on some
near-topical theme.   This is not just another pamphlet but
a pamphlet-with-a-purpose, a pamphlet so organised and
edited as to provide a working layout for a group discussion
on each selected theme.   Everyone will agree that there is no
shortage of urgent social, political, and economic topics in
the world to-day, and it is the job of the Bureau of Current
Affairs to set forth the issues with absolute detachment.   The
Bureau also issues on a wide scale visual aids of all kinds which
attempt to reduce current problems to the shape of pictures
and diagrams.   These vivid pictorial summaries of current
affairs are finding their way not only into barracks but into
factories, waiting-rooms on railway stations, and all other
places where people congregate in numbers.

Another section of the Bureau undertakes the job of training
leaders for group discussions.   Nothing that ABCA did in
war-time was more important than training young officers
in the difficult art of taking the chair, and the Bureau is
continuing this work.   The third department of the Bureau
provides reference facilities—a Reference Library, a Pamphlets Library, a Visual Aids Library, and so on.   A large house
in the centre of London (117 Piccadilly) has been provided by

F*

the Carnegie U.K. Trust, and it is hoped to make this house not only an office but a club for persons interested in the popularisation of current affairs.

The men and women behind this venture are not sentimentalists. They fully appreciate, for example, the perils of any popular craze, and the last thing they intend to do is to encourage a wholesale development of organised " nattering." If they have their way the Bureau will be pretty selective in its choice of customers for some time to come. It would prefer to nourish a limited number and type of discussion groups than to foster any rapid inflation in this relatively new field of mass education. In some potential spheres of activity there is room for much experiment before we shall know the capacity and the limits of civic education. The Bureau would like, for instance, to explore the feasibility of holding discussion groups in factories during working hours. There is, of course, a world of difference between " the King's time " and " the boss's time," and life in a camp bears little resemblance to life in a factory. Nevertheless it is known for certain that there are some large-scale employers willing to try out the experiment, on a modest basis, of allowing men and women an hour off for working-time discussion groups. And one does not need to be an industrialist psychologist to assert that the interlude for discussion will not necessarily reduce the output of those who take part. The Bureau of Current Affairs has no intention of setting up as a purveyor of lubricants recommended for reducing friction in industry, yet it does not reject the possibility that works-discussion might help to dissolve some of the prejudice and misunderstanding which abound on both sides in industry to-day. Many ABCA sessions in the Army became an open forum for the free discussion of the deficiencies of military life and organisation—and these exchanges never led to disaffection. We can at least say that well-informed discussion on matters of production, price-fixing, distribution, nationalisation and the like, would not darken the present general ignorance of those themes. Indeed, it might be said that in such innovations as Production Committees and Works Councils, a step has already been taken to ABCA-ising industry. The argument for conducting such systematic inquiries in working hours, on the job, is a powerful one. The significance of these matters in a man's daily life is, perhaps, increased if they are debated on the job and not in the four-ale bar. Citizenship, in many of its most vital aspects, is immediately related to the conditions of one's working life, and there is a case for considering some of the problems of citizenship in the place and the time where our working life occurs.

The policy of the Bureau, then, includes efforts to discover (with the co-operation of employers and workers) whether discussion groups are feasible in working hours—and, equally, whether (in suitable factories) discussion groups can be developed as a lunch-hour digestive or as a voluntary activity in firms which have an organised programme of community welfare. But apart from such explorations, there is no stint of opportunity for development in voluntary fields. It is predicted that there will be a considerable post-war growth of Community Centres, Youth Centres, Cadet Formations, British Legion branches, and similar movements, all of which are anxious to make current affairs an element in their programme, and within these movements the Bureau will find ample scope for trying out many methods and devices for making community discussion a vital and illuminating experience.

In some of its work the Bureau of Current Affairs will endeavour to promote public interest in national and international issues by a " direct exposure " method. Here again it will be developing a method well proved by ABCA in the Army. No camp institution better earned its keep (if it was well kept) than the Information Room or the current affairs hut, where the soldier could always find the pictorial delineation of topical issues. At his leisure he could browse over photographic exhibitions, study the week's ABCA Map Review, or observe in a variety of coloured charts and animated statistics the condition of the turbulent world. Much of the best education is done, so to speak, behind the pupil's back, and many a young soldier has assimilated the outline of world history or world geography not in the classroom but by wandering around his unit information room. The Bureau of Current Affairs hopes to expose British citizens to a similar pictorial influence. There are many strategic positions in everyday life for this kind of assault on ignorance, and it will be part of the Bureau's business to locate and use them. In this sense the Bureau will endeavour to infiltrate into public libraries, works canteens, railway stations, retail stores, and perhaps even the foyer of the local cinema. Its plan of visual aids is the most comprehensive ever undertaken, and one of the pioneers in this field to which the Bureau makes the readiest acknowledgment is the defunct Empire Marketing Board which did so much in its day to acclimatise our minds to a sense of kinship and responsibility for the British Empire.

This then is the rough outline of the enterprise upon which the Carnegie United Kingdom Trust has launched the Bureau of Current Affairs. The new organisation is " under " no Government department, nor does it receive a penny in State subsidies. It is non-political and non-profit-making, and any surpluses it may make upon its modest charges for publications and method-courses will be ploughed back into further disinterested development.

In launching ventures of this sort there is sometimes a hold-up while constitution and policy are being deliberated. But the Bureau of Current Affairs was able to start work before its final form of government had been devised. By placing the Bureau in the charge of a small provisional committee, the Trustees showed an agreeable sense of realism. It is no good " promoting " a body of this kind in thin air, and the best publicity the Bureau can command will be its own good deeds. The intention of the Trustees is that, in the near future, the Bureau shall attain some form of self-government. Here, indeed, is a venture with both feet on the ground and with some reason to believe that the road on which it sets forth leads to somewhere more tangible than a pious aspiration.

2. ARMY EDUCATION

ABCA was only the spearhead of a more comprehensive system of Army education which grew up during the war years. The first reinforcement to ABCA, which began to operate at the end of 1942, was the British Way and Purpose (B.W.P.), which was a background supplement to the rough-and-tumble discussion-group work of ABCA. The idea in B.W.P. was that after the ground had been broken in ABCA discussions, experts would be brought along to a unit usually supplied from civilian sources by the Regional Committees for Adult Education in the Forces—who would supplement the discussion form by set talks on a systematic series of subjects concerned largely with British conceptions and British institutions. B.W.P.

added a second compulsory hour a week to the Army's educational training. An even more ambitious plan was devised towards the end of the war in the Army Education Release Scheme, which laid down that from six to eight hours a week in all should be spent on compulsory education among the troops. This scheme gave a wide choice of " subjects " to men. For those who wanted to brush up their trade, or learn a new one, there was a wide choice of pre-vocational subjects designed to help a man on leaving the Army to feel that he had at least begun to fit himself for civilian employment. For other men, who had no anxieties about a job, there was an array of " cultural " subjects, including languages, philosophy, history, psychology, music, and the arts. One significant feature of this extensive project was that the Army trained its own instructors for the job, by taking men and women who had some rudimentary knowledge of a subject and putting them through a concentrated course enabling them to become at least adequate instructors of others. And at every stage the Regional Committees gave welcomed unstinting aid to all these ventures in improvised education. The Army Education Scheme was, at the worst, a good deal better than nothing at all. And it did give instruction to scores of thousands of troops in that restless and anxious period of awaiting demobilisation. Some parts of the Army Education Scheme need no such apologetic explanation. There were, for instance, the Formation Colleges, eight in all, which at home and abroad gave a compact residential course of educational training to thousands of the more advanced students—and gave them also an appetite for a residential education which is likely to make them keen supporters of the civilian equivalents of a Formation College.

From the foregoing pages it may be assumed that it was only in the Army that these educational schemes were carried out. Both the Royal Navy and the R.A.F. did, in fact, produce schemes based on those devised in the War Office, and in broad terms Services education followed the lines indicated here. But it would be wrong to let the reader suppose that the Royal Navy and the R.A.F. applied themselves with anything like the Army's determination to these educational tasks. The Navy, in particular, possessed certain advantages over the Army which should have enabled them to get first-class schemes in operation. The ship, after all, is a unit in which the men spent continuous days together and were, therefore, as much available for educational purposes as any other. If there was time, in the watch below, for playing the mouth organ and reading magazines, there was also time for an hour or two's compulsory education a week. The educational schemes operated in H.M. ships, however, were astonishingly few in number, and what little was accomplished occurred mainly on the shore stations. Both Malta and Gibraltar produced really effective educational schemes. In the R.A.F., on the other hand, there was some justification for the paucity of educational work. The main reason was the relative officer shortage on R.A.F. stations, so that it was impossible to arrange, as the Army did, regular group discussions of one officer to twenty or thirty men. But had the R.A.F. been educationally minded they might have found the means to get round this difficulty. There was no shortage of N.C.O.s in the R.A.F., and from these might have been recruited group leaders and elementary instructors on a considerable scale. In considering Services' education, therefore, it is fair to give the Army priority not only for its intention but for its achievement.

All three Services are to maintain and develop their educational schemes in the future, and it is evident that compulsory national services will not neglect the education of the young conscript.

V

1. THE ARTS COUNCIL

Another domain of popular education which has been prodigiously extended during the war is that of arts in general, and music in particular. Here two agencies may be selected as having had most to do with this advance. The first is the Arts Council of Great Britain, formerly known as C.E.M.A. (Council for the Encouragement of Music and the Arts). This organisation drew much of its pattern from a much smaller precursor (viz. the Art for the People scheme, inaugurated by the British Institute of Adult Education in 1934), but it was in 1940, of all years, when heavy raids on Britain had begun, that the Arts Council came into existence. In one sense it was a private enterprise, for the bulk of its funds came from the Pilgrim Trust. But the contributions of the Trust were matched by the Treasury, and within a couple of years the Treasury took over the financial responsibility for the Arts Council. The annual expenditure of the Arts Council is still a good deal less than half a million pounds. With this sum it circulates a remarkable total of art exhibitions, first-rate concerts, and first-rate play productions. Although the large towns get a fair ration of these pleasures, the Arts Council has always concentrated on taking the arts to the small towns and rural districts which, as a rule, never get the opportunity to enjoy a first-class concert, play, or art exhibition. The response to this movement has been extremely large, and to some extent the response can be decided by the great number of supplementary activities which have sprung up in the wake of the Arts Council's tours. They have instigated numerous local series of talks about the arts, and even more numerous trains of discussion groups, music clubs, etc. It takes a war to get such bold projects on the move. It cannot be denied that in war-time the Treasury is more amiable than usual to projects which can show that they have a morale effect on the population, and this was, indeed, one of the arguments whereby the Arts Council got access to Treasury funds. No doubt the work of the Arts Council has contributed to the morale of the population as a whole, but even more marvellous was the extent to which it roused and cultivated an interest in the common man for pleasures which had hitherto been beyond his reach. The Arts Council is still a very young movement indeed, and it can be expected within the next decade to make rapid progress. It is already, for instance, turning its attention to the problem of premises suitable for its activities in the smaller towns of England, and is said to be engaged now on a scheme for providing municipalities, at a relatively small cost, with a prefabricated Arts Centre, housing a concert, plays, and art exhibitions. All in all, here is a movement marking a real advance in the cultural life of Great Britain.

2. THE B.B.C.

It was in the late twenties that the B.B.C. decided that it had an educational as well as an entertainment mission. Urged by the organised bodies of adult education it attempted to interpret this mission by providing every afternoon talks, grouped into series, of a more serious educational kind. At the consumer end, the B.B.C. hoped to construct a system of discussion groups which were intended to take their agenda from the substance of the talk. Although most carefully and patiently nourished by the B.B.C., this self-conscious effort has not come to much, and it is doubtful, after the war, whether it will ever be revived. The full reasons for this comparative failure are too long to enter into here, but one of the more important of them is the inescapable fact that an invisible speaker, however excellent, is a less effective discussion-group leader than one who, for all his imperfections, is present in the flesh. Most of the other reasons have to do with the characteristic incapacity of adult education organisations to get together for any purpose whatever.

Two other educational features of the B.B.C. have, however, been an emphatic and large-scale success. The first is Schools Broadcasts, the second the Forces Educational Broadcasts. Each of these services had a clear instructional start. They set out to employ the resources of broadcasting to communicate hard facts about geography, history, science, music, English literature, and so on. They set out to teach, not to tickle passing interest, and the student who attends to them feels that he is getting definite instruction on the topic to which he has chosen deliberately to attend. Schools Broadcasts and Forces Educational Broadcasts have both developed such effective means of presentation that they are often as worth listening to for their ingenious form as they are for their informative content. This is particularly true of the Forces Educational Broadcasts, which began in the autumn of 1945 as a reinforcement to the Army Education Scheme for the Release Period. Thousands of soldiers are applying themselves with great diligence to the lessons in English, geography, current affairs, science, music, which are among subjects treated in the eighteen weekly broadcasts of the F.E.B. These two services of the B.B.C. became one of the most effective of systematic educational provisors in this country, and from the F.E.B. at least they can also claim to be reaching an audience which might not have become organised by any other agency. But apart from its deliberate education scheme, the B.B.C. is also accomplishing a vast educational mission in its day-to-day programme work. Any dispassionate observer must agree that the man in the street derives from the B.B.C. an immense amount of accurate and stimulating information about almost any subject under the sun. From such series as those of Jenifer Wayne (" This is the Law ") and Nesta Pain, the average citizen has become acquainted with a great range of subjects which he would have been inclined to dismiss as being too " serious " to read about for himself, or learn about in the evening institutes. Those, of course, who believe only in learning the hard way will disparage the easier approach which the B.B.C. provides, but it will remain incontestable that broadcasting has made millions aware of facts and principles which might not otherwise have come to their attention at all. In the field of current affairs, more than any other, has the B.B.C. brought home the issues to our fire-sides. And to this source, more than to any other, can be attributed the contemporary high level of the public's knowledge of world affairs and home affairs. If the cheap Press, which is so fond of baiting the B.B.C., could claim a similar record we might be more readily attentive to its scriptures on our broadcasting system.

The most spectacular educational effects of broadcasting, however, can probably be seen in the field of musical appreciation. With a most admirable sense of purpose the B.B.C. has not stinted a regular supply of " good " music, and it has devised numerous means of interpreting music to the man who presently finds his taste and his standard responding to what he hears. Such features as " Music Magazine " can claim to be among the most successful interpreters of music we have yet known in this country.

Within a few years it may be expected that television will be installed in most of our homes, and it may further be anticipated that through this medium the B.B.C. will be able to raise our standards in the visual arts as plainly as it has done in the realm of music. All in all, then, and more by indirect than by direct means, can the B.B.C claim to have become a powerful medium of adult education, and the fact that it hits its objective, so to speak, behind our backs makes it all the more effective a medium. In the air of British broadcasting there is a good deal of educational ozone, and though its percentage cannot be measured, its effect on public health cannot be denied.

VI

THE CINEMA

Although the cinema is older and more powerful in this country than broadcasting it cannot claim yet to have anything like the educational results of radio. It is for discussion whether things would have been different if the development of the cinema in this country had been entrusted to a public utility rather than left to private enterprise. These things go wrong not because they have any inherent wrongness in them, but because they get into the wrong hands ; the main reason why most of our films are so bad is not that they represent some low standard of what the public wants, but that they represent the cynical, profit-making, and semi-illiterate aspirations of the tycoons of the trade. It would be manifestly false to say that we wholly are starved of films of quality, but they remain a small percentage of the offering made to us week by week in the local cinema. Before the recent war the documentary producers, in a spirit of great faith and courage, had driven a small wedge into the commercial cinema. But as a rule they lacked the resources to compete on even terms with the entrenched hosts of the trade. If things had improved in this respect, credit must again go not to private enterprise but to Government leadership. Even its most petulant critics were disposed to admit that the Films Division of the late Ministry of Information did a good job. They were given the means, although all was on a modest scale, to produce the kind of documentary which in a small space of time could convey much useful and stimulating information on matters of geography, sociology, and current affairs. Both documentary and educational films have often been accused of dullness of presentation, and the charge is often true. But this contention proceeds not from any act of intent or production on the part of the documentary people, but from the chronic lack of resources with which they have usually been afflicted in this country. However, enough has been done to have shaken the cynics of the trade in their conviction that the public wants only entertainment in the cinema, and there are reassuring signs to-day that the region of the film world devoted to the advancement of adult education is gradually enlarging its frontals. In one final comment we can again contrast the powerful educational interest broadcasting has aroused in this country with the negligible one exercised by the film.

VII

The foregoing scale of changes in adult education between the two wars has omitted many references to work of promise. Surveying the period as a whole and with a due emphasis on wartime experience, one reaches certain main conclusions :

(1) The first is that adult education today is much more broadly based than it was at the beginning of this century, and that the base is tending to become broader still. Some observers, especially the older generation, regard this as a misfortune and are disposed to quote Gresham's Law as the inevitable consequence. They argue that the extension of the cruder interests of popular education will check the growth of those forms, like the University Tutorial Class, the University Extension Class, and the W.E.A. Class, whose purpose is to encourage adult students to make a serious study rather than to indulge in a mild interest, or practice a kind of hobby. Against this somewhat Calvinistic view it may be urged that a pyramid must have a base as well as an apex. The fact is that ordinary forms of adult education are by no means on the decline, and the W.E.A. reports an increase in its membership in the post-war period. In Army education it was discovered, moreover, that as the compulsory simple forms of adult education developed there came an increasing demand, from an increasing minority, for more thorough kinds of education in their own spare time. This seems to me the true answer. I believe that by broadening adult education at the base we increase the number of potential students for the harder kinds of adult education. The process of levelling the lump seems to me an essential one, and I regard the current growth of the humbler forms of adult education as a wholly desirable development.

(2) Throughout this century, in all forms of adult education, it has been found that the greatest progress is achieved when the education proceeds on some kind of community basis. To that conclusion may be added a more recent trend, viz. that men and women have developed higher " housing standards " in their leisure hours. Both the publican and the film distribu-

tor helped to create this increased concern for "housing standards," but adult education has lagged behind. One of the most imperative factors in adult education during the next few years will be the degree to which it can re-house itself. Among some of the older bodies of adult education the myth grows that an adult learns best if he constricts his portly forms inside the desks of an infants' school borrowed for an evening class. But this Spartan idea is an incorrect one. There are numerous prototypes now of what the premises should be for adult education. Here the Y.M.C.A. has a most creditable record, and there is no doubt that it attracts a great number of young people to its educational classes because they find they are conducted in premises of reasonable dignity and comfort— and close to such amenities as a canteen and a lounge. The L.C.C. is also conscious of this necessity. Just before the war it built the City Literary Institute, off the north end of Drury Lane, and it would be hard to find an institution more agreeable to this and more conducive to happy learning and good times. The Educational Settlements Association, although a small-scale body, was another organisation to learn the necessity to conduct adult education in premises which are a cross between a club and a college. Community Centres, by their name and nature, have been foremost in realising this conception, in principle if not always in fact. The Slough Community Centre is an obvious model, and the numerous schemes now in the offing promise that in time Britain will possess several Community Centres as spacious as can be desired. If adult education in all its forms is to thrive it is best likely to do so in premises where the spirit of conviviality is as apparent as the spirit of learning.

Some observers advocate a further development, i.e. the multiplication in this country of centres of residential adult education based on the lines of the Folk High Schools of Denmark. Much sentimental rigmarole has been written about the Danish Folk High Schools, an institution which is held in small regard to-day in the country of its origin, and which can be dismissed as an institution useful in its time and generation but entirely outmoded in the contemporary world. The glorifiers of the Folk High Schools forgot that Denmark is in the main composed of agricultural communities, the nature of whose work enables them to take time off, in slack periods of the year, to foregather as residential students. For industrial communities this pattern is about as inflexible as it can be.

There are other objections to the notion of residential adult education, which at best offers its poor deluded students (with apologies to Bisto) the odour, but not the gravy, of a higher education. On all accounts the better answer for this country seems to be a considerable increase of Community Centres in which a wide range of adult interests, from hobbies to the study of the classics, can be achieved by men and women during the couple of evenings a week of their busy lives which they are willing to devote to such activities.

Chapter XI

THE GREAT PHILANTHROPIC TRUSTS

by

HENRY A. MESS and CONSTANCE BRAITHWAITE

1. THE CARNEGIE AND PILGRIM TRUSTS

by

Henry A. Mess

THE philanthropic Trust is no new thing in English life. A large number of Trusts exist, many of them of considerable antiquity : some wealthy and well-disposed man or woman has left money or property, the income from which is to be distributed at intervals, usually intervals of a year, at the discretion of appointed trustees. The nineteenth century saw the foundation of such notable Trusts as the Peabody Trust and the Sutton Trust, both of which played considerable parts in the improvement of housing, whilst the early twentieth century saw the foundation of the world-famed Rhodes Trust, bringing students from all parts of the British Empire, from the United States of America and from Germany to Oxford. Most of the Trusts have been for specific purposes : often their benefactions have been confined to the inhabitants of one locality. The twentieth century has also seen the foundation of several Trusts, two of which have large funds at their disposal, which are singularly wide in the range of possible benefactions. The story of the operation of these Trusts, more particularly of the Carnegie United Kingdom Trust and of the Pilgrim Trust, is no small part of the story of voluntary social service during the last three decades, and their influence has also been felt in some spheres of statutory action.

The first to be founded of these great Trusts of wide range was the Carnegie United Kingdom Trust. The story of Andrew Carnegie is well known : the poor boy emigrating with his parents to America, making his way in business and amassing a large fortune. Andrew Carnegie gave away huge sums of money in his lifetime, and in 1913 he placed in the hands of trustees, whom he had chosen, Steel Corporation Bonds worth 10 million dollars. (The Carnegie United Kingdom Trust was not the only Trust which he endowed, but is the only one which need concern us here.) The original holding was converted during the first world war into British securities, yielding approximately £120,000 a year. According to the trust deed the trustees were " to assist pioneer projects of national scope by such means as come under the category of ' charitable ' according to Scottish and English law." The trustees were enjoined to bear in mind that the needs of the community are continually changing. The first official meeting of the trustees was in December 1913.

Andrew Carnegie had already given away in his lifetime very large sums of money, and especially in two directions ; he was interested in the provision of libraries and he was interested in the provision of organs for places of worship. The trustees found that these interests to some extent dictated their policy in the earliest days, but in each case they showed imagination and statesmanship in serving them.

With regard to libraries, the trustees commissioned Professor W. G. S. Adams, then Gladstone Professor of Political Science in the University of Oxford and now Warden of All Souls College, Oxford, to make a comprehensive survey and to report on public library provision. Professor Adams's report, published in 1915, which was of outstanding importance in the history of libraries in this country, showed that only 57% of the population was provided for, and that outside the great towns the provision was usually deplorable. (To this day it is sadly inadequate in many districts.) The deficiencies were, as might be expected, far greater in the country than in the towns : whereas 79% of the urban population had some library facilities, less than 2·5% of the rural population had them.

The Carnegie trustees took action on this report. So far as the towns were concerned they contented themselves at first with honouring a large number of promises which Mr. Carnegie had made. But in the country districts, where there was practically no provision at all, they decided to experiment in the supply of books. Of books, not buildings ; there was evidence in Professor Adams's report that in not a few cases where

Mr. Carnegie had provided a building, the maintenance of that building strained the resources of the recipients, and there was very little left to spend on books or on librarian's salary. Arrangements were made, therefore, to supply boxes of books from a central depot to village schools, the school teachers acting as volunteer librarians. The first experiments were made in two or three selected counties. In 1916 the Staffordshire County Council undertook the administration of such a scheme in its own area : and so well did this arrangement work, and so obvious was the need in other areas, that a number of other county education authorities applied to the trustees for grants. At this time county councils had no power to spend money themselves on library provision, so that all expenses had either to be defrayed by the Carnegie Trust or else to come out of the pockets of local persons who were sufficiently interested and public-spirited to meet them. The Public Libraries Amendment Act of 1919 made it possible for county councils to develop libraries in any district where the earlier Public Libraries Act had not been adopted, and to raise a rate for that purpose. The next sixteen years saw a partnership between the local authorities and the Carnegie Trust which resulted in the development of a fairly satisfactory village service, and of a much less satisfactory country town service, practically all over England. By 1935 the Carnegie trustees felt that their work was done, and their grants ceased.

In the case of towns the trustees, whilst fulfilling promises, confined themselves to making supplementary grants to small municipal libraries. Undoubtedly they did a good deal to stimulate municipal provision ; and they also did much to improve the status and salaries of librarians, since they always made it the condition of a grant that a minimum salary should be paid to a properly qualified librarian. They also made a grant to the Library Association, the professional association of librarians, and towards the foundation of a School of Librarianship. And they did a good deal to stimulate inter-library co-operation. In 1930 they made a grant which brought about a regional grouping of libraries in the north of England, with a scheme of mutual borrowing. Similar schemes have been brought into operation in other regions, and there is to-day a very considerable amount of lending of books between libraries, a facility for which a great many students have reason to be grateful. In 1933 the Carnegie United Kingdom Trust provided a building for the National Central Library, one of many organisations which owes much to the imagination and pioneering energy of Dr. Albert Mansbridge. The trustees also made grants to several special libraries, including the National Library for the Blind and the Seafarers' Educational Service, this last being another child of Dr. Mansbridge's fertile brain.

Summarising, the Carnegie United Kingdom Trust has been a prime agent in the building up of a rural library service ; it has contributed heavily to the building of a number of municipal libraries and to the stocking of many more ; it has helped to build up a number of special libraries ; it has inspired and made possible a well-integrated system of co-operation between libraries throughout the country ; and it has done much to raise the status and quality of librarianship.

A second great interest of Andrew Carnegie was in music ; in particular he had a great belief in the value of the church organ, and had given away in his lifetime no less than half a million pounds to provide, or to help to provide, church organs. The trustees did not share his enthusiasm, and beyond fulfilling outstanding promises amounting to £50,000 they did not pursue that line of benevolence. They set themselves instead to foster the love of good music in other ways. One of their earliest grants was to the Association of Musical Competition Festivals, which later became the National Federation of Musical Competition Festivals. They found that there was a shortage of published music of good quality, and in particular that contemporary composers of merit had great difficulty in getting work published on the ground that there was no market for it. A vicious circle needed breaking ; and the Carnegie United Kingdom Trust set themselves to break it by subsidising the publication of musical compositions, both old and new. Twenty-five thousand pounds was spent on subsidising the publication of works by contemporary composers, and another £16,000 was spent on producing editions of Tudor music. A most gratifying result of this subsidisation, in conjunction with other measures taken to foster an interest in good music, was that a few years later the trustees were able to state in their annual report that subsidies were no longer necessary, since the music publishers now found that the publication of good music was a commercial proposition.

Steps were taken to foster music in rural areas. One of the most effective of these was the subsidisation of concerts given by the Village and Country Towns Concerts Fund, under whose auspices villagers in Somerset and other counties listened to rendering of the works of Bach and of other great composers.

Towns as well as country districts profited by the grants to the Orchestral Loan Library, and by guarantees against loss which were given to small amateur choirs and orchestras, and by a grant made to the National Federation of Musical Societies for its administrative expenses.

The Old Vic theatre had for many years maintained against tremendous difficulties its task of supplying good performances of Shakespeare's plays, and of other classical plays, at cheap prices in an unfashionable part of London. In 1918 it found itself in dire straits, because the London County Council was demanding, very properly, costly structural improvements. At the same time it was much hampered by the deficiencies of its wardrobe. The Carnegie United Kingdom trustees made substantial grants towards the cost of meeting both these expenses. Seven years later the trustees enabled the Old Vic company to acquire the shell of Sadlers Wells theatre, a theatre of historic interest in what had become a poor part of London. Sadlers Wells, as is well known to all theatre lovers, has since specialised in opera, and it has also gained for itself a unique reputation as the only home of English ballet. The trustees have also subsidised a number of " Little Theatres " in different parts of the country. They made grants to the British Drama League, enabling it to obtain suitable headquarters and a central library ; and through the Rural Community Councils, themselves owing much to the generosity of the Trust, they contributed to the building up of village dramatic societies. If it is easier to-day for persons living in the poorer parts of London and of other cities, and persons living in the smaller towns and in rural districts, to see good plays occasionally, and for some of them to act in good plays themselves, it is in no small measure due to the help given by the Carnegie United Kingdom Trust. But no one who knows the situation can deny that an immense deal still waits to be done.

The biggest single allocation ever made by the trustees was in 1927, when £200,000 was assigned to aid the purchase of playing-fields. In this the trustees acted in co-operation with the National Playing Fields Association, on whose behalf a powerful appeal to the nation had recently been made by the Prince of Wales. The trustees claimed later that their contribution, together with the £60,000 supplied by the National Playing Fields Association, elicited at least £1,500,000 of other money, chiefly from local authorities, and resulted in 800 playing-fields, with a total acreage of 6,000 acres, being made available to the boys and girls of this country.

Another very big allocation was that of £150,000 during the quinquennium 1936 to 1940 for land settlement. In some ways this allocation differed from other allocations, chiefly in that it was well understood from the start that the total number of persons directly benefited would be small.

There have been many other benefactions of the Carnegie United Kingdom Trust, but it is not proposed to catalogue them. The chief forms of benefaction have been given, and sufficient has been written to indicate the main lines of the trustees' thought and policy. Their policy has been from the first carefully thought out and adhered to with much consistency. In the first place, the trustees have limited the range of their benefactions ; they state in one of their reports that " it is clearly better policy to concentrate on a small number of purposes which can be effectively carried out than to give inadequate assistance indiscriminately over a wide range of objects." In the second place, they have believed in continuity ; when they have decided to foster some form of social activity, they have done so as a rule over a number of years. From the beginning they have worked in terms of quinquennia, preparing carefully in advance a programme for each period. Thus from 1921 to 1925, and also from 1926 to 1930, they were specially concerned with Libraries, Music and Drama, Physical Welfare, and Rural Development. From 1931 to 1935 their main interests were Libraries, Music and Drama, Adult Education, Playing-fields. In the quinquennium 1936 to 1940 they subsidised heavily Music and Land Settlement. This does not mean that they confine themselves rigidly to these preselected interests during the quinquennium, but a substantial part of their income (about two-thirds) is earmarked for them. The policy for the quinquennium, and the conditions for grants, are announced well in advance, so that organisations who may benefit have time to prepare schemes. With regard to unallocated income, principles are laid down ; and the categories are stated of institutions and of purposes with regard to which applications cannot be entertained. The volume of useless applications is thereby reduced. Where the trustees do aid organisations they expect them to conform to a standard of efficiency, and they watch with considerable care the development of the experiments they make possible. It should be noted that the bulk of the activities subsidised *are experimental* ; the Carnegie United Kingdom Trust does not provide a permanent income ; its grants are terminable, and the organisations are expected during the period of subsidy to justify their existence sufficiently to earn public grants or to be able to raise their future income from subscriptions, or in some other way to become self-supporting. Of their quinquennial policy the trustees themselves say that it enables them " to achieve three purposes : (i) to announce periodically one or more definite experimental programmes based upon adequate preliminary investigation ; (ii) to compare results as experiments progress and to introduce appropriate modifications ; and (iii) to review the results towards the end of each successive period and decide whether an experiment has achieved its purpose or should be given a further trial period."

Limitation of range of benefactions, quinquennial programmes, terminable grants, some supervision of the experiments made : these have been the cardinal points of Carnegie United Kingdom Trust policy. It is to be noted that the Carnegie United Kingdom Trust seeks to get *its* policy carried out ; it is by no means content to subsidise organisations and programmes which can make out a good case for help. It is a formulator of plans, not merely an abettor of other men's plans. This policy, say the trustees in one of their annual reports, " compels the Trustees, instead of adopting the easy course of waiting to receive applications from miscellaneous sources, to make inquiries for themselves, and having decided that a given experiment is desirable, to seek out the organisation which is best qualified to put it to the test." Note the words "to seek out " ; the paragraph has the marginal heading " Choice of Agencies."

There can be no doubt that the Carnegie United Kingdom Trustees by following this carefully thought-out policy have made themselves one of the greatest shaping forces in the sphere of voluntary social service, and a considerable shaping force in the sphere of statutory social service, in this country. The County Library Service is mainly their creation, and we owe also to them many improvements in urban and special library provision and organisation. The network of rural community councils could scarcely have been created without their help. They have made a great contribution to the provision which enables ordinary men and women to enjoy and to practise the arts. These are their outstanding achievements, by no means exhaustive of what they have done or helped to do. Their work is a remarkable demonstration of what can be done by a small body of men who command a considerable but yet comparatively small income, and who use it with consummate skill. It remains to be said that since this small self-perpetuating body of men and women has such great influence on social development in this country, their moral responsibilities are correspondingly great, and each choice of a new trustee is a matter of national importance.

The Pilgrim Trust was founded in 1930 by Mr. E. S. Harkness, an American citizen, who wished to do something for the country of his ancestry, a country which was still suffering from the after-effects of the war in which it had spent its resources so freely. Mr. Harkness placed in the hands of a small body of trustees American securities valued at £2,000,000 and bringinging in an income of about £125,000. Both capital and income fluctuated a good deal in the following years. The trustees had complete discretion to use either capital or income for any purpose which came within the legal definition of " charity." Actually they have not touched the capital. The trustees' policy from the start was " to hold the balance fairly between objects which may be designated as social, and objects which relate to the nation's possessions." In the second category came such objects as the preservation or restoration of buildings of historic interest and the preservation of beauty spots, a valuable social service in the widest sense of that somewhat indefinite term. The objects within the first category were also those with which the Carnegie United Kingdom Trust, and other Trusts, were concerned ; and steps were taken at an early date to avoid overlapping.

Like the Carnegie United Kingdom Trust, the Pilgrim Trust thought it well to make clear categories of claims which it was not prepared to consider ; and the first annual report had a list of these :

(*a*) Those which belong to the sphere of the State or of public authorities, e.g. public health, large unemployment schemes, etc.

(*b*) Those of an eleemosynary character which are for the most part met by established charities with a popular appeal, e.g. hospitals.

(*c*) Individual applications for pecuniary assistance.

(*d*) Appeals on behalf of projects which are already receiving generous help from other Trusts.

(*e*) Appeals from churches and schools which desire to extend their premises or equipment, but which present no exceptional features of public importance.

To these the trustees added in the course of the next year medical research, but in later years they made exceptional grants to one or two bodies engaged in it.

The Trust was founded at a time of acute unemployment ; indeed, its foundation was stimulated by concern at the grave difficulties which this country was experiencing. The trustees turned their attention specially to the needs of those areas where unemployment was particularly bad. " The Trustees felt that they must respond to the repeated appeals which were reaching them to assist agencies which were working to counteract some of the worst effects of continued unemployment, and to prevent many places where moral and intellectual leadership is absent from sinking into despair."

The trustees accordingly subsidised Settlements and similar agencies working in the distressed areas ; they also subsidised the Society of Friends Allotments Scheme. Grants were made towards the salaries of organisers and instructors of various kinds. Belief in leadership and in the specialist instructor or adviser has marked Pilgrim Trust policy throughout. In the annual report for the year 1935 this is made explicit :

" Another feature of the year's policy, in the field of social work, has been the condition frequently imposed that a grant should be devoted specifically to the payment of the salaries of trained workers—wardens, club supervisors, and leaders—so as to guide and co-ordinate voluntary help in a district and secure the maximum benefit to all concerned in the undertaking."

The Pilgrim Trust has made a few big grants. In 1935 it gave £10,000 to Toynbee Hall on the occasion of its jubilee, and in 1936 it gave £10,000 to Birkbeck College to provide Common Room facilities. But in the main it has preferred to make many small grants, and this has been deliberate.

" In view of the economic conditions still prevailing," says the fifth annual report, " and in consideration of the success which has attended the distribution of small grants in many directions, the Trustees have seen no reason for departing from their practice of assisting on a moderate scale a large number of individual schemes of relief and social improvement."

Thus in 1934 the trustees allocated £51,210 to seventy-one different organisations, and some of these organisations were federal bodies which would have to redistribute their grants. In 1936 the trustees allocated £65,890 to eighty-four different organisations, some of them federal bodies. " We have learned," said Sir Josiah Stamp, speaking at Pontypridd in 1937, " that a very small key can open a big door, and we have tried to apply our grants so that they would act as catalysts or precipitants." In the allocation of their funds the Pilgrim Trust has shown a great catholicity of interests. The distressed areas and the work of the Settlements have clearly had a special place in its consideration, but it has also made grants to a great variety of organisations engaged all over the country in many kinds of social work. Thus in 1936 grants were made for the following among other purposes : the training of young girls for professional careers, the training of selected candidates for social work, training in case-work, the provision of camping holidays, the appointment of organisers of girls' clubs, medical research in the field of immunology, the equipment of nursery schools. Amongst the many bodies receiving help were the Musicians' Benevolent Fund, the Distressed Gentlefolks Aid Association, the Young Women's Christian Association, the Heritage Craft Schools, Morley College, the National Institute for the Deaf, the Midwives Institute.

The writer of this chapter, who had some experience of administering Pilgrim Trust grants, and who has watched fairly closely the administration of some of their other grants, thinks that the policy of wide distribution of small grants was carried too far. It is true that a small grant may attract other grants, may make the difference between success or failure of an enterprise. But it is not always so. It is the writer's view that in some cases the grants were too small to be effective, that one grant of £500 might have produced better results than two grants of £300.

A comparison of the Pilgrim Trust with the Carnegie United Kingdom Trust shows some interesting differences.

In the first place, the number of trustees is much smaller in the younger body, and they are on the whole persons of higher status. The composition of these powerful Trusts is obviously a matter of considerable social importance, and some comments are, therefore, worth while. My own view is that the Pilgrim trustees are too few and too remote from the organisations whose activities they support ; of the Carnegie trustees, on the other hand, it may be said that they carry a certain amount of dead weight of unimportant persons. What is desirable for Trusts such as these, and what is by no means easy to get, is a body of trustees who may be described as detached but not aloof, not identified too closely with any particular philanthropic society or philanthropic interest, but with something more than a paper knowledge of the field of voluntary social service. Both Trusts have been well served by their secretaries, to whom the nation, as well as the Trusts themselves, is much indebted.

Such criticism as has been made in this chapter is quite minor criticism. I do not think that it is possible for anyone to have watched the operations of these two Trusts, or to have read through the files of their annual reports, without a grateful realisation of the immense amount of good which has been done with the money they have dispensed. Much care and much thought has been put into their stewardship. When the social history of the last three decades comes to be written at all fully, the big part played by the Carnegie United Kingdom Trust and by the Pilgrim Trust will be realised.

A new group of Trusts has come into existence in recent years, those created by Lord Nuffield. They have already played a considerable part, especially in the field of medical and allied services and provision. It is likely that one at least of these Trusts will become of first-rate importance in a wider field. But the available records of their operations are not yet sufficient to enable us to submit them to such scrutiny as has been attempted in this chapter in the case of two earlier Trusts.

2. KING GEORGE'S JUBILEE TRUST

by

Constance Braithwaite

KING GEORGE'S JUBILEE TRUST provides an interesting contrast with the two Trusts already described. The first point of contrast lies in the fact that it was endowed not by an individual philanthropist but by the donations of large numbers of the British public and that it continues to be supported from year to year by these donations, so that it has a larger annual income than that derived merely from the interest on the original capital fund. The second point of contrast is that the Trust has, from the beginning, existed not for a wide variety of charitable purposes, at the discretion of the trustees, but for a defined object—the welfare of youth, in particular youth between the ages of fourteen and eighteen.

The Trust was inaugurated in the spring of 1935 by an appeal by the Prince of Wales for a national thank-offering on the occasion of the Jubilee of King George V, the proceeds to be devoted, at the desire of the King, to the welfare of the rising generation. The original appeals for the funds of the Trust were made very widely and were supported by the press, the wireless, and the cinema, and by many public officials and voluntary organisations. In addition to the donations received the Trust benefited by the profits on the sales of the official programme of the Jubilee Procession and on the sales of *His Majesty's Speeches* and by the organisation of flag days and other special events in connection with the Jubilee. The object of the Trust commended itself to a wide public, as was shown both by the support which it received from all parts of the United Kingdom and from overseas and by the large number of small donations. By the end of March 1936, when the original appeals were closed, the Trust had collected £1,018,000.

The Trust Fund was kept open for the receipt of annual subscriptions, donations, legacies, collections, etc., and in the years previous to the war the Trust aimed at collecting an annual income from these sources sufficient to maintain intact its capital of £1,000,000 despite a deliberate policy of expending more than the income derivable from that capital. While

G

the Trust did not succeed in realising this aim it did succeed in collecting substantial amounts each year. The receipts of the Trust in interest on its capital remained at about £31,000 in each of the three years 1936–9. Its receipts from sources other than interest were about £29,000 in 1936–7, £100,000 in 1937–8, and £20,000 in 1938–9. The amount received in annual subscriptions, including subscriptions under seven-year covenants, increased from about £6,000 in 1936–7 to £8,000 in 1938–9. The large increase in receipts in 1937–8 was due to the allocation to the Trust of the proceeds of various activities in connection with the Coronation of King George VI, including the profits from the sale of the official souvenir programme. At the end of March 1939 the total amount in the Trust Fund was £970,000.

The officials of the Trust were, in 1939, three trustees, an administrative council of eleven with a secretary, and one or more honorary wardens for each county in the United Kingdom. The wardens assisted the Trust by enabling it to obtain first-hand information, where required, of the local effects of its grants, of the needs of any particular district, and of the advisability or otherwise of adopting any given policy, and they also helped to maintain local interest in its activities.

The objects of the Trust are to advance the physical, mental, and spiritual welfare of the younger generation, especially those aged fourteen and upwards, and to encourage the growth and assist the maintenance of national voluntary organisations engaged in furthering these objects among boys and girls between fourteen and eighteen. The following description of the Trust's activities is based on its annual reports up to March 1939 and on a short statement issued by the Trust of its activities for the four years 1939–43. (As the Trust issued no annual reports after the war most of the following description is concerned with pre-war activities.)

The Trust decided on a bold policy of expenditure in its first four years : despite the fact that its regular income from investments was only about £31,000 a year it decided to spend £100,000 in each of three years up to 31st March 1939. This scale of expenditure was reduced in the four following war years, but between 31st March 1939 and 31st March 1943 nearly £154,000 was spent—an average of about £38,000 a year.

The expenditure of the Trust up to March 1939 (excluding

administrative expenses) can be divided into three classes—
expenditure on camping activities, certain special pieces of
work inaugurated by the Trust, and grants to organisations for
their general work.

Very soon after its inception the Trust spent £6,000 on aid
to camps in the summer of 1935, and up to March 1939 it had
spent a total of about £27,000 on camping activities. Grants
were given both to special camping organisations and to general
youth organisations, and in addition to these camping grants
some of the money from the general grants given by the Trust
was used by the youth organisations concerned for camping
activities. Grants were used in particular for the purchase of
equipment, for the improvement of camping sites, and for aid
to poor boys and girls to enable them to go to camp. The
Trust itself established a permanent camp near the sea in County
Durham, which was used for week-end conferences as well as
for camping.

The three main pieces of work inaugurated by the Trust
were a boys' hostel, a model youth centre, and a youth survey.
About £75,000 was spent on the establishment of King
George's House, a hostel in London for boys between fourteen
and eighteen. The two classes of boys catered for were boys
coming to London to work and homeless London boys. The
hostel was managed by the Boys' Hostels Association and provided many educational and recreational facilities. At the
end of 1938 there were 180 boys in residence. The Trust made
a grant of £8,000 for the establishment of a model youth centre
at Scunthorpe, Lincolnshire, with duplicate premises for boys
and girls and a canteen and gymnasium-hall for joint use. The
scheme was also assisted by the Borough Council and County
Council concerned, by the National Fitness Council, and by
local donations. Dr. A. E. Morgan was commissioned by the
Trust to make a systematic survey of the needs of the fourteen-
to-eighteen age group throughout the country and of the
means by which those needs were being met or should be met.
The results of this survey were published in 1939 in Dr. Morgan's
book *The Needs of Youth*.

From its inauguration the Trust has worked not to found any
new organisation but to extend the activities of existing organisations, and, outside the work already described, its main work in its
first four years was the allocation of grants to national organisa-

tions working for the welfare of youth. With the exception of a few grants made for special purposes these grants were made without conditions, and the organisations concerned were left free to spend and allocate them according to their discretion, reporting to the Trust on the uses made of the money. Nearly all these grants were made to national organisations, the number of organisations varying between twenty-three and twenty-six in the pre-war years. The organisations themselves spent the money received on behalf of their movements as a whole or allocated grants to their affiliated groups. The Trust reported in 1938 that " it is clear that they have been at great pains to ensure that their grants should obtain a maximum benefit for a maximum number of boys and girls over a maximum area. . . . Particular attention has been given to the geographical distribution of grants and the claims of every centre of activity in the United Kingdom have been scrupulously weighed." With regard to geographical distribution it is interesting to note that the Trust gave considerable assistance to youth work in rural areas, particularly in its grants to the Federations of Young Farmers' Clubs and to the Welsh League of Youth, and that several organisations assisted mentioned special aid given to work on new housing estates and in the depressed areas. The Trust did not confine its assistance to organisations dealing solely with young people under twenty-one : for example, it assisted the Boys' Department of the Young Men's Christian Association and aided the establishment of new hostels by the Youth Hostels Association.

The account given by the Trust in its annual reports of the uses made of its grants shows certain predominant types of expenditure by the organisations concerned. Many organisations used part of their grants to improve the training facilities for their youth leaders. This was recognised as of great importance and the prospect of financial assistance from the Trust over a period of three years made many training schemes possible. Another frequent form of expenditure of Trust grants was in improving area organisation, with a resultant widening of the geographical area of influence of the movement and increase in the number of youth groups. A third important type of expenditure was on the acquisition or adaptation of premises and the provision of equipment. A fourth form of expenditure was the provision of certain specialist services for the use of a movement as a whole, or in some cases of a group of allied movements. An interesting example of this was a scheme for the encouragement of handicrafts in girls' organisations which was to be administered jointly by representatives of eight organisations. The original intention of the Trust Council was that grants should be used for capital rather than for maintenance expenditure, but it is clear that a wide interpretation was given to this policy and that it was realised that not only the acquisition and improvement of property but also the development of organisation and the training of personnel could be regarded as of lasting advantage.

There is evidence that the Trust's grants enabled work to be done which resulted in large increases in the number of youth groups in the various organisations and in the number of members attached to these groups. For example, the National Association of Boys' Clubs reported a doubling of the membership of boys' clubs in the five years 1933–8, with more than double the number of clubs. There is also evidence that the financial benefit accruing to the movements concerned as the result of the Trust's grants was far larger than the amount of the grants. In allocating their grants the national organisations usually made assistance conditional on some part of the required sum being raised locally, often on a pound-for-pound basis. The Trust reported in 1943 that it had expended £425,000 in grants since its inception and estimated that, including the local financial support elicited by the grants, the total financial benefit was probably at least £600,000. The formation and activities of the Trust were important not only because of the direct financial aid it could give but also because it focused the interest of the public on the needs of youth and on the efforts being made to meet those needs.

Chapter XII

THE FINANCE OF VOLUNTARY SOCIAL SERVICES

by

HENRY A. MESS and CONSTANCE BRAITHWAITE

1. METHODS AND PROBLEMS OF FINANCE

by

Henry A. Mess

VOLUNTARY associations differ very much in the amount of their reserves. Many live from hand to mouth, many are overdrawn to the limit which their banks will allow. Usually, however, a well-established society manages to get some money behind it. There are societies with very large reserves ; one Scottish society has something like £60,000 reserve, or eight or nine times its annual expenditure. Many societies try to cash in on popularity and prestige at a favourable time. Thus the Boy Scouts raised an endowment fund in 1914 amounting to over £100,000. The National Federation of Women's Institutes raised an endowment fund of £12,000 in 1920. Reserves of this kind save the responsible officers from a great deal of petty worry and emergency money-raising and make a stable long-term policy possible. But also it is often said—and there are examples to support the view—that very large investments may lead to complacency and stagnation.

Some societies, especially big national societies, administer large sums of money, often incomes far in excess of their own income. This was notably the case with the National Council of Social Service at the height of unemployment. Obviously a voluntary organisation which administers money has a strong claim to some support from those whose agent it is. Some societies claim a percentage for administration, not infrequently 5% ; others trust that the goodwill and the prestige which the administration of trust money brings them will lead to increased support from the charitable public. It is my opinion that on the whole societies are too diffident ; they rarely claim as of right as large a commission as they might in justice take, and as the majority of donors would recognise to be reasonable.

Under the Finance Act of 1922 income devoted to charity for a period of at least seven years is exempt from taxation, a concession of great importance in view of the high rate of income tax ever since the middle years of the 1914–18 war. Many voluntary societies invite their subscribers to sign a covenant undertaking to give a certain amount annually for seven years ; the society is then able to recover tax. Thus, if income tax stands at 10s. in the £, for each subscription of £1 there can be recovered £1 in tax (£2 less 10s. in the £ = £1). There are a number of formalities to be complied with which have made recovery not worth while for small sums or by small organisations. The National Council of Social Service and some of the larger local Councils of Social Service and kindred bodies have special departments to deal with income-tax recovery. These enable a donor to covenant to give a fixed sum for a term of years ; he can give directions each year as to the societies which are to benefit. The scale on which this is done is well indicated by the fact that in 1939 the National Council of Social Service had 2,341 deeds of covenant on its books, and distributed £347,432. (It usually made a charge of 3% on sums distributed.) Subscriptions through deeds of covenant tend to have a steadying effect on the income of the recipient charities.

The community chest idea, so common in the United States, has not been accepted over here. There are, however, collecting agencies in Edinburgh, Glasgow, and Belfast ; in these cases the participating charities pay a fee to the organising body, usually a Council of Social Service, and their appeal appears in a handbook. There seems to be no great tendency for this method to spread.

Two important new forms of appeal to the general public have come into existence in the last twenty-five years or so. These are the flag day and the wireless appeal.

Flag days were introduced by the Lifeboat Association, whose example was quickly followed by other charitable societies. Poppy Day and Alexandra Rose Day are the best known flag days, each bringing in very large sums of money. Since 1916 the local police authorities have had power to regulate street collections. Watch committees usually demand evidence of the *bona fides* of a society, require to be satisfied that the money is needed, and require a statement of accounts after the day. The amounts collected vary with the popularity of the cause, the number and pertinacity of the collectors, and the weather. The importance of flag days in the budgets of the beneficiary societies varies very much. Poppy Day provides a substantial part of the funds from which the British Legion makes grants. Flag-day takings are a big item in the budgets of some local societies, e.g. some of the moral welfare societies and some district nursing associations. At one time the number of charities organising flag days was so great that there was something like a revolt on the part of the public, resulting in the grouping of kindred charities for purposes of flag-day appeal.

The potentialities of wireless for charitable purposes seem to have been exploited first in 1923, the earliest appeal being that of the Winter Distress League. Fairly early in the history of broadcasting it became necessary to regulate appeals, and for that purpose a Central Appeals Advisory Committee was set up by the British Broadcasting Corporation, with similar regional committees. On these advisory committees there sit, in addition to B.B.C. officials, outside persons with a wide knowledge of charities. The number of appeals does not exceed one national appeal and one appeal in each region per week, and in some weeks there is only the national appeal. Appeals are only allowed if the *bona fides* of the society is undoubted, and if the society can show its need of the money. The sums raised during a year are very great, ranging in 1938 in the case of national appeals from £580 to £42,103. Regional appeals naturally bring in smaller amounts, sometimes very small sums.

No convincing explanation has ever been produced of the variations in sums raised for various good causes, but those who are most familiar with the subject consider that the nature of the appeal, the celebrity of the person appealing, and the manner in which the appeal is made are the three chief factors. It is by no means the case that a popular figure or a great personage will always obtain a good result. Sincerity in the speaker and knowledge of and belief in the cause are indispensable for success.

Both the flag day and the week's good cause serve useful purposes. The former provides an easy way by which a large number of persons can give small sums of money ; the latter directs attention to a limited number of carefully selected societies. Both keep at bay the fraudulent society, and both guarantee that expenses of collection are kept reasonably low.

Another source of income for charities is the Sunday Cinema Entertainments Fund, a levy on the profits on Sunday opening of cinemas, made under the Sunday Entertainments Act of 1932. The fund itself may well be regarded as arising from an illogical compromise between two sets of views and interests. It certainly does provide substantial sums for charities. In the case of one Council of Social Service in a fairly large county borough, one-sixth of its income comes from this source. The procedure is that on the one hand cinema proprietors can nominate charities to receive grants, on the other hand charities can apply to the police to be put on a panel of recipients. Double approval is therefore necessary before a charity can benefit ; it must prove to the satisfaction of the police its usefulness and its need, and a limit is set to the amount a single charity may receive.

Many of the national and regional bodies ask affiliation fees from their constituent members, but it is seldom that any large income can be obtained in this manner. Wolf does not eat wolf, and the constituent societies are commonly as hard pressed as the organisation to which they affiliate. Affiliation fees are, therefore, often in the nature of token payments, small acknowledgments of services rendered and of solidarity realised. There are a few exceptions. The National Federation of Women's Institutes manages to collect not far short of £4,000 a year, some 40% of its total income.

A growing proportion of income comes from payments by the receivers of benefits. Settlements, community associations, clubs of many kinds make charges for various services which they render, amounting to substantial contributions towards the cost. As wages rise, and an increasing section of society is raised out of dire poverty, these contributions of beneficiaries to cost become more and more substantial. There has been a great growth of contributory schemes for hospitals and there are many similar schemes among district nursing associations.

Some organisations derive a considerable profit from trading. A well-run canteen can bring in a considerable income to a club. The Boy Scouts and the Girl Guides make a good profit on the sale of equipment and literature ; in the case of the

G*

Boy Scouts this has amounted in some years to little less than half of the headquarters' income. The profits on the Women's Institute magazine have in several years accounted for nearly 20% of the Federation's income. Letting of premises is another source of income ; but it may be a mark of weakness, as when financial stringency compels an organisation to give up the use of premises to such an extent that its work suffers. On the whole it may be said that a well-planned trading venture is a good method of financing voluntary social service.

Grants from statutory bodies have increased very much in importance during the last thirty years. In 1937 of 120 urban bodies functioning as Councils of Social Service or as Personal Service Societies, 49 were receiving grants from statutory bodies, the amounts ranging from £600 down to £10. Most of the grants were for specific purposes, but 21 of the bodies received grants which were not specifically allotted. Legislation since 1918 has made easier the making of grants, especially the Education Act of 1921, the Housing Act of 1936, and the Physical Training and Recreation Act of 1937. The establishment of the Development Commission has also been of importance. The sums disbursed have been in some cases very great. In 1936–7 the National Council of Social Service received £102,757 from the Ministry of Labour and £214,931 from the Commissioner for Special Areas to be spent, either directly by itself or indirectly by organisations to which it made grants, on unemployed welfare work.

Grants for specific purposes are sometimes by far the greater part of an organisation's income, and the organisation is in effect a non-statutory body to which a statutory body or bodies delegates tasks, supplying the means. Sometimes the non-statutory association is deliberately created by the statutory body : notable examples are the Land Settlement Association and the Rural Industries Bureau. One effect of the lightening of burdens by the modern state is that quite a number of the older institutions, e.g. some orphanages, are amassing big capital reserves.

With rising standards of efficiency and with the employment of professional staffs the proportion of income devoted to equipment and to salaries has risen a great deal, and the need for a steady income, or at least for a reliable nucleus of income, has become very much greater. Yet anyone who peruses a large number of reports will be struck by the insecurity in which many societies carry on their work.

As an example of the financial fortunes of a fairly important voluntary organisation we may take the history of the Central Council for the Care of Cripples. This was founded at the end of 1919, chiefly by the collaboration of a group of surgeons with the Invalid Children's Aid Association and the Central Council for Infant and Child Welfare. It was floated off with a grant of £750 from the latter body. As it had an honorary secretary and as office premises were provided rent free it managed comfortably on this sum for four years. A few small grants and small donations then carried it through another two years. The work then increased rapidly and in 1926 the honorary secretary was compelled by reason of ill health to resign ; the question of finance became more important. Expenditure jumped from £540 in 1926 to £927 in 1927. In 1929 things were beginning to look serious ; the Council needed a steady £1,000 a year, and donations and subscriptions were not much over £500 a year. In 1931 the Council was so poor that it could not afford to publish any new pamphlets and during the next few years it was " just able to keep its head above water " by means of special appeals and money-raising efforts. But this desperate struggle to keep going ended in 1935, when Lord Nuffield gave £125,000 to be used in the cause of cripples, of which £86,500 was to be expended by trustees on the advice of the Central Council. This gave such status to the Council and made its functions so necessary that it seems unlikely that it will again be in the position of being unable to afford the printing of a pamphlet.

The financial fortunes of this society have been described at some length as an interesting example of the way in which one voluntary association, whose work was of undoubted usefulness and which was able to command the approval of a good many influential persons, has had to cadge for the comparatively small annual income needed to maintain it in even partial efficiency. A thousand pounds a year is not a great income, but the Council appealed for it in vain over a good many years. One moral which may be drawn from this history is that it is still difficult to gain financial support from the public for a body whose main work is education and co-ordination.

What is one to say about such a financial history, which is

typical of that of a good many voluntary associations? The persistence and the resourcefulness are praiseworthy. Since presumably no statutory authority was willing and able to do the work, or to make a grant to enable it to be done, we must be thankful that the money was somehow raised to get it done. Yet one cannot help regretting the time and labour spent in money-raising by members and officials of the Council, who were diverted from the tasks which they were so anxious to perform. Nor can one imagine that associations do their best work when their future is in doubt; nor that salaried officials, however enthusiastic and single-minded they may be, can work at their best when it is an open question from quarter to quarter whether their employment and their salaries will continue.

Up to the outbreak of the 1914–1918 war there was no State supervision of charities except in the case of endowed charities, which were subject to some scrutiny by the Charity Commissioners or the Board of Education. There was, of course, liability to prosecution for fraud in case of gross dishonesty. Otherwise malpractices were kept in check by the vigilance of such bodies as the Charity Organisation Society and such newspapers as *Truth*, their chief weapon being publicity. A spate of new charities, many of them spurious, led to the passing of the War Charities Act in 1916, requiring the registration of all charities dealing with needs arising out of the war, and requiring the submission of accounts to the local registration authority. The Police, Factories, etc. (Miscellaneous Provisions) Act of 1916 gave powers to the police to regulate street collections (including flag-day collections). The Blind Persons Act of 1920 followed the precedent of the War Charities Act and extended registration to all those charities dealing with the blind. In 1939 a House to House Collections Act prohibited charitable collections from door to door except under licence. The War Charities Act of 1940 required registration of charities relieving needs arising out of the last war. But there is not as yet any general statutory regulation of charities.

The growth of central organisations has had a salutary effect in keeping up standards of honesty and efficiency, since most such bodies insist upon their affiliated members presenting their accounts in a proper manner and keeping within reasonable limits of economy and efficiency.

2. STATISTICS OF FINANCE

by

Constance Braithwaite

ANY account of the statistics of charitable finance is of necessity very incomplete because of the scarcity of collected information. The expenditure of public authorities and their collection of income must be approved by the representatives of the electors, and therefore accurate and inclusive information is collected and published. In contrast charitable organisations are in most cases responsible only to their supporters, and there is neither general publication of their accounts nor much assembling of information about the total expenditure and income of all organisations working in a particular field or a particular locality. Even in the cases in which there is public regulation of charities or of charitable collections there has been no publication of financial figures covering the whole country. Another difficulty confronting the inquirer is that charities vary in their systems of financial classification.

I made a study of the income of charities in England and Wales up to 1934, which was published as Section 2 of my book *The Voluntary Citizen*,[1] and much of what follows is based on that study. The reader is referred both to this book and to the original collections of figures described in this chapter for information in greater detail and for the necessary cautions with regard to the interpretation of the figures which there is not space to include here. Emphasis is laid on the income rather than the expenditure of charities, one reason for this being that figures of expenditure convey little meaning without a detailed knowledge of the type of activity of the organisation concerned.

On the basis of the available information I estimated that the total income of charities (excluding endowed charities) in England and Wales in 1934 was somewhere between £35 million and £50 million. If this estimate was correct it would mean an annual income of about £1 per head of the population, which was about the amount shown by the figures

---

[1] *The Voluntary Citizen: An Enquiry into the Place of Philanthropy in the Community,* Methuen, 1938.

for Liverpool charities quoted later in this chapter. Of the total income of charities I estimated that £3½ million to £5 million (10%) was received in legacies ; £14 million to £20 million (40%) in other charitable gifts ; £4½ million to £6½ million (13%) in interest and other forms of income from property ; and £13 million to £18½ million (37%) in receipts for services rendered.

In the same year the total income in England and Wales of the public social services (as included in the Treasury Return) was £435 million, of which £307 million was received from taxes and rates. Thus, on the basis of the above estimates, of the total receipts of both public and voluntary social services the voluntary social services received 7½–10%, and of the total receipts of these services from taxes, rates, and charitable gifts 5½–7½% was received in charitable gifts. It seemed likely that charitable expenditure was of small quantitative importance as compared with public expenditure in general financial relief to persons outside institutions and in the provision of education. In contrast there were fields of charitable expenditure in which there was little or no public expenditure, and there was evidence that in at least three social services both types of expenditure were important—hospitals, relief and welfare of the blind, and Homes for the young. Of the total expenditure on hospital services (excluding mental hospitals) 40% was expended by the voluntary hospitals, and of the part of that expenditure defrayed from taxes, rates, and charitable gifts 25% was defrayed from charitable gifts.

There are not available any recent general figures of the income of endowed charities. The Charity Commissioners (who control all endowed charities except those for educational purposes) estimated the number under their control in 1927 as about 80,000. The Board of Education estimated the number of endowed charities for education in 1934 as something less than 29,000.

My conclusions on the amount of receipts of charities and on the trends in recent years were based mainly on three sets of figures—those for voluntary hospitals in England and Wales, those for London and national charities, and those for Liverpool charities. Some of the points shown by these figures will now be described.

Voluntary hospitals probably receive larger annual receipts

than any other class of charity. They are widely distributed geographically and the service provided by them is approved by nearly everyone and supported financially by very large numbers of people. They are the only class of charity known to me for which reasonably inclusive figures for the whole country exist over a considerable period. For these reasons a study of their receipts is of interest, not only for its own sake, but also as an example of charitable finance.

Figures are available for all hospitals in England and Wales for the eighteen years 1924–41. These figures are those collected in the *Hospitals Year Book* (and its predecessor *The Voluntary Hospitals of Great Britain*) and those collected by the King Edward's Hospital Fund for London. There are various differences between the classification of the London figures and the classification of those for other parts of the country, and I have ignored some minor discrepancies due to these differences.

The total ordinary income of hospitals increased in every year except two over the whole period: it rose from £7·2 million in 1924 to £9·4 million in 1931, £12·1 million in 1938, and £14·6 million in 1941. Money income in 1938 was nearly 70% higher than in 1924 and " real income " (allowing for changes in the cost of living) was 90% higher. Until 1933 the price level was falling and " real income " increased considerably more than money income ; from 1933 to 1938 " real income " still increased, but with the considerable rise in the price level after 1939 the " real income " of hospitals fell, though their money income continued to increase. This illustrates a common feature of charitable receipts : their comparative stability in terms of money means that they do not adjust easily to changes in the price level, and charities therefore tend to benefit in times of falling prices and to suffer in times of rising prices.

The main classes of the ordinary income of hospitals are charitable contributions, income from investments, and receipts for services rendered. Charitable contributions rose from £2·6 million in 1924 to £3·2 million in 1938, with a fall to £3·0 million in 1941. They formed 36% of ordinary income in 1924 but only 26% in 1938. Income from investments rose from £1·3 million in 1924 to £1·6 million in 1938, forming 18% of ordinary income in 1924 and 13% in 1938.

The most striking change over the period in the constitution of the ordinary income of hospitals was the increase in receipts for services rendered. These receipts rose every year from £3·2 million in 1924 to £7·2 million in 1938 and £10·0 million in 1941. They formed 44% of ordinary income in 1924, 59% in 1938, and 69% in 1941. Up to 1936 the figures for hospitals outside London distinguished between three categories of receipts for services rendered—payments by individual patients ; payments from Contributory Schemes, Hospital Saturday Funds, etc. ; and " public services," including payments by public authorities and receipts from Approved Societies under the National Health Insurance Scheme. The figures showed that in 1936 of the total of £4·8 million received for services rendered 40% were receipts from individual patients (which had more than trebled since 1924), 47% were receipts from Contributory Schemes, etc., and 13% were receipts from public services. In peace-time the receipts of voluntary hospitals from public services were a comparatively unimportant source of income—in 1938 only £0·9 million was received by all hospitals in England and Wales, 7% of ordinary income. But in 1941 these receipts had risen to £3·8 million, 26% of ordinary income.

Statistics of ordinary income give a very inadequate picture of the importance of charitable gifts to hospitals. The reason for this is that in both 1924 and 1938 about a quarter of the total receipts of hospitals was in receipts outside ordinary income, and nearly all these receipts were in legacies and other charitable gifts. The proportion of total receipts received in charitable gifts of all kinds was 54% in 1924 and 45% in 1938.

The figures for legacies show considerable variation from year to year but the general tendency over the period was a rise in their amount. In the average of the four years 1935-8 they amounted to just under £2 million, of which £1·4 million were free legacies (i.e. legacies not earmarked for any particular purpose). Free legacies had risen from £0·9 million in the average of the four years 1924-7, an increase of 50%.

The total receipts of hospitals in the pre-war years had risen slightly less than their ordinary income : they rose from £9·8 million in 1924 to £16·2 million in 1938, an increase of 64% in money income and 84% in " real income."

In the first three years affected by the war total receipts continued to increase—from £16·2 million in 1938 to £17·1 million in 1941. But this increase was entirely due to the increase in receipts from public services, which rose from £0·9 million in 1938 to £3·9 million in 1941. The total of all other receipts of hospitals decreased from £15·3 million in 1938 to about £13·3 million in 1940 and 1941.

The figures of hospital receipts for the fifteen pre-war years showed clearly three facts—a steady rise in the amount of total receipts, a steady increase in the proportionate importance of payments for services rendered, and the fact that charitable gifts, while their proportionate importance decreased, remained a very important source of hospital income.

From 1908 to 1927 a series of figures of the finance of charities " in or available for the Metropolis " was included in the *Annual Charities Register and Digest* published by the Charity Organisation Society. These figures were again published for the years 1935, 1937, 1938, and 1939, but the later figures are in some ways not strictly comparable with the earlier series.

The figures include not only London charities but many national charities. Because of their scope they cannot be used as evidence of the amount of the total receipts of either any particular type of charity or of all charities in one locality, but they do throw light on the trends in charitable finance over a large block of charitable receipts.

The total receipts of the charities covered by these figures were £10·9 million in 1919, £15·0 million in 1927, and £14·7 million in 1938. Legacies remained a very constant proportion of total receipts, being 10% in the two years 1919–20, 9% in 1926–7, and 11% in 1938–9. Excluding legacies, the proportion of other receipts received in charitable contributions fell from 53% in 1919 to 45% in 1927 and 35% in 1938. The proportion received in interest rose from 14% in 1919 to 20% in 1927 and 26% in 1938. The proportion received in payments for services rendered rose from 32% in 1919 to 35% in 1927 and 39% in 1938.

In 1938 the five groups of charities listed below together received 89% of the total receipts of the charities covered by these figures, 89% of the charitable contributions other than legacies, and 85% of the legacies. London hospitals received

£4·7 million, of which £2·0 million was in charitable gifts (including legacies). Relief agencies received £2·3 million, of which £1·1 million was in charitable gifts. Charities for social and physical improvement received £2·3 million, of which £0·7 million was in charitable gifts. Homes for the young received £2·1 million, of which £1·3 million was in charitable gifts. Provident and benevolent charities received £1·6 million, of which £0·3 million was in charitable gifts.

Collected figures of the finance of charities in Liverpool are available for the twelve years 1923–34 and for some earlier years with regard to some items of finance. These figures were assembled by the Liverpool Council of Social Service and published annually in its quarterly journal. They refer to Liverpool charities, excluding purely endowed charities, and do not in general include the contributions of Liverpool residents to national charities.

The figures showed a total income (including free legacies) of Liverpool charities of £784,000 in 1923 and £858,000 in 1934. The rise during the period was not steady : the maximum figure was £971,000 in 1930. The total income amounted in 1931 to about £1 1s. 0d. per head of the population (income £905,000, population 856,000).

From an analysis of the statements of accounts on which the figures were based I estimated that in 1929 legacies accounted for 16% of total receipts, and that of receipts excluding legacies 29% was received in charitable contributions (7% in annual subscriptions and 22% in donations, collections, etc.), 19% was received in interest, and 49% was received in payments for services rendered (13% in public grants and 36% in other payments).

The published figures give information about three classes of receipts only—annual subscriptions, interest, and legacies. Annual subscriptions rose every year from £52,000 in 1919 to a maximum of £70,000 in 1927 and then fell every year to £50,000 in 1934. In 1929 they provided only 7% of total receipts excluding legacies, and only a quarter of the amount of charitable contributions.

In contrast the amount of legacies, while varying greatly from year to year, showed no particular trend over the period 1923–34. The amount averaged £115,000 a year over the whole period—13% of total income.

The amount received in interest increased by 32% from £128,000 (16% of total income) in 1923 to £169,000 (21% of total income) in 1934.

The Liverpool figures divide the charities covered into six groups, and it is interesting to note the proportion of the total income of all charities received by each group and the changes between 1923 and 1934. The groups which increased their proportions were hospitals and other medical charities from 40% to 42%, charities relieving permanent infirmity from 21% to 24%, and charities for social welfare from 7% to 10%. The groups which decreased their proportions were Homes and pensions charities from 24% to 19%, charities relieving temporary poverty from 5% to 1½%, and charities relieving moral infirmity from 3% to 2½%.

A set of figures for charities in Manchester and Salford for the year 1938 was prepared for the Manchester and Salford Council of Social Service and published in its quarterly journal. These figures were deliberately made comparable as far as possible with those for Liverpool.

The scope of the Manchester and Salford figures is similar to that of those for Liverpool except for the inclusion of endowed charities. Total receipts were £1,051,000, of which about £30,000 was received by endowed charities. Excluding endowed charities the receipts were about £1,022,000, amounting to about £1 1s. 6d. per head of the 947,000 population of Manchester and Salford. This resembles very closely the £1 1s. 0d. shown as the income per head of Liverpool charities in 1931.

Of the total receipts of all charities, including endowed charities, 9% was received in legacies, and of receipts excluding legacies 34% was received in charitable contributions (19% in annual subscription and 14% in donations, collections, etc.), 17% was received in interest, and 46% was received in payments for services rendered (17% in public grants and 29% in other payments). The proportion received from charitable contributions was rather higher than that in Liverpool in 1929, and the proportion received for services rendered was rather lower. The proportion received in interest was rather lower than in Liverpool in spite of the inclusion of endowed charities in the Manchester and Salford figures. But the broad picture of the sources of receipts of charities is strikingly similar in these two cities, particularly when allowance is made for the uncertainties in classifying certain items of receipts and for the interval of nine years between the dates of the two sets of figures.

This broad similarity is not, however, true of the distribution of receipts between different groups of charities. The Manchester and Salford figures divide the charities covered into six groups corresponding roughly, though not entirely, to the Liverpool grouping. The proportions of total receipts received by the various groups were as follows : hospitals and other medical charities 57%, charities relieving permanent infirmity 18%, relief agencies 8%, Homes 6½%, protective and preventive charities 3%, and charities for social welfare 7%. Medical charities received a much larger proportion of total receipts than in Liverpool in 1934, charities for permanent infirmity received a considerably smaller proportion, and Homes only a third of the Liverpool proportion.

One of the few sets of figures of charitable finance published by a public authority is the set of figures for street collections (including flag-day collections) in the Metropolitan Police District published annually in the *Report of the Commissioner of Police for the Metropolis*. The average amount collected each year for the fifteen years 1924–38 was £240,000, with an upward trend from an average of £223,000 in 1924–8 to an average of £252,000 in 1934–8. After the outbreak of war the amount collected more than doubled, averaging £530,000 in 1940–2 and rising to £634,000 in 1943.

It is obvious that the collected figures are too scanty for it to be possible to draw from them many conclusions as to the trends in the whole charitable finance of the country in the inter-war period. But in my opinion there is sufficient evidence for some conclusions.

There is little doubt that charities in general received a growing proportion of their total receipts in payments for services rendered, so that the function of charitable gifts was becoming more and more that of subsidising a service rather than that of providing its full cost. Nevertheless, both legacies and other charitable gifts remained important items in the receipts of charities.

There is little if any evidence from the collected figures for the fairly common assumption that the increase of taxation and the greater provision of social services by public authorities have had the effect of decreasing the amount of legacies and of other charitable gifts. The amount given in charity seems to have varied surprisingly little over the period if we consider all the concurrent changes in economic circumstances and public social policy which might have been expected to affect it.

Chapter XIII

THE PLACE OF VOLUNTARY SOCIAL SERVICE IN THE LIFE OF THE NATION

by
HENRY A. MESS

A. The Growth and Development of Voluntary Agencies and of Statutory Agencies

1. Statutory social provision has grown rapidly since 1906, and the opinion is sometimes expressed that with its further growth there will be a disappearance of the voluntary social service agencies. There are few signs of it as yet. The amount of voluntary social service in this country, judged either by voluntary contributions of money or by number of persons engaged in it, has probably been as great during the past twenty years as at any previous times—possibly greater ; we have no means of accurate measurement.

2. Certainly the salariat of the voluntary organisations has increased very much in numbers, in status, and in efficiency. There has been a striking transformation of voluntary social service ; it is conducted nowadays on a larger scale, with more science and less sentimentality, than formerly. The greater part of the administrative work is carried on by professional social workers, who tend more and more to be staffs analogous to the staffs of Government departments or of local authorities. They work under the direction of committees of unpaid persons, representing subscribers and others ; but their work is so skilled that their advice, like that of high permanent officials of the civil service or heads of departments of a local authority, counts for a great deal, and they have a considerable voice in shaping policy. Social work has become so technical that the members of committees of voluntary agencies can, for the most part, guide general policy only ; and many other voluntary social workers can be given only the simpler and subordinate executive tasks.

3. Whilst the salaried workers for voluntary agencies are

tending to assimilate to the staffs of statutory agencies, a reverse process has been taking place. Statutory agencies are becoming less rigid, more human in outlook, more ready to experiment. (One can cite some of the Public Assistance Committees, the Assistance Board, the Commissioners for Prisons.) The contrast between the spirit and the methods of voluntary agencies and of statutory agencies is less sharp than it used to be. And the contacts are closer and more frequent than they used to be. The newer social worker is continually in touch with a great variety of statutory officials ; and the newer statutory agencies make much use of voluntary workers and of voluntary agencies.

4. The statutory agencies which have grown up since 1906 have for the most part made provision in which voluntary agencies had previously experimented. Statutory provision has come into being piecemeal and without any definite plan or philosophy. In consequence, the field of social provision is divided between the voluntary agencies and the statutory agencies in a manner which cannot be explained on any logical principles. There seems to be no good reason why lighthouses should be provided by the State whilst lifeboats are provided by a voluntary society. It is not easy to explain why the provision and maintenance of hospitals should be divided as it is divided at present. Some suggestions as to a rational division of functions are made later in this chapter.

B. Types of Relationship between Voluntary and Statutory Agencies

The relationship between voluntary agencies and statutory agencies may take many forms, of which the following are the commonest.

1. In some cases a voluntary society is regarded very much as being *under the informal control of a statutory body*. This seems to be the case with some tuberculosis care committees, which are subsidised by local authorities and whose policy is largely under the direction of the Medical Officer of Health. The voluntary society is useful to him because it provides unpaid labour and because it is not bound by regulations, so that he can do through it things which he would find difficult or impossible to do in his official capacity.

This is a type of relationship which is regarded with dislike by most of those who have a wide knowledge of voluntary social service, and believe in its usefulness. A voluntary society should have genuine autonomy ; where that cannot be granted, it is better that the statutory body should take full responsibility and administer the service itself.

2. Another relationship is the *delegation of tasks* by a statutory authority to a genuinely independent voluntary agency. The N.C.S.S. is familiar with such delegation ; e.g. the delegation to it by the Ministry of Labour of the task of organising welfare work among the unemployed, the commission from the Ministry of Agriculture to stimulate the formation of Young Farmers' Clubs.

Much depends in such cases on the terms of the agreement between the two bodies. The voluntary agency should be assured both of sufficient freedom of action and of sufficient material and moral support. The statutory body requires to be assured that the main lines of policy will be consistent with its own, and that the administration is honest and competent.

3. In some cases the State recognises the *special interest and competence* of a voluntary society in some field, and gives it privileges and facilities. Good examples of this are afforded by the N.S.P.C.C. and the R.S.P.C.A. Whilst the State does not abrogate its responsibilities to children or to animals, and sometimes takes action through its own agents, it does recognise a special interest and a special competence of these societies, and it allows them facilities, e.g. their inspectors can prosecute. Similarly the Ministry of Education has allowed a privileged position to certain voluntary associations interested in adult education.

4. In a very large number of cases a voluntary society has its own policy and its own sphere of action, and there is an agreed (or well-understood) *division of labour* with the statutory body, each having its own field. For example, the Family Welfare Association and kindred bodies leave it to the statutory authorities to make such provision as lies within their powers, whilst they specialise in making provision for which no statutory authorisation exists.

Such a division of function is usually satisfactory, provided the boundaries are clearly drawn and clearly understood. A great deal of work has been done to make the necessary demarcations and to keep them up to date.

5. Another relationship is where a voluntary society plays the part of *informant or critic or petitioner*. Many voluntary societies make representations at times to statutory bodies ; sometimes they pass on information or views obtained or formed in the course of their work ; sometimes they exist solely for propagandist or vigilance purposes.

Any group of citizens has the right to inform or to criticise a statutory body ; and the members and officials of that statutory body will, if they are wise, welcome informed and honest criticism and profit by the information brought to their notice.

These important functions of information and of criticism could be discharged much better in many cases if adequate thought and care were given to them.

C. CRITICISMS OF VOLUNTARY SOCIAL SERVICE

The voluntary societies and their work are criticised by various sections of society on a number of grounds.

1. There is the complaint that the voluntary societies work *on too small a scale*, and with too small resources, to meet needs or to effect much.

There is considerable force in this contention, but (i) some of the voluntary bodies operate to-day on a fairly large scale, and (ii) where a widespread need is admitted, the statutory authorities should take the responsibility, and either meet it directly or delegate the task to voluntary societies, with adequate financial help given.

2. It is complained that the work of the voluntary societies is *sporadic*. There may be a strong society for the care of cripples in one town, but not in another ; one district may be overstocked with convalescent homes, whilst another district lacks them.

The answer is that the development of national functional societies and of regional councils is remedying this fast.

3. It is also said that voluntary societies are *unstable* ; they flourish and they decay, they cannot be depended upon for steady work over a number of years.

There is considerable force in this criticism. Voluntary societies are built up too much on strong personalities, often flamboyant personalities, and too little upon principles. It is by no means uncommon for an enthusiast to come along, to start an organisation (sometimes to the detriment of an existing organisation), for the new organisation to flourish for a few years and then to fade away.

Remedies must be sought chiefly in two directions : (*a*) steady insistence on principles, and the building up of loyalty to them rather than to personalities ; (*b*) again in the work of the national functional councils and the regional councils. But the difficulty is a serious one ; powerful personalities are often undisciplined and often unco-operative ; and further, success in voluntary social service depends much on success in money-raising, and those who raise money easily are not always those who spend it well. A good deal of the difficulty arises from the ingrained British objection to thinking out principles. Here, as in some other fields, the voluntary societies might give a lead.

4. Other complaints are that voluntary organisations are *ill-equipped, understaffed*, that they *sweat their employees*, that they are *inefficient*.

All of these charges have had much truth in the past ; in some of them there is still a measure of truth, but it is decreasingly so. The best societies are moderately well equipped, their offices do not compare badly with a number of Government and local authority offices. Nor are the best societies seriously understaffed. That employees are poorly paid is still on the whole true, though salary scales are rising and pension schemes are multiplying, and there are now a fair number of higher posts carrying moderately good salaries. But it cannot be denied that there is a bad tradition to live down. As to the charge that voluntary societies are inefficient, it is difficult to get standards of comparison, but it may be doubted whether they get less accomplished per pound and per person employed than does the average business firm or the average municipal office.

That standards of efficiency are rising is due in considerable measure to (*a*) the creation and development of national functional bodies and of regional bodies ; (*b*) the rise of associations of professional social workers ; (*c*) the training provided by universities in conjunction with professional associations ; (*d*) the widespread growing appreciation of the value of skilled and scientific social work.

5. Complaints are also made that the voluntary societies are *snobbish* and *patronising*. It is a complaint which is crystallised in the stigmatising use of the term Lady Bountiful. To large numbers of the working classes, to the majority (probably) of active trade unionists and active members of the Labour Party, to many others who are strongly democratic in outlook, the voluntary charitable society is anathema.

Few who are well acquainted with voluntary social service are likely to deny that a considerable amount of this criticism is justified. With regard to the first of these charges, that of snobbishness, one has only to glance through a number of annual reports to see that the offices of highest honour are given overwhelmingly to the rich and the titled, more particularly to the latter. It can be pointed out in extenuation that the attitude of the voluntary societies is part of the attitude of the nation. When the social stratification of the nation changes, when its valuations change, then the change will be reflected in the voluntary societies. But this is not a full reply. Deference to the rich and the titled is carried further in the field of voluntary social service than in most fields of national life.

With regard to this matter there will be very different views within the ranks of those engaged in voluntary social service. Some are content to accept the precedences which have been given in the past in this country. These will see little objection to present practices. They must expect to encounter the criticism and hostility of those who are discontented with the present social order. Others (amongst whom the writer of this chapter places himself wholeheartedly) deplore this toadying to the rich and the titled, and think that the voluntary societies would do well to purge themselves of it. They think that many of these honorary officers have nothing substantial to recommend them, and that they are a dubious asset to their societies. They feel, with the critics, that toadying in the field of the social services helps to perpetuate the evil in the life of the nation.

With regard to the second point, the charge of patronising, it is perfectly true that the giving of help can injure both donor and recipient. The relationship is a dangerous one, and those who enter into it need to be on their guard. But the danger would not necessarily disappear altogether if all voluntary provision were replaced by statutory provision. A statutory official can be as offensive, can enjoy and abuse his power, as an official of a voluntary society can do. What, however, is of importance is that provision should be given as a right wherever this can be done with due respect to other considerations, such as the maintenance of the will to self-support and to the prevention of the evils which render provision necessary.

6. Finally, it is said that voluntary provision is *unnecessary*. Most of the needs would not arise in a well-ordered society ; or, if they should arise, they would be better met by statutory provision.

With regard to the first point, practically every social worker and supporter of social work will agree that where need can be eliminated, it should be eliminated. Opinions will differ as to how far and how quickly it is possible. Voluntary societies may well be asked to scrutinise their work, and to take care lest any of it be palliating evils at the risk of prolonging them. But doubt may well be expressed whether in any society which can be conceived, needs arising out of misfortune or misconduct will entirely cease. Certainly present-day society would be in a deplorable condition if all voluntary service ceased.

The consideration of the second point, whether all need might be met more satisfactorily by statutory provision, brings us to an examination of the case which can be made for the superiority of the voluntary social services over statutory social services in some fields. It is certain that there is at present a great deal of need which is not met by statutory provision ; it is at least likely that there will be needs to be met for many years to come. What advantages can be claimed for voluntary social service ?

D. The Advantages of Voluntary Social Service in some Fields

1. Voluntary societies can work more *flexibly*. Statutory agencies can only do what they are specifically authorised by legislation to do. Further, they are for the most part bound to work to rule and scale, and they cannot easily make nice adjustments to individual cases. Voluntary societies are not so closely bound, though, of course, they are accountable to their subscribers for the administration of their funds. It is

easy to over-stress the difference ; modern statutory administra-
is in many cases much more flexible than statutory administration used to be ; and to some extent, rigidity of administration
is a question of scale rather than of voluntary or statutory
administration. But, broadly speaking, it is still true, and is
likely to remain true, that voluntary agencies have the advantage where individualised dealings are desirable.

2. Voluntary societies can *experiment* more easily, for the
same reasons ; though again the contrast must not be over-
stressed ; there are signs that the State and local authorities
are capable of imagination and of enterprise. But in the main
they can only experiment in spheres of proved need. The first
attempts to meet ill-diagnosed needs by unproved methods
have almost always been made by voluntary societies ; and it
is likely to be so in the future, certainly in the near future.

3. Voluntary societies can act in *controversial* matters. An
outstanding example of this is the birth-control clinic. Lauded
by some, to others it was of the devil. It was extremely difficult
for the State to take action in view of the doubts of a large
number and the fierce opposition of a substantial minority.
But those who believed that birth-control clinics were a good
thing were at liberty to try them out, and did so.

4. Voluntary societies can operate *schemes to supplement* statutory provision. This is of importance in relation to our class
structure. The provision which the Poor Law or the Assistance Board makes for an unskilled labourer is unsuited for an
artisan, still less to a middle-class man or woman who falls into
distress. There are many who will wish to see appropriate
help given, and that can be given by voluntary societies (e.g.
the Distressed Gentlefolks' Aid Association).

Moreover, many men and women will want to help especially,
and more fully than the State is likely to help, those who have
something in common with them which creates an emotional
bond. This may be a common school, a common regiment, a
common profession. It would be difficult, if it were desirable,
to prevent them from giving expression to this wish ; and it is
natural that there should be organisations for the purpose
(e.g. Actors' Benevolent Fund, the various regimental funds).
It may be that there will be no need for such bodies in the
future, but the time is certainly not yet.

5. Several writers have called attention to the importance

of *international charities*, by which men and women of one country relieve distress in another country. It is not easy, though it may not be impossible, for states to undertake such tasks.

6. Certain kinds of *redemptive work* are done specially well by voluntary societies, inspired by and inspiring religious enthusiasm. It is not easy for statutory agencies to inspire or to use religious enthusiasm, and such work is best left to voluntary societies (Salvation Army, Josephine Butler Home, etc.). The statutory agencies can keep in close touch with such bodies and can give them both material and moral support, as they do in the case of the Discharged Prisoners' Aid Society and other bodies.

It is true that a certain amount of work formerly done by powerful personalities under religious inspiration is now done by persons psychologically trained ; we trust less to religious conversion and more to psycho-therapy. The two are not necessarily antagonistic, not necessarily divorced. But on the whole the future lies with science, and a larger part of this work may fall within the statutory field (e.g. the police-court missionary is being replaced by the probation officer). But for the present, and probably for a good while to come, voluntary societies can do some work in this sphere which statutory agencies cannot do.

7. Voluntary agencies can often promote *mutual aid* schemes by means of a little help in the early stages. This help may take the form of stimulation, of advice, of direction ; it may be financial help. It is probable that as gross poverty is eliminated, mutual aid schemes will become more and more important. It is impossible to think of a form of society in which they will not play some part, perhaps especially in the field of culture. The most extreme democrat can scarcely object to the giving of time and of skill (if not of money) to stimulate and to improve mutual aid. The social worker of a more equalitarian age would correspond in some ways to the Stakhanovite of contemporary Russia. Already a good deal of social service is of this nature, and the proportion of it increases.

8. It is most important in a democratic society that active citizenship should be widespread. Whilst only a comparatively few persons can take direct part in the work of the statutory authorities, it is possible and desirable for a much greater

number to watch that work intelligently and to contribute to its efficiency. This can be done through voluntary associations which collect and transmit information and make known their views. Tenants' Associations, Ratepayers' Associations (though unfortunately their attitude is too often limited and negative), Community Councils, afford examples of bodies exercising such functions to-day. There is room for great improvement and great development in this sphere of work.

In the light of these criticisms and these enconiums it should be possible to envisage a more logical division of functions between statutory agencies and voluntary agencies than exists to-day. Where large-scale provision is generally recognised to be necessary, and where it is of a kind which can be standardised without great difficulty and without hardship to individuals, that provision should be the responsibility of the State, and it is probable that in most cases it should be directly administered by the State. Where flexibility, experiment, supplementation or an exceptional degree of self-devotion are necessary, there is a strong case for the voluntary society, though this need not preclude State co-operation. Social work whose desirability is a matter of strong controversy must usually be left to voluntary societies. International charities are at present an appropriate sphere for voluntary action. The promotion of mutual aid schemes usually requires action by a voluntary body, though again this does not preclude State action. Information services may be provided by either statutory or voluntary bodies ; but criticism and propaganda depend for their value on complete independence of the bodies criticised or stimulated.

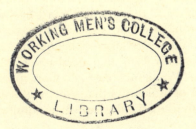

Chapter XIV

THE TRAINING AND RECRUITMENT OF
SOCIAL WORKERS

by

GERTRUDE WILLIAMS

I

ALTHOUGH it was beginning to be generally accepted by
the end of last century that constructive aid was more valuable
than haphazard charity, there was no such general agreement
that this work requires carefully trained workers. Sympathy,
generosity, and a " capacity for getting on with people " were
widely regarded as adequate equipment for social work and
there was a comfortable assumption that knowledge of what to
do to help and how to do it would come " naturally " to those
who possessed these personal qualities. True, such great
figures as Octavia Hill and Sir Charles Loch did not hold this
view. Though Octavia Hill always insisted that the right
spirit was the prime essential for good work she was equally
emphatic that this was no substitute for knowledge and much
of her time was spent in training her assistants. " It is of no
use," she said, " to have the right spirit if the technical matters,
all the sanitary and financial arrangements, are in a mess.
Beware of well-meant failures," and the C.O.S. very soon after
its foundation began to organise courses of lectures for some of
its workers. But it was not until 1890 that there was any
attempt to provide some wider education for social workers in
general. " We feel strongly," said the Warden of the Women's
University Settlement in Southwark, who was primarily responsible for this move, " that the last word has not been said on
many of the problems before us, that we have still a great deal
to learn, that there are many phenomena not satisfactorily
accounted for, many facts that need co-ordination and to be
reasoned upon. We should like to do more in the future towards
the elucidation of difficulties than we are able to do at present.
The old idea that goodwill is sufficient equipment is, happily,

dying out ; we have begun to realise that . . . we need the guidance of principles and the strength of experience."

The short course of lectures organised by the Settlement marked the beginning of the formal training of the social worker ; but it was soon apparent that a more integrated course of study was required than the Settlement could provide and in the following decade Schools of Social Studies were established in London, Liverpool, and Birmingham. Though from the first there was an informal connection with the universities, these schools were independent bodies and it was not until 1908 that Birmingham University created a precedent by accepting full responsibility for the training of social work students.

Others followed suit but by the beginning of the first world war training courses were still in their infancy. A period of rapid development, however, began largely as a result of the war itself. Then, as in the recent war, there emerged all sorts of exceptional problems, consequent on the strains and stresses of military and industrial mobilisation, and there was a greatly increased demand for people with the knowledge and experience to cope with them. The Ministry of Munitions, in particular, was faced with many difficult adjustments that sprang from the large-scale substitution of female for male labour in the munition factories and, desperate for " welfare workers," offered grants to selected students to take intensive training courses provided by the universities. The interest in social problems, in general, was much heightened and many proposals were put forward for building a " land fit for heroes." All such schemes demanded at least a nucleus of trained personnel and gradually most of the universities accepted the responsibility of providing them.

But it is one thing for the universities to organise Schools of Social Study and quite another thing for employing bodies to require their workers to have attended them, and we are still far from the position when any specific training—whether provided by the university or any other institution—is considered an essential prerequisite for work in the social services. It has taken time and experience for the value of a sound education to gain recognition, and even though, by now, more and more emphasis is coming to be laid on the importance of adequate preparation for work of this type, there is not as yet

H

any complete agreement on the form that that preparation should take.

There is at present, therefore, a wide variety in the kinds of training for different branches of social work and considerable variation in the degree of importance placed on it by employing bodies. To a certain extent, no doubt, this elasticity is due to the lack of an adequate supply of highly qualified applicants for the rapidly increasing number of jobs offered in the expanding services. The low salaries that were common until very recently were no inducement to men and women to engage in a long and expensive training; and even those organisations that were convinced of the value of a sound preparation for their work were obliged to employ many who fell below their desired standard. As always, poor pay and poor qualifications formed a vicious circle; it has been difficult to insist on high qualifications while the rewards were so slight, and difficult to demand higher pay while so many unqualified persons could get jobs. Nothing has been more important in this respect than the development of professional organisations whose fight to establish more reasonable standards of pay and conditions of employment has done much also to fix recognised standards of qualification. Such associations, for example, as those in labour management and hospital almoning have gone a long way towards professionalising the spheres of work with which they are specially concerned. By arranging their own training courses they have made it possible for those wishing to enter the service to gain a professional qualification which, through their work as employment agencies, they could try to enforce on employers; and to a quite considerable extent they have been successful in doing so. But while their influence is extensive and growing it has not been sufficient to shut out entirely from employment those who do not possess the qualifications recognised by the professional association.

In these circumstances it is impossible to give any account of the training of social workers that could rightly be thought to be of general application. There is no common agreement that training is necessary and there are differences of opinion on what training should consist of amongst those who combine to believe it essential. There are still some employing bodies that work on the principle that common sense and a pleasant personality comprise the total of what is needed ; there are others that lay stress on experience of the conditions of life in the homes of the poorer sections of the community ; there are some who place their faith in evidence of a good general education, such as the possession of a university degree whatever the subject of study, and trust to the experience on the job to provide any special knowledge required ; there are some who put most value on a specialised training for a specific type of work ; there are others who prefer more general knowledge of social conditions ; and there are still others who believe that a general knowledge of the social background is necessary as a foundation but that this must be followed by a more specialised professional training.

Yet, in spite of this bewildering variety, certain definite trends in opinion are discernible. In the first place, it is true to say that on the whole the case for training of some sort has been established. There are very few responsible bodies that are now prepared to maintain that social work requires only the right personality. The right personality remains the prime essential as it always has been ; but it is coming to be universally admitted that, by itself, it is not enough. And in the second place, the belief is growing that a university course in social studies provides the best foundation on which specialised knowledge and experience can be built.

An attempt will be made in this section to give a summary of the different kinds of training that are available at present, leaving to a later part of the chapter a discussion of the problems that have arisen. The courses to be described can be grouped into three classes : (1) university courses ; (2) professional training designed to follow a university course ; (3) professional training which is not related to a university course. The first consists of integrated courses planned expressly to qualify people for social work or for degrees which though not vocational in character are considered a particularly valuable educational preparation for such work ; the second comprises such specialised training as that for Labour Management, or Hospital Almoning or Youth Leadership ; while the third includes such courses of training as those for House Property Management or Occupational Therapy.

Of university courses the most usual is one which lasts two years and leads to a certificate (or diploma) in Social Science (or Social Studies)—the name differs in different universities.

As each university is autonomous there can be no standardised form of training, but as a matter of fact the various schools of social study have come to have a marked family resemblance. This development is due partly to the logic of circumstance and partly to the activities of the Joint University Council of Social Studies and Public Administration which was founded in 1918 to provide a common meeting-ground for discussion and has done much to establish common standards of training and qualification.

Although social study courses are vocational in character the universities do not interpret this in any narrow sense ; there are, however, two respects in which this aspect is dominant. First, as regards the selection of students. There is no question that if the " right spirit " without knowledge is not enough, knowledge without the " right spirit " is equally inadequate. Social work demands certain qualities of character and temperament, lacking which nothing of much value is likely to be achieved ; and no school of social study is willing to accept any candidate simply because he can show that he has reached some prescribed academic standard (e.g. matriculation). Whether or not a successful method has been evolved for determining if a potential student has, in addition, got the necessary personal qualities is certainly open to question (it is a point that will be discussed later), but there is no doubt that every school thinks it essential to make the attempt. In the early years of development perhaps rather undue stress was put on the personality factor, or perhaps it would be more correct to say that too little stress was put on the need for a good intellectual equipment. It was recognised that many people would make excellent workers in the field even though they were not the type to win scholarships. But experience has proved that the responsible worker needs real intellectual ability if he is to deal constructively with the multifarious problems with which he will be confronted, and although a loophole is generally left for those few exceptions who are practical geniuses but cannot pass examinations, most schools now demand that entrants should be of matriculation, or sometimes Higher School Certificate, standard.

It is a remarkable fact, and one that adds considerable complexity to the situation, that social science courses which are thus open to some extent to those without any definite academic standing are accepted also as post-graduate training. There are many people who are anxious to have a good general education before embarking on their life work ; there are many also who do not respond to the attractions of work in the social service field until they are brought into contact with the wider and more stimulating life of the university and realise the many different kinds of work for which it is possible to qualify. Such students can be assumed to have trained and cultivated minds by the time that they have graduated and can be expected to master the special subjects of study required for social work with greater ease than those coming direct to the social study courses. Graduates are therefore generally allowed to take the certificate course in a little more than one year, though in some universities this privilege is confined to those who have graduated in some cognate subject. The session is then usually devoted entirely to academic work and practical experience is gained partly in the vacations and chiefly during a period of continuous field work when the lecture courses have been completed. Teachers in social studies departments are thus given the extremely difficult assignment of providing courses of lectures which are sufficiently stimulating and advanced in matter and method to be of value to graduates and which are at the same time intelligible to the younger student with no special training behind him. This wide variation in previous equipment is one of the reasons why so much stress is laid on tutorial work. In most schools of social study seminars play a large part in the academic side of the course and this enables the individual capacities and interests of the students to be taken into account more than is possible in a series of lectures.

The practical work, to which reference has just been made, is the second feature of social science training which has a vocational importance. The practising social worker requires more than a wide general knowledge of social affairs ; if he is to do his job efficiently he needs also to develop the right techniques and this can come only from practice. A great deal of all social work consists of talking to people, and interviewing is a specialised craft—perhaps even an art. The social worker, in the same way as the doctor, will fail unless he can gain the confidence of his client ; he must learn to pick out the significant detail from a spate of irrelevancies ; he must develop the faculty of thinking quickly what step to take while apparently listening sympathetically to what is being said ; he must have the trained observation to enable him to notice much more than is stated. These are skills in which learning can come only by doing, and every course of training consequently places great emphasis on practical work. In most qualifying examinations practical work ranks with the academic subjects and the candidate who fails to get a satisfactory report on this part of the examination is not awarded the certificate.

The form taken by the practical work varies necessarily with the facilities offered by the region in which the university is situated and the field of work in which the student hopes to practise, but some experience in what has now come to be known as " family case-work " is generally thought to be basic. Such agencies as the Charity Organisation Society[1] or Personal Service Societies afford the student an insight into social conditions and fundamental problems which cannot easily be gained in any other way. In most other forms of social work the organisation comes into contact with only one facet of the client's life and interests ; but a great many of the problems with which the specialised worker—as, for example, the youth leader or the hospital almoner or the labour manager—has to deal cannot be properly understood without an intimate knowledge of family relationships and home circumstances. The appointment of hospital almoners is in itself a recognition on the part of the hospital of how little medical science alone can do to heal the patient whose mind is torn with anxiety over what is happening at home, or indeed whose illness may actually be the outcome of unhappy family relationships. Similarly, the youth leader who has no knowledge of the houses of his club members or who is not aware of the limiting circumstances of their lives has little chance of creating a harmonious and developing community life in the Youth Centre ; and the same applies to the labour manager whose knowledge of the workers he is supposed to serve is confined to the factory. Each individual is the centre of a whole network of social and group relationships which shape his life and mould his out-look ; and of these the family is undoubtedly the most fundamental. No other form of work gives so much opportunity as family case-work to see the individual " in the round " and to appreciate the quality of the social fabric into which his life is woven.

[1] Now the Family Welfare Association.

There are other advantages. Part of the price we have to pay for expanded statutory social services is the increased tendency to divide people up into categories with appropriate classified rights, and there are, indeed, many routine situations which can best be met by routine methods. But no form of practical experience teaches more quickly and more effectively than family case-work the infinite variability of human beings. In this way the student learns more thoroughly than by any other means how rarely the individual problem can be solved by the stock answer. The unspecialised character of such work has the further merit that it familiarises the student with the complicated network of social agencies, both voluntary and statutory. He gradually learns their particular scope and functions and comes into contact with them as working models instead of as museum exhibits. The proprietor of Dotheboys Hall may have carried to excessive lengths the principle that practical application of knowledge is the best teacher, but it undoubtedly has its points. Most of us are so deficient in imaginative power that we do not realise the living quality of an institution until we have seen it in action. This familiarity with different organisations is often thought so valuable that some schools of social study insist that students should spend some time in a settlement where they have an opportunity to become acclimatised to a new social environment, but the number of vacancies is not sufficient to open this form of experience to everybody.

Apart from case-work, practical training varies according to the interests of the individual student ; such, for example, as club work or in the office of an Employment Bureau, but for the most part the more specialised practical experience is gained during the later professional course rather than during the basic university period. In addition to the work in which the individual takes part there are numerous visits of observation whose purpose is to give a more concrete background to the lectures.

On the academic side the courses place much more emphasis on providing a good liberal education than on vocational training. True, the profession for which the student hopes to prepare is kept in mind in the choice of subjects of study ; but both the content of lecture courses and the method of teaching and discussion are designed to develop powers of analysis and judgment. The courses of instruction vary, of course, from one institution to another, but Social Economics, Social History, Social Administration and Machinery of Government are common to all, whilst Social Psychology and Social Philosophy are almost as general. Universities have a habit of retaining the name of a series of lectures while intro-ducing revolutionary changes into the content, and one cannot, therefore, always be certain of the nature of a course by looking at its official title. Nevertheless it is probably true that the majority of social studies courses, however they may divide the " subjects," cover more or less the same ground. They aim at giving the student, on the one hand, some grasp of the socio-economic structure of society with a more detailed knowledge of the social agencies which affect the standards of living of the community's members, and on the other hand, at developing an understanding of the behaviour of the individual in his various group relationships.

A two-year course of study cannot do more than introduce students to subjects as wide as these, and even when a good deal of time is devoted to tutorials and seminars in which discussion of particular problems can help to carry the student further, it has to be recognised that it is not possible to do more in the time than to establish a solid foundation on which more specialised training can be built. It is not surprising, therefore, that the emergence within the social field of highly specialised activities such as labour managemenet or psychiatric social work has led to the development of specialised professional training. To a certain extent this development is due to the desire of which mention was made earlier ; the organised practitioners in the different branches of work are eager to establish recognised standards of qualifications, and specialised training is therefore generally undertaken by the appropriate professional body. The Institute of Hospital Almoners, the Institute of Labour Management, the Family Case-workers' Association, and the National Association of Girls' Clubs and Mixed Clubs, all organise training courses for those who wish to offer themselves for employment in their special fields. In all these professions the student is expected to have taken a social science course at the university before entering the special training. In most cases this is naturally the certificate course in social science but graduates who have taken degrees in social science subjects are accepted without the certificate, though preference is usually given to those who have managed to gain some experience of practical work during the university vacations.

Of recent years there has been considerable development in degrees in social science and sociology. In one or two universities there has been established a degree course which is on the same lines as the certificate but carries the academic studies to a higher level, and practical work is as integral a part of the course as it is in the certificate. But this is unusual. Degrees in economics or sociology may cover a large part of the same ground as the certificate courses—though, of course, more intensively—but they are not intended to be vocational studies and do not offer any organised practical experience as part of the degree course. Moreover, the approach is different. The sociology degree in the University of London, for example, is not primarily concerned with English conditions but with the analysis and comparison of social institutions of different civilisations from which some understanding of the factors governing social development may be derived. But the knowledge of social structure and the analytical training that the student receives in such a course are one of the finest preparations that could be devised for social work or social research. Those students who know from the outset of their university life that they wish to go on afterwards to prepare for professional social work may give up their vacations to gaining necessary experience, and are then allowed to enter directly on the specialised training.

It is usual, though not essential, for those who wish to enter professions for which a special professional qualification is needed, to be selected by the professional bodies during their university course, and when this is done the student is often advised to choose the particular options offered in the course which are thought to be most valuable in the chosen career. Thus hospital almoners are urged to study psychology and physiology, labour managers industrial history and law, and so on.

In one fairly newly organised professional training the responsibility rests with the university instead of the professional body, though here too the latter is represented on the committee which supervises the course. This exception to the general

H*

practice is for psychiatric social work, the recognised qualification for which is the Mental Health Certificate offered by the London School of Economics and the University of Edinburgh. In both, a certificate in social science or appropriate degree is the essential qualification for admission to the course.

In the types of training dealt with so far the Departments of Social Studies of the universities play a large part. The certificate or a degree in social subjects comprises either the whole or the basic training for work. But there is a third category which follows a rather different line. The Society of Women Housing Managers, for example, arranges its own courses of training without any co-operation from the universities. Students with university qualifications are preferred but no restrictions are laid down as to the subject of study. A degree is welcomed as evidence of intellectual ability but it is not thought that the content of the degree course is of prime importance, and those without academic qualifications are accepted for training. In some others, such as Occupational Therapy or Church Moral Welfare, the training courses, which are generally fairly short, are entirely specialised and no regulations are laid down as to the previous qualifications of candidates for admission.

II

What changes, if any, are needed in the training of social workers? We have now had a sufficiently long period of organised courses to be able to judge how far we have developed on the right lines and whether any fundamental changes are required to meet new needs. This section is devoted to a discussion of some of the problems that call for consideration.

The planning of any course of professional training depends primarily on two things: (1) what you want to achieve; (2) the type of person you have to deal with. When we are considering the training of social workers we have a further question—Is there a profession which we can rightly call " social work " ?   There are, of course, a large number of occupations which can be grouped together under that heading, but is the kind of work done in them sufficiently homogeneous to justify them being considered as parts of the same profession ?   This question is fundamental because the answer we give to it determines whether or not it is possible to devise any course of training which can be accepted as basic preparation for all such forms of work.

The question is very much more difficult to answer now than it would have been twenty years ago, because the nature of social work has undergone such important changes. At the end of the first world war social work was almost entirely concerned with the casualties of community life. Voluntary social services came into existence to help those who for one reason or another were not able to maintain themselves on the level demanded by public opinion. In the general philosophy of the time in which the early societies were founded it was assumed that the majority of people would continue to lead their independent lives without any contact with formally constituted organisations. It was the underprivileged, the unfortunate, and the incompetent to whom assistance was offered in the form of advice, encouragement, education, or financial help. This kind of service is still needed and given, but not on the same scale as it was before the great expansion of routine social benefits which has characterised the present century. A great many of those who would have been in need of private benevolence are now kept from distress by unemployment and sickness benefits or by old age pensions. But no routine benefit can ever be devised to meet the infinitely varied demands made by individual circumstances ; as its name implies it is concerned only with what may be looked on as the common denominator of needs. And although social legislation now provides statutory resources for the common vicissitudes of life, there is still a wide field in which the peculiar problems of the individual can be solved only by the patient care and friendliness and assistance which the voluntary body can so well provide. The work of such agencies is therefore as necessary and valuable as ever, but its scope is no longer so extensive. Attention has come, nowadays, to be focused more on the social organisation which can prevent distress from occurring rather than directed to the methods of curing it when it has occurred. Social work, in fact, is developing along the same lines as medicine. People who fall ill must, of course, be cured and doctors must be trained to know how to recognise diseases and prescribe remedies for them ; but more and more of the work of the doctor is gradually coming to be positive and preventive rather than curative. It is the aim of the doctor to discover the way of life and the kind of environment in which people can grow healthily rather than to cure them when they have allowed themselves to become ill ; and in the same way the emphasis of social work is coming to be to foster a healthy growing social life rather than simply to pick up and succour the casualties. Community Centres and Youth Clubs, Play Centres, Marriage Guidance Councils, Discussion Groups and Neighbourhood organisations cater not only for the under-privileged or the incompetent, but for the normal member of society. They develop from the growing realisation that a community is a closely woven fabric in which threads of many different colours and textures are necessary to make up the pattern. It is only by the provision of a great variety of opportunities for free association for different purposes that individuals can discover and develop their capacities. To an ever-increasing extent nowadays social work is concerned with constructive rather than remedial work, and this gives point to the question : How far are the knowledge, technique, and qualities required for work in this field the same as those for the more widely known type of work which is mainly devoted to the help of the individual social casualty ? Can the same course of training be an adequate preparation for both ?

The question can best be tackled by considering first the reason for grouping different types of occupation as " social work." Why do we customarily accept the warden of a Community Centre as engaged in social work but exclude the officer in charge of the municipal sewerage system ? Both are serving the community ; both are playing a part in enabling a number of people to organise their group life satisfactorily. Yet as a matter of practice we imply some distinction between them by labelling one " social work " and not the other. There is, of course, one sense in which all work which does not definitely infringe accepted codes of social behaviour can be included in social service. Advertisers, indeed, make great play with this notion and the grocer and the bootmaker claim with some justice that they serve the public, but in fact we all recognise that the ulterior motive of profit makes a distinction between their activities and those of the public servant. This distinction is not intended to imply any adverse criticism of the profit motive, but the fact that their work is not, and does not claim to be, disinterested and that the public benefit is the means to an end rather than the end in itself, puts it into a different category from that of work whose prime objective is public welfare. It is based on different philosophical assumptions. We can say then as a first point that any work done primarily for private profit is automatically excluded from social work.

But this distinction does not hold in the two professions named, since both the warden of the Community Centre and the municipal sewerage officer have the public welfare as the objective of their work. This brings us, I think, to a second necessary qualification of social work, i.e. that it involves personal relationships. The municipal sewerage system is undoubtedly constructed primarily for the public benefit but the officer in charge of it need have no knowledge of or contact with the persons making use of it. He supervises the provision of certain facilities and his main concern is to see that these facilities are adequate in amount and efficient in operation ; his interest is in the object provided, not in the people who make use of it. It is because this impersonal element predominates that we rank sewerage as a public utility and not as social work.

But there are other kinds of work which do involve personal relationships and which we yet customarily exclude from social work ; e.g. the work of the secretary of the Carlton Club might justly be compared with that of the Community Centre warden. Here, I think, we have to admit that there is no precise and definite line of demarcation which can be permanently maintained. The distinction depends on what is generally accepted in the opinion of the day as part of the minimum standard and what is not so regarded. An efficient sewerage system is assumed by everybody to-day to be an essential element in urban civilisation ; its provision is taken for granted and everybody in the area makes use of it without question. If opportunities for social intercourse and for the development of a richly varied and harmonious network of social relationships were considered to be as integral a part of group life as the need for efficient sewerage, so that every community made provision for one as much without question as provision for the other, the wardenship of a Community Centre would no longer be ranked as social work any more than the secretaryship of the

Carlton Club. The organisation would be the conventionally accepted way of satisfying a recognised common need. But at present the Community Centre is not in this position. There are millions of people whose lives and interests are so impoverished that they have never realised the enjoyment and value to be gained from such corporate activities and who would not have the slightest idea how to set about providing for them even if they had. The Community Centre is designed to help those who would be unable to make provision for themselves, either individually or collectively, to enjoy a full and balanced community life, and it is in this respect that it differs both from the sewerage system and the Carlton Club, though one of these is a public utility and the other a private association. It is not initiated and controlled entirely by itself for itself. Here we have the common element in all social work ; it is that help is given to increase the social well-being of those who would not be able to do this for themselves without some assistance. It does not matter whether the help is given to the individual to cope with his moral, social, or economic problems, or whether it provides the environment, equipment, inspiration, and encouragement by which a whole group may enrich their reciprocal social relationships.

Social work may be defined then as any activity which, through personal relationships and without consideration of profits, endeavours to increase the welfare of those who, whether individually or collectively, are unable to reach the desired social standard unaided. It is only necessary to give a general definition of this sort to make it plain that there are certain basic requirements in the equipment of anybody preparing to undertake such work. Nobody can hope to be of any assistance to anybody else, whether individual or group, unless he has a good deal of sympathetic understanding of two things : he must know what folk are like, how their minds and emotions work and what are their principal preoccupations, and secondly, he must have some knowledge of the social pattern and moral values of the people he is trying to help. No amount of well-wishing can take the place of knowledge and understanding in these two spheres.

Here then is the answer to the question with which we started : there is undoubtedly so large a common element in all social work as to justify a common basic preparation for those who wish to train for it. And the determination of this common element gives us also a good deal of guidance as to the form this basic preparation should take—knowledge of the individual and knowledge of the society into which he has to fit.

In the majority of social studies courses to-day a very considerable amount of attention is given to both these subjects. Most courses lay stress on psychology and economic and political organisation and generally endeavour to train the student to understand something of the social background of the people with whom he will later be concerned. Where, perhaps, changes in this respect are required is in developing a greater degree of integration in these studies. A student may learn a good deal about the workings of the human mind in a general way and may have acquired considerable knowledge of the organisation and structure of industry or of the laws governing a man's responsibility for his dependants, and yet never appreciate such factors in social life as, for example, the incalculable importance of group loyalties in industrial disputes or the effect of a particular local tradition in establishing the scales of social values or the strength of family ties in certain situations. Sociologists are gradually building up more knowledge of the importance of cultural patterns in determining the responses made by individuals to the various situations with which life confronts them, with the result that we are gaining a clearer understanding of social structure and social processes. Much of this knowledge and understanding is needed by the social worker ; particularly now, with the changed emphasis of social work. When the concern was primarily with the individual the social organisation was generally taken for granted and effort was directed to helping the individual to take or recover his own place within that organisation. Even then, however, sounder knowledge would have prevented many blunders, for too many workers were inclined to condemn a cultural pattern or set of social values simply because they happened to be different from their own. A greater awareness of the diversity of social patterns and groupings might have prevented much ineffectual effort. But now that the focus has changed and so much more attention is given to the development of the social organisation itself, this subtler understanding of the nature of society is absolutely imperative.

This is not to say that no social worker can be of any value in the field of practical work unless he is an expert sociologist, but that he is likely to make fewer serious blunders and to do much more constructive work if he knows something of the structure of society and has some idea of the ways in which communities change and develop. As Miss Jennings pointed out in the chapter on case-work, the efficient case-worker who tried to make the best possible plan for the family of the man with the broken leg probably caused immense suffering and may have done irreparable psychological injury to the young children whose family life she broke up. The present case-worker has learned to appreciate the great importance of family life and would not, probably, make such a mistake. But the housing reformer has only just begun to realise the similar fundamental value of long-standing ties of neighbourliness and friendly association in the slum areas he is so anxious to demolish and that the new housing estate—pretty, well-planned, and hygenic as it may be—may spell psychological starvation and frustration of the social needs of the individuals transferred to it.

Such knowledge of human relationships can, of course, be gained in many specialist studies—for example, in social psychology and social economics—but it is so important a foundation that it deserves a place to itself, in addition to the courses now usually provided. Even a fairly general and elementary course, devoted specifically to the study of the structure of society, would do much to accustom the student to think of society as a functioning, growing organisation of which the individual is an integral constituent, rather than a backcloth against which he stands out in relief.

In the first section of this chapter attention was drawn to the fact that the universities have never allowed the vocational character of training courses for social work to exercise too strong an influence ; their aim is to develop certain mental qualities rather than to be content with the accumulation of an amount of factual information. The social worker must, of course, have a sound and detailed knowledge of social services and social agencies, both statutory and voluntary, as an essential part of his equipment ; but he needs much more than this. If the definition of social work given above is accepted, the primary concern of the social worker must be to diagnose correctly the needs of the individuals and groups to whose welfare he is trying to contribute, before he can begin to formulate a plan to do so. The mental qualities that are most needed, therefore, are the analytical power that enables one to grasp the salient features of a situation and the constructive ability to mobilise available resources to deal with it ; and much of the academic part of the course is concerned with cultivating them. But there is another function which can be expected of the social worker and one which so far has received much less recognition—and that is, he should learn to see the thing he is dealing with in its general relationships so as to use his detailed knowledge and experience to shape the policy of the future. The great social workers of the past certainly accepted this as a major part of their work. Octavia Hill, for example, was never content to confine herself to improving the housing conditions of the few families with whom she came in contact, though this was the side of the work she most enjoyed ; but she used the experience she gained in this way to devise long-term plans for a fundamental amelioration of working-class housing as a whole. But on the whole the majority of social workers have failed to take the long view or to see the wood as well as the trees. That this is so is evidenced by the dearth of literature produced by those working in the field. One would have expected a wealth of social records and documented commentaries from the persons working in the many new fields into which trained social workers have penetrated during the last twenty years, but in fact very little has emerged. There is, indeed, a very wide gulf between the social researcher and writer on the one hand and the practical social worker on the other ; yet it should obviously be to the social worker that the researcher should ordinarily turn for a great deal of his material. This lack must evidently be due to some defect in the training of the social worker who has not developed the faculty of recognising the value of the factual material with which he comes into daily contact. How many labour managers, for example, or hospital almoners or housing managers or family case-workers have thought of keeping careful records of the incidence of certain factors which they find continually recurring in the course of their work so as to try and discover underlying causes or to devise a long-term policy which would more adequately meet the situation ? That they have not done so is evidence that the training they have received has not developed that faculty—at once analytical and creative—which enables one to see a small detail as part of a complicated pattern, or the universe in a grain of sand.

The fault may lie, however, not so much in the training as in the type of student who ordinarily offers himself, or more often herself, for the courses ; and it is necessary to turn our attention to a consideration of this question. How far have the departments of social study been successful in attracting suitable recruits for social work ? Where entry to the profession has been by way of a degree in sociology or social science, or in some other subject followed by a period of special training, there has been as great a proportion of high ability as is found in a cross-section of any other walk of life. But the majority of students are to be found in the certificate or diploma courses and it is more difficult to generalise about these, though there has been a good deal of criticism on two grounds. It is argued, first, that the average level of ability has not been sufficiently high in view of the importance of the work to be done, and secondly that the students are too young and immature to benefit by the training or to be capable of responsible work even after completing it. How much truth is there in these criticisms, and, if they are well founded, is there a remedy ?

It must be admitted at once that there is a considerable amount of justification for both contentions, though it is certain that they have not nearly as much foundation now as they used to have. It is, unfortunately, true that a very large number of people are still ignorant of what is comprised by social work. They still think of it as consisting in taking charitable gifts to the deserving poor or helping with a class of girls and boys at Sunday School, and are inclined, therefore, to think it suitable work to fill in the leisure time of women who have not much to do, or as a dumping ground for anybody who wishes, or needs, to take up some paid work but shows no special capacity or interest in any of the well-established professions. Unhappily, a large proportion of headmistresses and other advisers of youth are to be found in this category, particularly in those localities where social work has not been very highly developed, and their ignorance of the variety, complexity, and expertise of social-work occupations has often led them to steer into this profession only those whom they despaired of fitting into any other niche. This situation is altering very rapidly as the value and interest of various branches of social work are becoming more widely known, largely owing to the efforts of the professional associations and their insistence on recognised qualifications. But it takes a long time for a faulty idea to die and there are still too many candidates for admission to social science departments whose main claim consists of " being good with people," a claim which, when analysed, often enough means that the candidate has pleasant manners, dislikes teaching, and does not know in what other way to set about earning a living.

It should, of course, be the work of the department of social science to sift the sheep from the goats and select those who are likely to be suitable workers. The difficulty is to find the way to do it. It was emphasised in the first section of this chapter that all universities, and indeed all bodies connected with training, lay great stress on the importance of selecting students on personal qualities as well as academic attainment. But it would be foolish to pretend that they have yet discovered any really successful way of doing so. Neither written reports and testimonials nor an interview of fifteen to twenty minutes can do more than eliminate those who are likely to prove hopeless misfits, and so far no other method of selection has been devised. It may be that in the future we shall be able to trust more to the results of intelligence and aptitude tests, but that time has not yet come. Despite the great development in these tests due to their widespread use in the Services, they are still very much in the experimental stage for anything more than the classification of people into wide categories. They cannot as yet be used for pinpointing. Moreover, the test of the candidate's capacity is only half the problem. It is equally important to establish what qualities are most essential to the work ; and job analysis—particularly of work demanding such a combination of temperamental as well as intellectual qualities as social work—has not yet reached a stage where we can feel confident that selection of students can be left to the findings of a routine test.

The prospect for the future is, however, not nearly so bad as it seems at first sight. In fact, the position is rapidly righting itself. Until fairly recently the monetary rewards offered for social work were so negligible that the profession had little appeal except to those whose selfless devotion to their fellow men made them oblivious of personal gain. But as one section of workers after another has become organised there have been established standard conditions of pay and conditions of employment which compare quite favourably with those of many other professions. This development has had two important consequences : first, standards of pay necessitate recognised standards of qualifications which, in a sense, advertise the profession to the world so that those planning their future have them in mind as possible alternatives worth consideration ; and second, the better conditions and pay compete with those offered by older professions to attract a larger share of the available ability. The effect of these changes is already noticeable and is likely to increase.

There is, however, one factor which may continue to have a depressing influence unless revolutionary changes are made in the usual methods of staffing social service organisations. Although the pay and conditions of the rank and file have been so notably improved there remains one serious difference between social work and most other occupations. Social work is, in fact, probably unique amongst professions in the slight degree of movement that exists between the lower ranges and the higher. In most types of employment the entrant of capacity can expect to have opportunities to rise to more responsible and better-paid jobs as his experience and knowledge grow, but it is rare for any branch of social work to offer any avenue of promotion to the rank and file, however able they may prove to be. There is a great gulf between the higher administrative grades of most agencies and the practical worker in the field, and it is still extremely unusual to find any trained social worker amongst the more highly paid officials. Until recognised channels are established whereby those of special ability who enter the ranks can hope to rise into the higher levels of administration and policy, it is unlikely that the profession will attract those of first-class quality.

The problem of the age of recruits for social work—the subject of the second serious criticism—bristles with difficulties. Responsible social work demands a knowledge of life, a maturity of judgment, and an understanding of human relationships that can come only with time, however well endowed one may be with innate capacity. H. W. Nevinson, in his delightful account of his early days at Toynbee Hall with Canon Barnett, tells a story of a young woman who came to work in the Settlement and who, being warned of the complexity of different " cases " submitted to her care, replied confidently, " Character presents no difficulty to me ; I took a First in Moral Philosophy at Cambridge." No doubt a very few weeks sufficed to make her more humble. No amount of intellectual attainment or " book knowledge " can compensate for the lack of that kind of understanding that comes only with experience. So much of social work, particularly on the individual side, consists in giving advice which will help people to find their feet in the complex relationships of modern life ; there is something impertinent in this attempt on the part of a young, untried, and inexperienced fledgling. But it is not only the practical work that presents a difficulty. To somebody who has known nothing of the trials and sorrows that the world can bring, many of the topics discussed in the academic courses have little meaning. There is no question that the value of the training would be immensely increased if students were older and more mature before entering on it. In particular, their appreciation of the social problems dealt with would be much greater if they were obliged to spend an intervening period between school and university in some form of paid work which involved them in the task of making ends meet on their earnings, holding down a job, getting on with workmates and the like.

But it is not only students intending to take up social work who would be benefited by such an interlude. A very strong case could, in fact, be made out for the demand that at least one year of outside paid work should be an essential prerequisite to entry to any university course, and not merely to the department of social studies. But unless it were made compulsory, or at least customary, for all it is doubtful if it would be practicable to insist on it for social science entrants alone.

The age of dependence has lengthened so greatly during the last half century that the burden on parents has become extremely heavy and few could be blamed for refusing to allow their children to choose social work as their profession if it entailed a much longer period than other professions before complete economic independence was reached. The force of this argument is made even stronger when it is remembered that the majority of trained social workers are women who customarily expect to leave paid employment, for a time at least, when they marry and begin to have children. Most women expect to marry in their twenties and if they could not begin their professional training until twenty-one or twenty-two they would complete it only at the moment they expected to retire from professional work. In such circumstances it is fairly certain that a large proportion of those of ability who might, as far as their special interests were involved, have been anxious to enter social work, would have chosen the next profession on their list of preferences if it enabled them to qualify and earn at a much earlier age.[1]

There are probably always to be found a number of older students who are ready to abandon the career on which they have already begun in order to train for something of such abiding human interest as social work and in the post-war years there is no question that there are and will be many such. But in this case there are two particularly favourable circumstances —first, many have been coming out of the special form of national service in which they have spent the war years and anyway would be faced by a break in the continuity of their working lives; and second, there are special financial facilities offered to many groups which helps them over the cost of both the break and the new training. But as a long-term policy it seems unlikely that the main body of those offering themselves for training in social work can be much different in age from entrants to other professions. As it is, most universities insist that those beginning social science courses shall be at least nineteen, which is a year more than the age at which undergraduates in general enter on other courses of study. As a further period of specialised professional training is required for most branches of work a fully qualified social worker cannot begin earning before the age of twenty-two, and there seems little likelihood that the majority of parents will be prepared to maintain their daughters to a later age than this, or that daughters for their part will be willing to remain economically dependent at an age when all their friends are out in the world.

[1] This was certainly true of the nursing profession. Voluntary hospitals used to refuse to admit probationers below the age of twenty-one but as alternative openings for educated women began to offer themselves it was found that many of the best recruits had been creamed off by the time they reached that age and consequently the hospitals have been forced to lower the age of entry.

There will, of course, be some whose professional career is likely to be prolonged beyond that of the average woman and who will be prepared to return at a later age for specialist training, as is the case now, for example, with those interested in psychiatric social work or probation work. But it looks as if we must reckon, in the future as in the past, that the majority of entrants to courses must necessarily be drawn from those of nineteen and twenty years of age.

The place of practical work in training has been left to the end because it is so closely related to this question of age. The aim of practical training is threefold : (*a*) to give the student an opportunity of learning something of the lives and homes of people of a different environment and experience from his own ; (*b*) to learn the methods and techniques of organised help ; and (*c*) to become familiar with the various agencies, both statutory and voluntary, with which his own work must be integrated. If the majority of students in training for social work were drawn from the wage-earning groups of the population the first of these aims could be very rapidly achieved, for although it would still be necessary to get a wider experience of conditions in different localities and amongst people of different wage levels, the student would be already aware of many of the problems and preoccupations that play a dominant part in working-class lives. The shadow of insecurity, the narrow margin of resources, the lack of space and privacy for individual hobbies and interests in a small house or rooms, the sacrifice involved in apprenticing a child or accepting a scholarship, and the neighbourliness in times of sickness or distress, would all be matters of one's own domestic experience which would form the background to additional knowledge. But as a matter of fact most students are drawn from the middle ranks in the population. Until recently local authorities insisted that scholarship holders should enter on a degree course, and although many have relaxed this regulation during the last year or so it is as yet too soon for the change to have had any appreciable effect. In consequence, social work students have been confined to those who could afford to pay their own way through college and this has inevitably excluded those from the smaller-income classes.

To a marked extent, therefore, the earlier months of practical work are taken up in absorbing the knowledge of conditions of life in an environment with which the student is wholly unfamiliar. The difficulty of " thinking oneself into somebody else's life "—which is an essential of good social work— has been intensified by the higher degree of social segregation which has developed in this country during the present century. One result of the increased motor and electric transport facilities has been the movement of the better-off members of society away from the shops and factories where their incomes are earned into " high-class residential neighbourhoods," and nowadays a large proportion of young people grow up in what are virtually one-class localities. The middle-class girl who has grown up in such a suburb may reach the end of her teens without ever having seen a working-class home at close quarters and must spend a considerable time in acquiring the sort of knowledge which she would have absorbed imperceptibly if her own adolescence had been spent in a different environment. This is not training in any vocational sense of the term ; it is simply an essential prerequisite for such training and would be largely unnecessary if the student had had an interval between school or university in which she had worked in a factory or shop and lived among her fellow workers on the wages she had earned.

Learning the technique is obviously made more difficult by this ignorance on the part of the student, for those responsible for her work hesitate to leave her to cope with a situation in which the blunders she may make affect other people's lives. Yet the practice of social work cannot be learned solely by observation ; learning must come by doing, and it is only by having to deal with a problem under the guidance of a more experienced person that the student can gradually master the principles of her work. Not until she is faced with the knotty problem of what to do about Mrs. Smith or Mr. Jones, with the acute realisation that it is imperative that something *must* be done, and quickly, does she begin to appreciate fully the complexity of human difficulties and how very rarely Mrs. Smith or Mr. Jones fit into the neatly classified categories with their appropriate remedies that she has learned about in her lecture courses.

Some part of the blame for the difficulties encountered by the student in her practical work must be put down to the lack of integration between the academic and practical sides of the training which is, at present, the most serious defect of social science courses. In one or two university centres this criticism no longer applies ; a joint board has been formed consisting of members of the university social science department and representatives of the principal agencies which accept students for training, and here the theoretical and practical sides of the course can be carefully welded into a coherent and integral whole. But these are rare exceptions and for the most part the bewildered student remains completely unaware that there is any vital connection between the subjects she is studying at the university and the human problems with which she is trying to deal in her practical work.

In part the difficulty is inherent in the situation since the university is bound to take advantage of facilities for training in organisations which are quite independent of it, and not only the correlation but the quality of the training may leave much to be desired. Both the philosophy and the methods of social service change as time goes on, but this does not mean that every officer of every agency is entirely up to date in either ideas or technique. Even such humdrum matters as office organisation, correspondence and filing, the conduct of meetings, and the hundred and one mundane but extremely important details of running an organisation, may be inefficient or slipshod, but the university has no authority to investigate them or to alter them if they are not up to the standard that would be wished for. In some universities an effort is made to bridge the gulf between academic and field work by the appointment to their own staff of a tutor whose special function it is to correlate the two sides of the course ; but even this is not a complete solution. Even a person with wide experience in the field gets rapidly out of touch with current practice if he leaves practical work on his appointment to the university, and though at the outset he may enliven his discussions with the fruits of concrete know-ledge, as the years go on he may come to be completely out of date and ignorant of both the changing spirit and the new methods of work. Sometimes by means of two half-time appointments, one in the field and the other in the university, the practical tutor keeps abreast of developments on both sides, but in a university with many students this necessitates a very large staff of tutors if every student is to have the benefit of their expert guidance. How valuable such a method can be has been well demonstrated by the developments in the training for Mental Health and Youth Leadership work, in both of which the practical work done by the students is under the continual supervision of tutors who are themselves experienced practising workers. The solution of the problem for the general course is largely, as so often, a question of finance. If the university is prepared to finance a sufficiently large staff the appointment of several practical work tutors can do much to enable trainees to get full value out of both sides of the course ; but so far this is exceptional.

There is still another difficulty which makes the practical work a less valuable element in the course than it could be, and this is the frequent lack of ability to teach on the part of the officials of the agencies who act as supervisors of practical work. In part this too is financial in origin. In some under-staffed organisations the harassed official is herself so over-worked that she can do little else than rope in the students as cheap assistants and leave them to find out the principles as well as they can as they go along, and the only remedy is for universities to be prepared to pay enough for the facilities afforded them to enable the agency to allow the official to devote a good deal of her time to her teaching duties. But the principal difficulty is not really one of finance. Although many supervisors take their teaching work seriously and are anxious to give of their best to the students committed to their care, they rarely have any skill in this work and cannot explain what they are doing in such a way that the student gets a real grasp of its essentials. The lack of integration between academic and practical work has its repercussions here too, for often enough the official has only the haziest idea of the subjects taught or is unaware of the stage the student has reached, so that she expects a degree of background knowledge and capacity far beyond what the student has to offer.

Many of the organisations that play the largest part in the practical work training are painfully aware of their deficiencies, and it is due to their initiative that a move has recently been made to " train the trainers " by evolving the techniques by which students can most successfully be introduced to different fields of work. This would be a welcome step in any case but at the moment its importance cannot be exaggerated, in view of the great expansion in the demand for qualified workers.

In the past students have been placed with a few recognised organisations whose officials have, at least, a good deal of experience in dealing with the problem. But the number of students that can be accommodated by any one office is strictly limited and at present the intake of students to the universities is necessarily kept down to the places available for practical work training. It is only if the universities can feel confident that there are sufficient organisations willing to and capable of taking students for practical work that they can hope to increase the number they admit, and this could be so if it became accepted policy for supervisors to qualify for the work. There are a great many agencies specialising in interesting pieces of work where students could gain valuable knowledge and experience, provided that the officials who would be responsible for supervising their work could be guaranteed to have some capacity for teaching as well as their own particular expertise. If the societies undertake to ensure that their officers are trained as fully to supervise students as to do their own social work, the opportunities for practical training could be greatly extended and enable a larger supply of qualified workers to be more quickly forthcoming. Such a solution of the problem does, of course, require money. Voluntary societies cannot be expected to use the time and energies of their officers on training university students unless the universities are prepared to pay for their services. But while finance is important it is by no means the chief element in the situation ; what is most urgently required is a greater realisation of the imperative need to integrate academic and practical training into a coherent whole so that what the student learns in the university and in the field illustrate and illuminate each other.

But however complete and satisfactory the overhauling of the courses may be, it is essential to accept their limitations. Even the best organisation cannot make a course of training lasting two years able to turn out fully qualified social workers capable of undertaking responsible work. Particularly is this the case if, as has been argued, the majority of the students are young. So much of the time has to be spent in learning something about life itself and so much more to know something of the workaday world that an insufficient amount remains to gain experience in varied fields and to practise the different techniques required. Most of the subjects studied in the university demand a considerable amount of reading, thinking, and discussion if any real value is to be derived from them, and this means that inevitably the emphasis must be put on the theoretical rather than the practical side during the second session. Most social workers are very hardworking, and once they have entered professional life they find it difficult to get the solid blocks of time and the access to libraries and tutors which are available to them while they are at college, so that it is worth while to take advantage of their college life to try to grasp some of the fundamental principles involved in the kinds of work to which they propose to devote themselves. But the amount of time that this leaves for practical work is not enough for them to acquire the thorough mastery of the job that they should have if they are to be placed in fully responsible positions. It is no wonder then that the certificated student often finds it difficult to get placed when she first leaves college, for most employing bodies are unwilling to take the risk of allowing her to gain her experience at their expense.

For many branches of work the student undertakes a further course of professional training which consists mainly of practical work in the field under expert guidance, and this is tending to become more and more the practice as one type of social work after another organises itself and standardises its rates of pay and corresponding qualifications. But it is open to question whether this is the wisest path of advance. There is very real danger that social work will become too departmentalised and will consist of parallel professions with very little connection with one another. It has been the argument of this section that, apart from the narrow " craft " element in social work, the basic knowledge and personal qualities are common to all. Whatever the particular type of work a real understanding of what folk are like and of how society is made up is needed, and the wider and more varied the experience of different kinds of work the fuller and more profound this understanding is likely to be. It is much to be desired, therefore, that workers should move from one branch of work to another and enlarge their knowledge of the many facets of individual and social life. The Ministry of Education has taken a wise step in urging those who enter the Service of Youth to consider it as a short-term occupation and be prepared to transfer to some other work, such, for example, as that in Community Centres, before they get too old to enter wholeheartedly into the pleasures, trials and preoccupations of youth. Very much more needs to be done along these lines. As it is there is sometimes a tendency for the devoted worker in one branch of work to lose a sense of proportion and to fight with almost too great a zeal for the expansion of the service with which he has identified himself. And also this narrow specialisation means general loss ; much of the insight into the lives of people that is gained by a detailed daily contact with one of their activities can be most profitably used in attacking problems of quite a different nature, but this valuable source of knowledge is lost when there is so little interchange between various fields of work. If there were more movement from one type of work to another there would be less difficulty in seeing people in the round or in appreciating the innumerable bits and pieces that go to make up the mosaic of life.

There is a further aspect of this that needs to be considered. As new ground is broken there is a need for workers with imagination and initiative to undertake jobs whose possibilities are still unexplored and for which there cannot be any recognised qualification or preparation. There is less chance of finding such people if the established branches of work have become so completely separated that elasticity has been lost. Social work, in common with most other parts of the employment market, needs to encourage a much greater degree of flexibility amongst its personnel so as to allow of easier mobility from one job to another than is customary to-day. At present this mobility is prevented by the highly specialised post-certificate professional training in two ways : first, it narrows the student's interests, and second and more important, the professional bodies which organise the training are the recognised employment bureaux in their respective fields and place all their weight against the employment of those who have not taken their training.

It is necessary, therefore, to devise some form of post-certificate experience which enables the young worker to gain confidence and skill without leading him into too narrow a channel. That something is required is not in doubt. The newly certificated student is rarely capable of undertaking responsibility, for social work deals with such important and often such intimate aspects of people's lives that the 'prentice hand cannot be trusted too largely. In big organisations, where there are many officials of differing grades of responsibility, the difficulty can be overcome by appointing the newly qualified person to an assistant's post where he can learn to apply his knowledge and get a proper sense of his own limitations under the expert guidance of his seniors. This is, indeed, the way in which the newly qualified doctor learns his trade—by a series of hospital jobs in which his responsibility is related to his growing experience. But there are very few branches of social work in which this is a practical solution to the problem, for in most the number of qualified personnel is so small that there is no place for assistants. The only way out of the difficulty seems to be to reproduce as nearly as possible the lines of such apprenticeship jobs by the institution of a third year of training in which the student devotes the greater part of his time to practical work in a number of selected fields, with perhaps a bias towards the particular type of work in which he feels a special interest. By the third year he would be both sufficiently mature and sufficiently educated to take full advantage of the experience offered him, and the opportunity to follow a job through over several weeks without the constant interruptions made by the demands of academic work would enable him to grasp the essentials of the field work much more rapidly.

For such a scheme to be practicable it would, of course, be necessary for the professional bodies to be prepared to recognise this less specialised third year as an alternative to their own courses. A joint body representing the university and the principal organisations could well establish the types of work that should be included so as to give the student experience of different sides of his future clients' lives which would be valuable whatever the special field in which his later employment lay. Such a non-specialised professional training could do much to widen interests as well as to create that greater degree of mobility in the world of social work which would be so great an advantage to all.

One further development is needed if mobility is to be achieved—a better organisation of the employment market in social work. The rather narrow sectionalism to which reference has been made is due only partly to the highly specialised training—it owes its origin in part also to the lack of any central clearing-house for workers and jobs. There are at present three methods by which employing bodies and potential workers are brought together. In those branches of work which have become highly organised, e.g. hospital almoners, family case-workers, labour managers, youth leaders, etc., the professional associations have waged a very successful battle to control their respective labour markets. It is becoming increasingly customary for employing bodies to notify their needs in the knowledge that they will be put in touch with those who possess the qualifications they wish for. The associations have done, and are doing, a notable piece of work in this way which enables them at one and the same time to get their members quickly into jobs and to ensure that posts are filled by those with recognised qualifications. The second method is by advertisement ; both the special periodicals and the weekly and daily press usually carry a number of notices of vacant posts, but on the whole these relate to the less specialised forms of social work and, in particular to those for which no professional association has yet come into being. Thirdly, a very large number of posts are filled through personal contacts, that is, by the chance that somebody on the managing committee happens to know a suitable person who may be persuaded to fill the vacant post. At first sight this third method sounds wholly bad because it seems to savour too much of nepotism, but there is, in fact, much to be said for it, especially in new and experimental kinds of work. As the field of work expands and new agencies are established to cope with new problems, the work to be done is necessarily so much the subject of improvisation that it is impossible to know beforehand exactly what kinds of qualifications will prove most suitable. What is needed above all at that stage is courage, initiative, vision, and a profound belief in the work itself. The techniques have still to be evolved as well as the policy, so that it is not possible to find persons who are already experienced ; they must be drawn from other occupations. No other way of doing this except through personal knowledge has yet been devised. At the same time it must be realised that this method of recruitment has severe limitations since it depends on the double coincidence that those looking for staff happen to know suitable people among their acquaintance and also have the insight to sort them out. How comparatively rare it is for both knowledge and spotting talent to be combined is evidenced by the number of misfits in high places in social work.

Each of these three methods has its advantages but all need supplementation. The first is very efficient within its own boundaries but prevents mobility ; the second and the third are haphazard in varying degrees and can draw on too narrow a field of selection. The outstanding need of the moment is for the establishment of a Bureau of Social Service to act as an employment agency covering all branches of social work. The initiative could best be taken by some co-ordinating body such as the National Council of Social Service or the British Federation of Social Workers, but it would be essential for efficiency that the management should be widely representative of different sections of the profession.

Two things would be essential for the success of such a Bureau : first, all those who are qualified by specific training or relevant experience should be encouraged to register with the Bureau so that employing bodies could notify their vacancies with the confidence that they were thus being put in touch with all available personnel ; and second, those in charge must have a wide and thorough knowledge of the kinds of work done in the various types of occupation. These are important because the work of the Bureau should not be taken to be simply to bring together those with vacancies and those without jobs, though this in itself is a valuable function ; but there is a more serious and, in a sense, a more constructive piece of work to be done. Owing to the specialisation obtaining nowadays, those who are already in work in one field never hear of opportunities in another, and through ignorance of what is required rarely think of offering themselves if they do hear of them. Yet the experience they have gained and the qualities they have developed may be exactly what is needed in the vacant post. It should, therefore, be one function of the Bureau to keep this in mind and to circulate notices of suitable vacancies to those who are already employed if they believe that their experience is likely to prove the right background for the job. In this way the Bureau might overcome two difficulties at the same time : it would undoubtedly increase the flexibility of the social service labour market and it would also help to narrow the gulf (to which reference was made earlier) which separates the rank and file of the various social work professions and the higher administrative and policy-making jobs.

INDEX

ABCA. *See* Army Bureau of Current Affairs

Actors' Benevolent Fund, 211

Adam, Sir Ronald, 158

Adams, Professor W. G. S., 173

Adolescents, 129, 130 ff. *See also* Youth

Adoption Association, the National Children's, 121

Adoption of Children Acts, 121

Adoption Society, the National, 121

Adult Education, British Institute of, 3, 165

After care, children's. *See* Care committees

Aged, the. *See* Old age and Old people

Agriculture, Board of, 150. *See also* Ministry of Agriculture

Air-raid precautions, 36

Allotment schemes, 32, 45, 180

Almoners, hospital, and almoning, 31, 58, 216, 217, 220, 223, 231, 245

Andrew, Miss Clara, 121

Annual Charities Register and Digest (C.O.S.), 3 *n.*, 199

Anti-Gambling League, National, 3

Anti-Vivisection Society, 3

" Approved " schools. *See* Schools

Arethusa training ship, 119

Army Bureau of Current Affairs (ABCA), 155

Army education. *See* Education

Army Educational Corps, 163

Army Education Release Scheme, 163, 166

Art exhibitions. *See* Arts Council of Great Britain

Art for the People Scheme, 165

Arts centres. *See* Arts Council of Great Britain

Arts Council, 77

Arts Council of Great Britain (formerly CEMA), 103, 164 ff.

Assistance Board, 89, 105

Associated Council of Children's Homes, 111, 119

Association of Infant Consultations, 107

Association of Infant Welfare and Maternity centres, 110

Association of Nursery Training colleges, 110, 111

Babies Welcomes, 108

Baby Week Council, National, 110

Ballet, English, 176

Barker, Sir Ernest, 69, 74

Barlow, Sir Thomas, M.D., 128

Barnardo, Dr., 23

Barnardo's homes, 118, 125

Barnett, Canon, 56, 235

B.B.C., 166–8, 190 ; brains trusts, 157 ; Central Appeals Advisory Committee, 190 ; talks to villagers, 102 ; " To Start You Talking," 142 ; under-twenty clubs, 142

Beauty spots, preservation of, 179

Becontree, 69

Bedford College, social science department of, 140

Benevolent Fund of N.C.S.S., 92, 93

Beveridge Plan, 14

Billeting, 37

Birkbeck College, 181

Birth control, 211

Blacksmiths and modern machinery, 89–90, 104

Blind, national library for the, 175 ; residential homes for the, 63 ; training of the, 25

Blind Persons Act of 1920, 194

Board of Education. *See* Education

Board of Guardians (now Public Assistance Committees, q.v.)

Board of Guardians, Jewish. *See* Jewish

Boys and girls, work among, 129 ff.

Boys' Brigade, 130

Boys' clubs (*see* Clubs) ; National Association of, 81, 89, 133, 187

Boys, hostels for. *See* Hostels.

Braithwaite, Constance, vi, viii, 81, 172, 183, 195

British Drama League, 103, 176

British Federation of Social Workers, 246

British Legion, 161, 190

British Restaurants (Study by N.C.S.S.), 94 *n.*

Brynmawr (Jennings), vi, 41, 45

Buildings of historic interest, 179

Bureau of Social Service, suggested, 246

Butler Act, 1944

B.W.P. (British Way and Purpose), 162–3

Cadet forces, cadet formations, 148, 161

Cadets, Red Cross and St. John Ambulance, 141

Caldecott community, the, 126

Cambridge Evacuation Survey, 37

Cambridgeshire, Huntingdonshire and the Isle of Ely Community Council, 100

I

Camping, holiday camps, camping sites, etc., 75, 130, 132, 181, 185

Canteens, circulating, 63

Care committees, 20, 21, 22, 62, 114, 115

Carnegie, Andrew, 172 ff.

Carnegie House, 110

Carnegie United Kingdom Trust, 71, 83, 84, 99, 100, 102, 103, 104, 134, 136, 153, 159, 162, 172 ff.

Case work, 31, 35, 55 ff. *See also* Family case work

Catholic Child Welfare Council, 119

C.E.M.A. *See* Arts Council of Great Britain

Central Association for Mental Welfare. *See* Mental welfare

Central Council for Infant and Child Welfare, 110, 193

Central Library, National

Chadwick, Edwin, 96

Chairmanship, training in (ABCA), 156, 159

Charities, endowed, 30 (*see also* Finance) ; international, 212, 213 ; registration of, 194 ; State supervision of, 189, 190, 194

Charity Commissioners, 194, 196

Charity Organisation Society. *See* C.O.S.

Child guidance, 34, 65, 66

Child Guidance Council, 110, 123, 124

Child Welfare Council, Catholic, 119

Children, adoption of, 120, 121 ; boarding out, 123, 124 ; delinquent, 123–4, 126 ; homes for, 66 ; illegitimate, 119 ; maladjusted, 123 ; neglected, orphan and destitute, 117–19, 121, 123 ; probation of (*see* Probation) ; welfare of, 9, 10, 19, 20, 21, 22, 23, 24, 25, 61, 62, 64–5, 106–28. *See also* Boys and Girls, Care committees, Invalid children, Juvenile advisory committees, Juvenile labour exchanges, Orphans

Children's allowances for unmarried mothers. *See* Unmarried mother, the

Children and Young Persons Act of 1933, 123, 124, 126

Children's Country Holiday Fund, 116

Children's homes, 117–18 ; Associated Council of, 111, 119

Church Army, 125

Church of England Waifs and Strays, 118, 119

Cinema, the, 168–9

Citizen, The Voluntary (Braithwaite), 195

Citizens' Advice Bureau, 36, 38, 66, 81, 90, 91

Citizens' Advice Bureau in Great Britain and Advice Centres in Liberated Europe (N.C.S.S.), 91 *n.*

Citizens' Advice Notes, 91

Citizens, citizenship, 30, 132, 149, 152, 156, 158, 161, 212–13

Citizenship, National Union of Societies for Equal, 152

City Literary Institute (L.C.C.), 147

Civic Centre, the, 78

Civil Defence, 71

Clinics, ante-natal, 108, 109 ; baby, 108 ; birth control, 211 ; child guidance (q.v.), 30, 65, 124, 125 ; dental, 114 ; for the examination of child offenders, 124 ; infant welfare, 19 ; marriage guidance, 34 ; tuberculosis, 63

Clubs, boys', girls' and/or adolescents', 30, 33, 81, 116, 130, 132, 187 ; community service, 88, 89, 93, 97 ; family, 35 ; for old people, 77 ; for unemployed, 32, 36, 41–54, 86 ; for wives and daughters of unemployed, 51 ; mixed (*see* National Association of Girls' Clubs and Mixed Clubs) ; occupational (*see* Community service clubs) ; " under-twenty " (B.B.C.), 142 ; women's, 51 ; works, 129 ; young farmers', 154–5 ; youth, 226

Coalfields Distress Fund, 1927, 41

Colleges, County, 142

Commissioner of Police for the Metropolis, report of, 202

Commons, Open Spaces and Footpaths Preservation Society, 3

Commonwealth fellowship, 64

Commonwealth Fund of America, 124

Communal feeding, 94 *n.*

Community associations, 71, 72, 82, 83, 85 ; consultative council of, 72 ; and community centres, definitions of, 73, 78 ; federations of, 72, 78 ; National Federation of, 72, 74, 77, 83

Community centres, 30, 35, 38, 69 ff., 148, 149, 153, 161, 170, 226, 227 ; and associations committee, 71, 83, 85 ; buildings, 76 ; financing of, 73, 75 ; organisation and leadership, staffing and management, 76, 77 ; relationship to local authorities, 77

Community Centres (Ministry of Education pamphlet), 72, 74

Community councils, 48, 78, 81, 87, 99, 100 ff., 104, 154, 176, 213 ; definition of, 83

Community service movement, 94

Community wardens, organisers, etc., training of, 72, 75, 76

Concert parties, touring, 103

Concerts, Village and Country Towns, Fund, 176

Convalescent homes, 63

Co-operative guilds, 34

C.O.P.E.C., 32
Cormack, Miss, 65
C.O.S. (Charity Organisation Society, now Family Welfare Association), 14, 15, 16, 18, 31, 56, 60, 61, 194, 199, 206, 214, 220
Cottage homes, 118, 119
Council for Industrial Design, 77
Council for the Preservation of Rural England, 3 n.
Council for Voluntary War Work, 86
Councils of Social Service, 78, 87, 189, 191, 192, 200. *See also* National Council of Social Service.
Courts, children's. *See* Juvenile courts
Craft work, 97
Creech-Jones, Violet, vi, 106
Crippled, the, 25, 63
Cripples, Central Council for the Care of, 193
Crusade of Rescue, 125
Current Affairs, Bureau of, 159 ff.
Current affairs hut (army), 161
Curtis, Miss Myra, 119

Davies, Walford, 47
Day nurseries. *See* Nurseries
Deaf, National Institute for the, 181
Deaf, training of the, 25
Degrees in economics, social science and sociology, 223
Delinquents, young, 24
Demobilised men. *See* Ex-service men
Development Commission, Development Commissioners, 83, 84, 90, 100, 103, 104, 192
Directory of Health and Social Welfare, Todd's, 109 n.
Discharged Prisoners Aid Society, 212
Discussion groups, 157 ff., 160, 165, 166, 226
Dispersal (Study by N.C.S.S.), 94
Displaced persons in Europe, 97
Distressed areas. *See* Special areas
Distressed Gentlefolks' Aid Association, 181, 211
District Nursing Committees, 33
Drage, Geoffrey, M.P., 3 n.
Drage Return. *See* Expenditure on social services
Drama, documentary (A.B.C.A.), 156 ; joint committee for, 103 ; rural, 99, 102–3, 176
Drama League, British, 103, 176
Durant, Ruth, 70 n., 79
Durham Community Council, 48

Education (*see* Blind, Cripples, Mentally Defective, W.E.A.) ; Acts, 36, 72, 73, 75, 76, 77, 84, 85, 114, 115, 130, 135, 139, 142, 145, 192 ; adult, 37, 38, 46, 94, 102, 146 ff. (*see* W.E.A.) ; army, 162 ff., 169 (*see* A.B.C.A. and B.W.P.) ; Board of, 37, 82, 100, 110, 113, 124, 135, 136, 138, 139, 144, 194, 196, 206 ; continued, 129 (*see* Education, adult) ; Government White Paper on, 94 ; Ministry of (*see* Ministry) ; of unemployed, 46 ; rural, 99 ; Services (*see* Army, Royal Navy, R.A.F.)
Education (Administration Provisions) Act, 1907, 20
Education Journal of, 158
Education (Provision of Meals) Act, 1906, 20
Educational Settlements Association, 83, 170
Empire Marketing Board, 162
Employment exchanges, 32 ; juvenile (*see* Juvenile)
Encyclopaedia of the Social Services, 1 n.
Epileptic, the, 58
Evacuation, evacuees, 37, 66
Evening schools and institutes, 131 (*see* Education, adult)
Expenditure on social services, 4, 9 (*see* Finance)
Ex-service men, 26, 32, 67

Fabians, the, 10
Family case work and workers, 15, 220 ff., 231, 245
Family Caseworkers' Association, 222
Family welfare, 61, 62, 66
Family Welfare Association (*see* C.O.S.)
Fathers' evening conferences, 108
Faversham Report on the Voluntary Mental Health Services, 25
Festivals, musical and dramatic, 103, 104
Films Division, Ministry of Information, 168
Finance Act, 1922, 188
Finance, methods and problems of, 81, 89, 188 ff.
Fire prevention, 36
Fisher Act, 1918, 113, 142
Fitness Act, National, 1937, 94
Fitness campaign, Fitness Council, National, 75, 103, 136, 137, 185
Flag days, 189–90, 194, 202 (*see* Street collections)
Folk high schools of Denmark, 170–1
Forces Educational Broadcasts (F.E.B.), (*see* B.B.C.)
Formation colleges, army, 163
Foster parents (*see* Children)
Fraser, Lovat, 123
Friendly societies, 34
Friends, Society of, 32, 41, 45, 125, 180

Games. *See* Play, Recreation

I*

Gilwell Park, 133
Girls and boys, work among. *See* Boys and Girls, Adolescents
Girls' Clubs, National Association of, 140
Girls' Clubs and Mixed Clubs, National Association of, 222
Girls' Clubs, National Council of, 134
Girls' Friendly Society, 129, 131, 134
Girls Growing Up, vi
Girls' Life Brigade, 131
Gisburne House, 126
Government and public funds, distribution by N.C.S.S., 93
Government in Transition (Percy), 4 *n.*
Group organisation, 76
Grundy, Dr. F., 108
Guardians, boards of. *See* Public assistance committees
Guides, Girl, 30, 129, 130, 135, 191
Guilds of Help, 80, 87
Gymnasiums, 75

Handicrafts in girls' organisations, 187
Harkness, Mr. E. S., 179
Health Insurance, National. *See* Insurance
Health, Medical Officer of, 205
Health visitors, 66
Hereford Rural Community Council, 100
Heritage craft schools, 181
Hill, Octavia, 12, 56, 66, 214, 231
Holiday camps. *See* Camps
Holidays, country. *See* Children's Country Holiday Fund
Holidays, international. *See* School Journeys Association
Holidays (study by N.C.S.S.), 94
Home helps, 63
Home Office, 24, 124, 126, 130
Homes, for the aged, 63 ; Josephine Butler, 212 ; special, for children, 66
Hop Scotch Inn, St. Pancras, 115
Hospital almoners (*see* Almoners) ; Institute of, 222
Hospital clinic, the, 63
Hospital finance. *See* Finance
Hospital Fund, King Edward's, for London, 197
Hospital Saturday funds, 198
Hospitals Year Book, 197
Hospitals, the Voluntary, of Great Britain, 197
Hostels Association, Boys', 185
Hostels for boys, 185
Hostels, youth. *See* Youth
House property management, training for, 217
House-to-House Collections Act, 1939, 194

Housewives' service, 37
Housing, 34, 35, 69, 99, 230, 231
Housing Acts, 69, 74, 75, 76, 145, 192
Housing Authorities (Rent Collectors), 66
Housing estates, 79
Housing managers, 231

Industrial Design, Council for, 77
Infant and Child Welfare, Central Council of, 110, 193
Infant Consultations, Association of, 107
Infant Mortality, National Association for the Prevention of, 110 ; National Association for the Prevention of, and for the Welfare of Infancy, 107 ; National Association for the Prevention of, and the Promotion of the Welfare of Children under School Age, 128
Infant welfare, 107 ff. *See also* Children, welfare of, Clinics
Infant Welfare and Maternity Centres, Association of, 110
Information rooms, army, 156, 161
Insurance, Insurance Act, 1911, 13 ; national, 38 ; National Health, 24, 32, 198 ; sickness (*see* National Health) ; unemployment, 26, 32
Intelligence and aptitude tests, 233
International common room for social workers, 97
Invalid Children's Aid Association, 24, 110, 193

Jennings, Hilda, vi, 28, 55, 230
Jephcott, Pearl, vi, 129
Jewish Board of Guardians (Children's Homes), 118, 119, 125
Jubilee Trust, King George's, 136, 183–7
Juvenile Advisory Committee, 22
Juvenile courts (children's courts), 65, 123, 125, 126
Juvenile delinquency, 64, 130 ff.
Juvenile employment and employment exchanges, 22, 115
Juvenile instruction centres, 136
Juvenile Organisations Committee, Central, 130

Keep Fit movement, 134
Kensington Baby Clinic, 108
Kent Council of Social Service, 102
Kent Rural Community Council, 100, 102
Kindergartens, 20
King Edward's Hospital Fund. *See* Hospital
King George's House, 185

King George's Jubilee Trust. *See* Jubilee Trust
King, Harold, vi, 69

Labour exchanges. *See* Employment exchanges
Labour management, labour managers, 216, 217, 220, 223, 231, 245
Labour Management, Institute of, 222
Labour, Ministry of. *See* Ministry
Labour Party, 51, 209
Land settlement, 177
Land Settlement Association, 103, 192
Legitimacy Act, 1936, 120
Leisure, 35. *See also* Holidays, Education, Recreation
Librarianship, school of, 174
Libraries, provision of, 102, 159–60, 173 ff.
Library Association, 174
Library, National Central, 175 ; National, for the Blind, 175 ; orchestral loan, 176
Library Service, County, 179
Life Brigade, 129
Lincolnshire Community Council, 101 *n*.
Literary Institute, L.C.C. City, 147, 170
Liverpool Council of Social Service, 200 ff.
Local Government Act, 111
Loch, Sir Charles, 58, 214
London Charity Organisation Society. *See* C.O.S.
London County Council, 20, 21, 61, 69, 116, 121, 126, 147, 170, 176
London Diocesan Council for Youth, 133
London Marriage Council, 66
London School of Economics, 140, 224

Macdonald, Margaret, 108
Maes-Yr-Haf, 41
Mallet, Sir Bernard, 4, 5
Manchester and Salford Council of Social Service, 200 ff.
Mansbridge, Dr. Albert, 146, 175
Marriage Council, London, 66
Marriage guidance clinics, 34
Marriage Guidance Council, 226
Maternity and child welfare (*see* Infant welfare, Children, Clinics) ; National Council for, 110, 120, 124
Maternity and Child Welfare Act, 110
Maternity benefit and the unmarried mother, 120
McMillan, Margaret, 112
McMillan, Rachel, 112
McNair Report on the Supply of Teachers and Youth Leaders, 140
Meals, provision of. *See* Education
Mechanics' institutes, 46
Medical inspection, school, 21, 114

Medical missionary, 3
Medical officer of health, 205
Medical research, 180, 181
Medico-social services, 58–9, 62–3
Mental deficiency, 25, 63
Mental Deficiency Act of 1913, 25
Mental health, 63, 66 ; certificates, 224 ; National Council for, 67, 124 ; training, 240
Mental hospitals, 65
Mental Hygiene, National Council for, 124
Mental Health, training, 240
Mental Welfare Association, 25
Mental Welfare, Central Association for, 124
Mess, Henry, vi, vii, 1, 40, 69, 84, 96, 99, 172, 188, 204
Methodist Youth Movement, 141
Midwives' Institute, 181
Middleton, Mary, 108
Milk depots, 107
Milnes, Nora, vi, 8
Ministry of Agriculture, 100, 206 ; Education, 35, 72, 74, 75, 84, 86, 103, 141, 142, 147, 150, 242 (*see* Education, board of) ; Health, 38, 66, 69, 83, 100, 107, 108, 109, 111, 120 ; Information, 168 ; Labour, 44, 49, 89, 92, 134, 192, 206 ; Munitions, 215
Missionary, medical, 3
Missionary societies, foreign, 3
Moral welfare associations, 63, 224
Morant, Sir Joseph, 96
Morgan, Dr. A. E., 129, 185
Morgan, John, vi, 80
Morley College, 181
Mortality, infant, 108
Mothers, schools for. *See* Schools
Music, concerts, etc. *See* Arts Council of Great Britain, B.B.C., Andrew Carnegie
Musical appreciation, 167
Musical Competition Festivals, Association of, National Federation of, 175
Musical societies, grants in aid of, 103
Musical Societies, National Federation of 176
Music and rural community councils, 102–3
Music festivals, 103
Musicians' Benevolent Fund, 181
Music magazine, 167
Music schools, rural, 103
Mutual aid, mutual aid schemes, 1, 6, 212
Mutual Registration of Assistance, 60

N.A.G.T.C., 140
National Adoption Society, 121 ; Anti-

Gambling League, 3; Assistance, 38; Association for the Prevention of Infant Mortality, 110; Association for the Prevention of Infant Mortality and for the Welfare of Infancy, 107; Association for the Prevention of Infant Mortality and the Promotion of the Welfare of Children under School Age, 128; Association of Boys' Clubs, 81, 89, 133, 187; Association of Girls' Clubs, 140; Association of Girls' Clubs and Mixed Clubs; Association of Parish Councils, 104; Baby Week Council, 110; Central Library, 175; Children's Adoption Association, 121; Children's Home, 118, 119; Council for Maternity and Child Welfare, 110, 120, 124; Council for Mental Health, 67, 124; Council for Mental Hygiene, 124; Council for the Unmarried Mother and her Child, 120, 127; Council of Girls' Clubs, 134; Council of Social Service (*see* N.C.S.S.); Federation of Community Associations, 77, 84; Federation of Musical Competition Festivals 175; Federation of Musical Societies 176; Federation of Women's Institutes, 188, 191; Federation of Young Farmers' Clubs, 89; Fitness Act, 1937, 94; Fitness Campaign, National Fitness Council, 75, 103, 136, 137, 185; Health Insurance (*see* Insurance); Institute for the Deaf, 181; League for Health, Maternity and Child Welfare, 110; Library for the Blind, 175; Playing Fields Association, 177; Old People's Welfare Committee, 86; Organisations, Standing Conference of, 86; Society of Children's Nurseries (formerly National Society of Day Nurseries), 110, 111; Union of Teachers, 142; Union of Societies for Equal Citizenship, 152; Union of Women's Suffrage Societies, 152; Voluntary Youth Organisations, Standing Conference of, 85, 86, 130; Youth Committee, 138; Youth Organisations (*see* Youth)

N.C.S.S. (National Council of Social Service), 27, 32, 35, 36, 37, 42, 46, 47, 48, 49, 50, 51, 52, 53, 54, 71, 72, 73, 74, 79, 80 ff., 120, 130, 134, 153–4, 188, 189, 192, 206, 246; annual reports, 86–7, 88, 96; international and overseas relations, 96, 97

Needs of Youth, the (Morgan), 185

Neighbourhood centres and relationships, 35, 77–8

Neighbourhood organisations, 226. *See* also Community

New Estates and Community Councils, Paper No. 1 (N.C.S.S.), 73

New Estates Community Committee (N.C.S.S.), 71

Nottinghamshire Community Council, 101–2

N.S.P.C.C., 121–3, 206

Nuffield College Social Reconstruction Survey, 65 *n.*, 99

Nurseries, Children's, Society of, 110, 111; day, 20, 109, 110, 111, residential, 117

Nurseries and Nursery Schools (Creech-Jones), vi

Nursery classes in elementary schools, 113

Nursery nurses, training of, 111

Nursery schools. *See* Schools

Nursery School Association, 110, 111, 113

Nursery Training Colleges, Association of, 110, 111

Nursing profession, the, 236 *n.*

Occupational clubs. *See* Clubs, community service

Occupational therapy, 217, 224

Old age, old people, 63, 77, 86

Old People's Welfare Committee, National, 86

Old age pensions, 16, 32, 225

Old Vic, 176

Orchestral Loan Library, 176

Organs for places of worship (Carnegie Trust), 173, 175

Orphans, 23. *See also* Children

Opera, 176

Our Towns, 37, 94

Out of Adversity (N.C.S.S.), 89

Oxfordshire Rural Community Council, 99

Parent-teacher associations, 66

Parish councils, 81

Parish Councils, National Association of, 104

Peabody Trust, 172

P.E.P. Report on the British Social Services, 3 *n.*, 4

Personal service societies, 192, 220

Physically disabled persons, 58. *See also* Blind, Cripples, Deaf, Epileptic, Tubercular

Physical training, 73, 130, 136–7. *See also* Recreation

Physical Training and Recreation Act, 38, 75, 76, 136, 137, 145, 192

Pilgrim Trust, 103, 134, 165, 179–82

Play centres, 115–16, 226

Playing fields, 75, 176–7

Playing Fields Association, National, 177
Play therapy, 125
Police Court Mission, 125
Police, Factories, etc. (Miscellaneous Provisions) Act of 1916, 194
Political Quarterly, 99
Poor Law, 13, 61. *See also* Public Assistance
Poor Law Commission, 10, 58, 60, 80
Poultry, schemes for unemployed, 45
Preservation of Rural England, Council for the, 3 *n.*
Pre-service societies (A.C.F., S.C.F., A.T.C.), 140–1
Prisons, Commissioners for, 205
Probation of Children, 123, 124
Probation officers, probation system, probation work, 123, 212, 237
Probation service, 62
Professional associations of social workers, professional bodies, 216 ff., 222, 223, 233, 245
Production committees, 160
Provident maternity clubs, 108
Psychiatric social work and workers, 34, 64, 65, 66, 224, 237
Public Assistance committees, 44, 123, 205. *See also* Assistance Board
Public Assistance, Inter-Departmental Committee on, 90
Public health services, 20
Public Libraries Amendment Act, 174

Quakers. *See* Friends, Society of

R.A.F., education in, 157, 164
Ratepayers' associations, 213
Reconstruction for Peace, Oxford Conference on, 81
Recreation, adolescent, 130. *See also* Adolescent, Playing fields, Camping, Holidays, Youth
Red Cross, 102, 109, 141
Regional Commissioners for Civil Defence, 87
Regional officers of N.C.S.S., 87
Reformatory schools. *See* Schools
Rehabilitation centres, 63
Rehousing. *See* Housing
Relief Abroad, Council of British Societies for, 97
Relief work, international, 97
Rent collectors for housing authorities, 66
Resettlement advice centres and service, 37, 92
Rest centres, 36
Rhodes Trust, 172
Rhondda Valley, 41
Richmond, Mary, 64

Royal Navy, education in, 157, 164
Royal Sanitary Institute, 111
R.S.P.C.A., 206
Rural community councils. *See* Community councils
Rural Disfigurement and its Remedies, 99
Rural industries, 81, 89, 99, 104, 154
Rural Industries Bureau, 192 ; Report on Work of, 104 *n.*
Rural Industries Equipment Loan Fund, 89–90, 104–5
Rural life, problems of, 99
Rural Organisations Council, 99
Rural social service. *See* Social service, rural

Sadlers Wells Theatre, 176
" Save the Children " campaign, 9
" Save the Children Fund," 110, 113, 116, 117
Salvation Army, 125, 212
Sawston Village College, 102
School care committees. *See* Care committees
School dinners, 62
School Journey Association, 117
School for Mothers, St. Pancras, 107–8
Schools, approved, 24, 125, 126 ; broadcasts (*see* B.B.C.) ; camp, 93 ; for mothers, 107, 108 ; nursery, 20, 112–14, 181 ; for producers of plays, 102 ; reformatory, 24 ; rural music, 103 ; of social studies, 215
Scottish Council of Social Service, 87
Scouts, scouting, 30, 85, 97, 129, 130, 135, 191, 192
Scunthorpe, Model Youth Centre, 185
Seafarers' Educational Service, 175
" Service of Youth," 137, 138 ff., 242
Service of Youth circular (Board of Education), 37, 138
" Service of Youth " literature, 140
Service welfare officers, 67
Settlements, educational, association, 83
Settlements, residential, 35, 60, 116
Settlements, Residential, British Association of, 83
Settlement, Women's University, in Southwark, 214–15
Shaftesbury homes, 119
Simey, T. S., 4 *n.*
Slough Community Centre, 170
Smallholdings for returned soldiers, 99
Social Centre, Slough, 137
Social Diagnosis (Richmond), 64
Social science, social studies, sociology, certificates, degrees and diplomas in, 217, 223 ; courses and training (*see* Universities)
Social Service, British Institute of, 80 ;

Bureau of, suggested, 246 ; Councils of, 81, 87, 153 (see also N.C.S.S.) ; definition of, 1 ff. ; growth of, viii ; National Council of (see N.C.S.S.) ; rural, 81, 99

Social Service in Rural Areas (Mess), 99

Social Service Review, 80 n.

Social services, public ; statutory, vii, 3 ; voluntary, vii

Social Studies and Public Administration, Joint University Council of, 218

Social studies, schools of, 215

Social study (N.C.S.S.), 94

Social work, definition of, 228 ; training for ; special workers, training of, 124, 139–40, 214 ff. (see also Training centres)

Social workers, selection of, 232, 233

S. & S.F.A., 13

S.S. & A.F.A., 67

Southwark, women's university settlement in, 214–15

Special areas (distressed areas), 29, 134, 180

Special Areas Act, 1932, 145

Special areas, " adoption " of, 50 ; commissioners for, 49, 52, 89, 93, 134, 192 ; staff fund for, 49

Staffordshire County Council, 174

Stamp, Sir Josiah, 181–8

Standing Conference of National Organisations, 86

Standing Conference of National Youth Organisations. *See* Youth

Statutory agencies, relations with voluntary, 204 ff.

Stapeley House, 87

State, Children's Association, the, 123

Street collections, 189, 190, 194

Suffolk Community Council, 101 n.

Sussex Community Council, 101 n.

Sunday Cinema, Entertainments Fund, 191

Sunday Entertainments Act of 1932, 191

Sutton Trust, 172

Swimming baths, 73

Teachers, National Union of, 142

Teachers, visiting, 66

Technical colleges. *See* Education, adult

Tenants' associations, 70, 213

Theatres, assisted by Carnegie Trust, 176

Times Educational Supplement, 140

Tow Law, 45

Town and Country Planning Association, 3 n.

Town planning, 79

Townswomen's guilds, 35, 148, 152

Toynbee Hall, 181, 235

Training centres (ABCA), 156

Training centres for disabled adults, 63

Training, for house property management, 217 ; for mental health work, 240 ; for occupational therapy, 217 ; for professional careers, 181 ; of club leaders, 133, 134 ; of scout masters, 133 ; of social workers, 60, 181 (see Social workers) ; of staff for children's homes, 124 ; of youth leaders, 186, 217, 240

Truth, 194

Tubercular, the, 58

Tubercular persons, workshops for, 63

Tuberculosis clinic, the. *See* Clinics

Tyneside, 43, 44, 45

Tyneside Council of Social Service, vii

Unemployed, 88 ; education of, 46 ; men's centres, 35 (see Clubs) ; training of, 17 ; welfare work among, 49, 50, 51, 206 ; wives and daughters of, 50, 51 ; women, 50

Unemployment, 180 ; post-war, 40, 41

Unemployment Assistance Board, 32, 44

Unemployment benefit, 49, 51, 225

Unemployment insurance. *See* Insurance

Unemployment, post-war, 40, 41

United Nations, 97

Units, Civil Defence, 71

Universities, extra-mural departments, 36, 102 ; training in social science, 60–1, 215 ff.

University Extension Class, 169

University Extension Movement, 146

University of Birmingham, 215 ; of Edinburgh, 224 ; of London, vii, 223

University Tutorial Class, 169

Unmarried Mother, National Council for the, and her Child, 120, 127

Village, colleges, 99, 102 ; committees, 81, 84 (see Rural) ; halls, 81, 84, 99, 103, 104 ; social life, 81

Villagers, plays by, 99. *See also* Drama

Voluntary Citizen, The (Braithwaite), vi, 195

Voluntary social services, advantages of, 210 ff.

Voluntary Social Service (Cormack), 65, 99

Wages in Modern Industry (Milnes), vi

Waifs and Strays. *See* Church of England

Ward, Mary, Settlement, 115

War and social services, 8, 9, 86

War Charities Acts, 194

War Office, 156, 164

War Relief and Personal Service, Conference on, 81

Watling (Durant), 70 *n.*

Watling, 70, 79

Watling Residents' Association, 70, 71

Waugh, Benjamin, 121

Webbs, The Sydney, 10

Welfare, old people's. *See* Old people

Welfare workers, 66, 215 ; on new estates, 66

Welfare work, training for leadership in unemployed, 49. *See also* Service welfare officers

Welsh League of Youth, 129, 186

Wickwar, W. H., 3 *n.*

Widows, 17

Williams, Gertrude, vi, vii, 214

Williams, W. E., vi, 146

Winter Distress League, 190

Wireless appeals, 189, 190

Witten, Rev. John H., 119 *n.*

Women Housing Managers, Society of, 224

Women's institutes, 83, 148, 150–2, 154, 192

Women's Institutes, National Federation of, 188, 191

Women's organisations, co-ordination of, 86

Women's Public Welfare Group of N.C.S.S. (q.v.), 37, 86, 94

Women, unemployed. *See* Unemployed

Women's Suffrage Societies, National Union of, 152

Women's Voluntary Services (W.V.S.), 13 *n.*, 36, 37

Worcestershire Rural Community Council, 100

Workers' Educational Association (W.E.A.), 30, 36, 41, 46, 102, 142, 146 ff., 169

Works councils, 160

World Association for Adult Education, 3 *n.*

Y.M.C.A., 36, 97, 129, 130, 148, 170, 186

Young farmers' clubs, 129, 154–5, 186, 206

Young Farmers' Clubs, National Federation of, 89

Young Offenders (Carr-Saunders, Mannheim, Rhodes), 132 *n.*

Youth activities, youth movements, 33, 37, 38, 77, 85, 86, 130, 141

Youth centres, 161, 185, 220 ; colleges, 148 ; hostels, 129 ; leaders, 220, 245 (*see* McNair Report) ; leadership, training for (*see* Training) ; organisations, foreign, 142 ; organisations, inspection of, 139 ; service of (*see* Service of Youth) ; service organisers, 138 ; welfare of, 183 ff. (*see* Clubs, Camping, Service of Youth) ; Welsh League of, 186

Youth Committee, National, 138

Youth Hostels Association, 89, 186

Youth, London Diocesan Council for, 133

Youth Organisations, Standing Conference of National Voluntary, 85, 86, 130.

Youth, The Needs of (Morgan), 185

Y.W.C.A., 36, 129, 148, 181

The International Library of
SOCIOLOGY AND SOCIAL RECONSTRUCTION

Editor: KARL MANNHEIM
Late Professor of Education in the University of London

PLAN OF THE LIBRARY
Sections

Sociology of Education, p. 2

Sociology of Religion, p. 3

Sociology of Art and Literature, p. 3

Sociological Approach to the Study of History, p. 4

Sociology of Law, p. 4

Criminology and the Social Services, p. 5

Sociology and Politics, p. 5

Foreign Affairs, Their Social, Political and Economic Foundations, p. 6

Migration and Re-settlement, p. 7

Economic Planning, p. 7

Sociology of the Family and Allied Topics, p. 7

Town and Country Planning. Human Ecology, p. 8

Sociological Studies of Modern Communities, p. 9

Anthropology and Colonial Policy, p. 9

Sociology and Psychology of the Present Crisis, p. 10

Social Psychology and Psycho-analysis, p. 10

Approaches to the Problem of Personality, p. 11

Philosophical and Social Foundations of Thought, p. 11

General Sociology, p. 12

Foreign Classics of Sociology, p. 12

Documentary, p. 12

KEGAN PAUL, TRENCH, TRUBNER & CO. LTD.
68-74 Carter Lane, London, E.C.4

SOCIOLOGY OF EDUCATION

Education after School
by C. STIMSON   *In preparation.   About 15s.*

The Problem of Punishment in Education
by EWALD BOHM   *In preparation.   About 21s.*

Mission of the University
by ORTEGA Y GASSET. Translated and introduced by HOWARD LEE NOSTRAND
                                                          7s. 6d.

Total Education: A Plea for Synthesis
by M. L. JACKS, Director, Department of Education, Oxford University
                                   Second Impression.   10s. 6d.

Education in Transition
A Sociological Analysis of the Impact of the War on English Education
by H. C. DENT   *Fourth Impression.   12s. 6d.*

The Reform of Secondary Education
by H. C. DENT   *About 15s.*

Education for Adults: A Study in Transition
by T. MACKAY MURE   *About 10s. 6d.*

Who Shall Be Educated? The Challenge of Unequal Opportunities
by W. LLOYD WARNER, Prof. of Anthropology and Sociology, Member of Comm. on Human Development, Univ. of Chicago; ROBERT J. HAVIGHURST, Prof. of Education, Member of Comm. on Human Development, Univ. of Chicago; MARTIN B. LOEB, Inst. of Child Welfare, Univ. of California, at Berkeley   *10s. 6d.*

The Social Psychology of Education: A Sociological Study
by C. M. FLEMING, Ed.B., Ph.D., University of London Institute of Education   *Fourth Impression.   7s. 6d.*

German Youth: Bond or Free
by HOWARD BECKER, Professor of Sociology, University of Wisconsin
                                               Illustrated.   18s.

2

The Museum: Its History and Its Tasks in Education
by ALMA S. WITTLIN, Dr. Phil. *In preparation. Illustrated. About 21s.*

SOCIOLOGY OF RELIGION

The Sociology of Religion
by JOACHIM WACH   *About 10s. 6d.*

The Economic Order and Religion
by FRANK KNIGHT, Prof. of Social Sciences, University of Chicago,
and THORNTON W. MERRIAM, Director of U.S.O. Training, Nat.
Council of the Y.M.C.A.   *15s.*

SOCIOLOGY OF ART AND LITERATURE

Sociology of the Renaissance
by ALFRED VON MARTIN, translated by W. L. LUETKENS
                                    Second Impression. 8s. 6d.

Theatre, Drama and Audience in Goethe's Germany
by W. H. BRUFORD, M.A., Professor of German, University of
Edinburgh   *In Preparation. About 25s.*

Chekhov and His Russia: A Sociological Study
by W. H. BRUFORD, M.A., Professor of German in the University of
Edinburgh   *About 21s.*

The Sociology of Literary Taste
by LEVIN L. SCHÜCKING. Dr. Phil.   *Second Impression 7s. 6d.*

Men of Letters and the English Public in the 18th Century, 1660-1744. Dryden, Addison, Pope
by ALEXANDRE BELJAME. Edited with an Introduction and Notes
by Prof. BONAMY DOBREE. Translated by E. O. LORIMER *About 21s.*

SOCIOLOGICAL APPROACH TO THE STUDY OF HISTORY

The Aftermath of the Napoleonic Wars: The Concert of Europe—An Experiment

by H. G. SCHENK, D.Phil. (Oxon)

Illustrated. 16s.

Progress and Disenchantment: A Study of European Romanticism

by H. G. SCHENK, D.Phil. (Oxon)

Illustrated. About 21s.

SOCIOLOGY OF LAW

The Sociology of Law

by GEORGES GURVITCH, Ph.D., LL.D., Prof. of Sociology, University of Strasbourg, France. With an Introduction by ROSCOE POUND, Prof. of Jurisprudence, late Dean of the Faculty of Law, Harvard University

18s.

The Institutions of Private Law and Their Social Functions

by KARL RENNER, President of the Austrian Republic. Edited with an Introduction and Notes by O. KAHN-FREUND, Ll.M., Dr. Jur., Lecturer in Law, University of London

About 10s. 6d.

Legal Aid

by ROBERT EGERTON, Hon. Sec. Legal Sub-committee Cambridge House, Solicitor of the Supreme Court. With an Introduction by D. L. GOODHART, K.C., D.C.L., Ll.D., Prof. of Jurisprudence, Oxford

2nd Impression. 10s. 6d.

Soviet Legal Theory: Its Social Background and Development

by RUDOLF SCHLESINGER, Ph.D., London

2nd Impression. 16s.

CRIMINOLOGY AND THE SOCIAL SERVICES

Theory and Practice of a Family Court
by CARL BIRNBAUM, formerly Professor of Psychiatry, Berlin University, and John Otto Reinemann, Dr. Jur., formerly Municipal Councillor in Berlin   *In preparation. About 15s.*

Juvenile Delinquency in an English Middletown
by HERMANN MANNHEIM, Lecturer in Criminology in the University of London   *In preparation. About 18s.*

Mental Health in a Rural Area
by Dr. MAYER GROSS   *In preparation. About 15s.*

Criminal Justice and Social Reconstruction
by HERMANN MANNHEIM, Dr. Jur., Lecturer in Criminology in the University of London   *15s.*

The Psycho-Analytical Approach to Juvenile Delinquency: Theory, Case Studies, Treatment
by KATE FRIEDLANDER, M.D., L.R.C.P. (Edin.), D.P.M. (Lond.), Hon. Psychiatrist, Inst. for the Scientific Treatment of Delinquency; Clinical Dir., W. Sussex Child Guidance Service   *18s.*

Voluntary Social Services since 1918
by HENRY A. MESS, late Reader in Social Science in the University of London in collaboration with Constance Braithwaite, Nora Milnes, John Morgan, Violet Creech-Jones, W. E. Williams, Pearl Jephcott and Hilda Jennings. Edited by GERTRUDE WILLIAMS, Lecturer in Economics, University of London   *About 21s.*

SOCIOLOGY AND POLITICS

Social and Economic Movements: A Handbook to the Understanding of the Modern Political Scene
by H. W. LAIDLER   *In preparation. About 30s.*

The Analysis of Political Behaviour: An Empirical Approach
by HAROLD D. LASSWELL, Professor of Law, Yale University School of Law   *21s.*

5

Dictatorship and Political Police

The Technique of Control by Fear by E. K. BRAMSTEDT, Ph.D. (London)

15s.

Nationality in History and Politics

by FREDERICK HERTZ, Author of "Race and Civilisation"

Second Impression.   25s.

FOREIGN AFFAIRS, THEIR SOCIAL, POLITICAL AND ECONOMIC FOUNDATIONS

Patterns of Peacemaking

by DAVID THOMSON, Ph.D., Cantab., Research Fellow of Sidney Sussex Coll., Cambridge; E. MEYER, Dr. rer. pol., and A. BRIGGS, B.A., Cantab.

21s.

French Canada in Transition

by EVERETT C. HUGHES, Professor of Sociology, University of Chicago

15s.

State and Economics in the Middle East

by A. BONNE, Dr. œc. publ., Director, Economic Research Institute of Palestine

About 25s.

Economic Development of the Middle East

An Outline of Planned Reconstruction by A. BONNE, Dr. œc. publ., Director, Economic Research Institute of Palestine

Second Impression.   12s. 6d.

Federalism in Central and Eastern Europe

by RUDOLF SCHLESINGER, Ph.D., London

30s.

The Danube Basin and the German Economic Sphere

by ANTONIN BASCH, Dr. Phil., Columbia University

18s.

The Regions of Germany

by R. E. DICKINSON, Reader in Geography, University College, London

Second Impression.   10s. 6d.

MIGRATION AND RE-SETTLEMENT

Settlement in Underpopulated Areas
by JULIUS ISAAC, Ph.D. (London).   *In preparation.   About 18s.*

Economics of Migration
by JULIUS ISAAC, Ph.D., London. With an Introduction by Sir ALEXANDER CARR-SAUNDERS, Director of the London School of Economics   *18s.*

Co-operative Communities at Work
by HENRIK INFIELD, Director, Rural Settlement Inst., New York
                                                        15s.

ECONOMIC PLANNING

Retail Trade Associations
A New Form of Monopolist Organisation in Britain, by HERMANN LEVY, Author of "The New Industrial System"   *Second Impression. 15s.*

The Shops of Britain: A Study in Retail Trade Distribution
by HERMANN LEVY   *About 21s.*

The Price of Social Security—The Problem of Labour Mobility
by GERTRUDE WILLIAMS, Lecturer in Economics, University of London
                                       Second Impression.   12s. 6d.

SOCIOLOGY OF THE FAMILY AND ALLIED TOPICS

The Family and Democratic Society
by J. K. FOLSOM, Professor of Sociology, Vassar College
                                       In preparation.   About 30s.

Nation and Family
The Swedish Experiment in Democratic Family and Population Policy
by ALVA MYRDAL   *2nd Impression.   21s.*

The Sociology of Women's Work

by GERTRUDE WILLIAMS, Lecturer in Economics, University of London

About 15s.

Adolescence

Its Social Psychology: With an Introduction to recent findings from the fields of Anthropology, Physiology, Medicine, Psychometrics and Sociometry

by C. M. FLEMING, Ed.B., Ph.D., University of London Institute of Education

About 15s.

TOWN AND COUNTRY PLANNING. HUMAN ECOLOGY

Social Background of a Plan: A Study of Middlesbrough

Edited by RUTH GLASS. Illustrated with Maps and Plans

In preparation. About 30s.

City, Region and Regionalism

by ROBERT E. DICKINSON, Reader in Geography, University College, London. With Maps and Plans

21s.

The West European City: A Study in Urban Geography

by ROBERT E. DICKINSON, Reader in Geography, University College, London. Illustrated, with Maps and Plans. *In preparation. About 21s.*

Creative Demobilisation

Vol. I. Principles of National Planning
By E. A. GUTKIND, D.Ing.

Vol. 2. Case Studies in National Planning
Edited by E. A. GUTKIND, D.Ing.

Second Impression. 21s. each

Revolution of Environment

by E. A. GUTKIND, D.Ing.

Illustrated. 30s.

The Journey to Work

by K. LIEPMANN, Ph.D., London. With an Introduction by Sir Alexander Carr-Saunders, Director of the London School of Economics

Second Impression. 15s.

8

SOCIOLOGICAL STUDIES OF MODERN COMMUNITIES

Negroes in Britain
A study of Racial Relations in English Society
by K. L. LITTLE, Ph.D., London   25s.

Co-operative Living in Palestine
by HENRIK F. INFIELD, Director, Rural Settlement Inst., New York
Illustrated. 7s. 6d.

ANTHROPOLOGY AND COLONIAL POLICY

The Sociology of Colonies: An Introduction to the Study of Race Contact
by RENÉ MAUNIER. Translated from the French by E. O. Lorimer
In preparation. About 42s.

Malay Fishermen: Their Peasant Economy
by RAYMOND FIRTH, Prof. of Anthropology, University of London
Illustrated. 25s. net

Peasant Life in China
by HSIAO T'UNG FEI, Ph.D., London   *Fourth Impression. Illustrated. 15s.*

A Chinese Village: Taitou, Shantung Province
by Martin C. Yang   *About 15s.*

Hsinlung Hsiang
A Field Study of Peasant Life in the Red Basin, West China
by ISABEL CROOK and YU HSI-CHI   *About 21s.*

A Japanese Village: Suye Mura
by JOHN P. EMBREE, Visiting Assoc. Prof. of Anthropology, University
of Chicago. With an Introduction by A. R. RADCLIFFE-BROWN,
Professor of Social Anthropology, Oxford University
Illustrated. 18s.

The Golden Wing: A Sociological Study of Chinese Familism
by LIN HUEH-HWA, with an Introduction by RAYMOND FIRTH
About 15s.

9

SOCIOLOGY AND PSYCHOLOGY OF THE PRESENT CRISIS

War, Love or Money: A Psychological Study of European Culture Patterns
by H. V. DICKS, M.D., M.R.C.P.   *In preparation.   About 21s.*

Diagnosis of Our Time
by KARL MANNHEIM   *Fourth Impression.   10s. 6d.*

Farewell to European History or the Conquest of Nihilism
by ALFRED WEBER   *About 30s.*

The Fear of Freedom
by Dr. ERICH FROMM   *Fourth Impression.   15s.*

SOCIAL PSYCHOLOGY AND PSYCHO-ANALYSIS

Psychology and the Social Pattern
by JULIAN BLACKBURN, Ph.D., B.Sc. (Econ.), Lecturer on Social Psychology, London School of Economics   *Second Impression.   10s. 6d.*

The Framework of Human Behaviour
by JULIAN BLACKBURN, Ph.D., B.Sc. (Econ.), Lecturer on Social Psychology, London School of Economics   *12s. 6d.*

Individual Development in Society
by JULIAN BLACKBURN, Ph.D., B.Sc. (Econ.), Lecturer on Social Psychology, London School of Economics   *About 10s. 6d.*
(Three independent volumes supplementing each other)

A Handbook of Social Psychology
by KIMBALL YOUNG, Professor of Sociology, Queens College, New York   *Second Impression.   21s.*

Sigmund Freud—An Introduction
A Presentation of his Theories and a discussion of the Relationship between Psycho-analysis and Sociology by WALTER HOLLITSCHER, Dr. Phil.   *8s. 6d.*

Social Learning and Imitation
by NEAL E. MILLER and JOHN DOLLARD of the Institute of Human
Relations, Yale University   *15s.*

APPROACHES TO THE PROBLEM
OF PERSONALITY

The Cultural Background of Personality
by RALPH LINTON, Professor of Anthropology, Columbia University
                                                              10s. 6d.

The Feminine Character. History of an Ideology
by VIOLA KLEIN, Ph.D., London. With an Introduction by KARL
MANNHEIM.   *12s. 6d.*

The History of Autobiography in Antiquity
by GEORG MISCH. Translated by E. W. DICKES   *About 21s.*

Personality and Problems of Adjustment
by KIMBALL YOUNG   Demy 8vo.   *About 30s.*

PHILOSOPHICAL AND SOCIAL FOUNDATIONS
OF THOUGHT

Homo Ludens
by Professor J. HUIZINGA   *In preparation.   About 21s.*

The Ideal Foundations of Economic Thought
by W. STARK, Dr. rer. pol., Dr. Jur.   *Second Impression.   15s.*

**The History of Economics in Its Relation to Social
Development**
by W. STARK, Dr. rer. pol., Dr. Jur.   *Second Impression.   7s. 6d.*

America: Ideal and Reality
The United States of 1776 in Contemporary European Philosophy by
W. STARK, Dr. rer. pol., Dr. Jur.

The Decline of Liberalism as an Ideology
by J. H. HALLOWELL   *12s. 6d.*

Society and Nature: A Sociological Inquiry
by HANS KELSEN, Formerly Prof. of Law, Vienna and Geneva, Department of Political Science, University of California   *21s.*

Demographic Material Appearing in the Transactions of the Royal Society in the 17th and 18th Centuries
Edited by Dr. R. R. KUCZYNSKI   *In preparation.   About 15s.*

Population Controversies of the Eighteenth Century
Edited by DAVID GLASS, Ph.D.   *In preparation.   About 15s.*

GENERAL SOCIOLOGY

A Handbook of Sociology
by W. F. OGBURN, Professor of Sociology, University of Chicago, and
M. F. NIMKOFF, Professor of Sociology, Bucknell University   *25s.*

FOREIGN CLASSICS OF SOCIOLOGY

Wilhelm Dilthey: Selected Readings from his Works and an Introduction to his Sociological and Philosophical Work
by H. A. HODGES, Prof. of Philosophy, University of Reading   *10s. 6d.*

From Max Weber: Essays in Sociology
Translated, edited, and with an Introduction by H. H. GERTH and
C. W. MILLS   *About 21s.*

DOCUMENTARY

Changing Attitudes in Soviet Russia
Documents and Readings concerning the *Family*
Edited by R. SCHLESINGER, Ph.D., London   *About 21s.*

Changing Attitudes in Soviet Russia
Documents and Readings concerning *National Autonomy and Experiments in Administrative Devolution*
Edited by R. SCHLESINGER, Ph.D., London   *About 21s.*

Changing Attitudes in Soviet Russia
Documents and Readings concerning *Foreign Policy*
Edited by R. SCHLESINGER, Ph.D., London   *About 21s.*

All prices are net

THE WESTMINSTER PRESS, LONDON, W.9